LATIN AMERICAN

TRADE PATTERNS

LATIN AMERICAN
TRADE PATTERNS

by

Donald W. Baerresen

Martin Carnoy

Joseph Grunwald

The Brookings Institution *Washington, D.C.*

© 1965 by

THE BROOKINGS INSTITUTION

1775 Massachusetts Avenue N.W. Washington, D.C.

Published October 1965

Library of Congress Catalogue Card Number 65-27966

PRINTED IN THE UNITED STATES OF AMERICA

BY GARAMOND/PRIDEMARK PRESS, INC., BALTIMORE, MD.

THE BROOKINGS INSTITUTION is an independent organization devoted to nonpartisan research, education, and publication in economics, government, foreign policy, and the social sciences generally. Its principal purposes are to aid in the development of sound public policies and to promote public understanding of issues of national importance.

The Institution was founded December 8, 1927, to merge the activities of the Institute for Government Research, founded in 1916, the Institute of Economics, founded in 1922, and the Robert Brookings Graduate School of Economics and Government, founded in 1924.

The general administration of the Institution is the responsibility of a self-perpetuating Board of Trustees. The trustees are likewise charged with maintaining the independence of the staff and fostering the most favorable conditions for creative research and education. The immediate direction of the policies, program, and staff of the Institution is vested in the President, assisted by the division directors and an advisory council, chosen from the professional staff of the Institution.

In publishing a study, the Institution presents it as a competent treatment of a subject worthy of public consideration. The interpretations and conclusions in such publications are those of the author or authors and do not purport to represent the views of the other staff members, officers, or trustees of the Brookings Institution.

Foreword

WHILE ACTUAL PROGRESS in the economic integration of Latin America has been slow and prospects may not look bright at the moment, pressures are mounting to improve the present machinery for a free trade area and to push forward toward the economic union of the region. Concurrently, there is a rising awareness of the need for further knowledge about the effects of regionwide trade and investment policies. Various inter-American agencies, such as the Inter-American Development Bank, the United Nations Economic Commission for Latin America, and the Secretariat of the Latin American Free Trade Area, are now engaged in research along this line.

At Brookings, a new program of economic and social development studies in the Foreign Policy Studies Division, which is under the direction of H. Field Haviland, Jr., gives particular emphasis to examining the problems of the economic integration of Latin America. Research in this area is divided into two major aspects: studies of trade problems and studies concerned with investment policies. This monograph provides some background data and material for projects in the first category. The Brookings Institution is also coordinating studies which deal with the investment allocation in the Latin American Free Trade Area. That project is being undertaken jointly with nine Latin American research institutions.

The present study is primarily intended as a compilation of pertinent statistics which, when properly expanded and continued, will aid in the evaluation of the effects of the new trade arrangements in Latin America. In order to enhance understanding of current trade patterns and the problems involved in changing them, Chapter II provides a brief historical review. A commentary on the tables is contained in Chapter III, while further lines of research are indicated in Chapter IV. The Foreign Policy Studies Division is now engaged in following up some of the research suggested in this study.

The monograph was originally designed by Donald W. Baerresen under the guidance of Joseph Grunwald of the Brookings senior staff, who is responsible for the program of economic and social development within the Foreign Policy Studies Division. Baerresen, who was a research associate at the Brookings Institution from August 1963 to September 1964, was able to prepare a nearly completed first draft before joining the staff of the Organization of American States. Subsequently, Martin Carnoy, who replaced Donald Baerresen as research associate, and Joseph Grunwald modified the text and revised and expanded the statistical materials. Changes were made to take into account the new materials and the suggestions of the reading committee and other persons. The reading committee consisted of Harvey Perloff of Resources for the Future, David Pollock of the Economic Commission for Latin America, and Walter S. Salant of Brookings. The authors are grateful for the helpful suggestions of this group. In addition, valuable comments were received from John Adler of the International Bank for Reconstruction and Development, Eduardo Figueroa and Raul Rey Alvarez of the Inter-American Development Bank, Isaiah Frank of the School of Advanced International Studies of the Johns Hopkins University, and William Turnage of the Bureau of American Republics Affairs, Department of State. The following colleagues at Brookings have read the manuscript at various stages and have been of great assistance: Robert E. Asher, Robert Brown, Lawrence B. Krause, and Philip Musgrove. Jane Lecht edited the manuscript. Furthermore, the authors wish to express their appreciation to Field Haviland, Director of Foreign Policy Studies, without whose encouragement this study would not have been possible.

The study was financed by a Ford Foundation grant. The views expressed in the study are entirely those of the authors and do not necessarily reflect the views of the persons consulted during its preparation, the Ford Foundation, or the Brookings trustees, officers, or other staff members.

ROBERT D. CALKINS
President

July 1965
Washington, D.C.

Contents

Foreword vii

PART ONE. *Perspective and Analysis*

1. INTRODUCTION 1

2. HISTORICAL SURVEY 7
   Colonialism: 1500-1820 7
   Integration into World Markets: 1820-1914 13
   World Wars and Depression: 1915-1945 19
   Postwar Years and Institutionalized Development: 1946-1963 . . . 28

3. TRADE PATTERNS 39
   General Trade Patterns of LAFTA Countries,
   Bolivia, and Venezuela 43
   Individual Analysis of LAFTA Countries 45
   Individual Analysis of Bolivia and Venezuela 55

4. CONCLUSIONS 58

PART TWO. *Trade Statistics*

NOTE ON SOURCES 67
BASIC TABLES 74

Bibliography 325

Summary Tables

A. The Share of Principal Trading Countries in the Imports and Exports of Latin America, Selected Years, 1910-1941   20
B. Latin America: Population, Exports, and Capacity to Import, 1929-1939   22
C. Imports from and Exports to Latin America as a Percentage of Imports from and Exports to the World, by Country, 1934-1938 and 1946-1951   28
D. LAFTA Import Index for All LAFTA Countries, 1960-1961 and 1962-1963   63
E. Categories of Latin American Exports   68-69
F. SITC Code Corresponding to Categories of Table E   70-71

Basic Tables

GENERAL LATIN AMERICAN TRADE (Pages 74 to 80)

I.   World and Latin American Foreign Trade, 1934-1963
II-a.   Latin American Exports and Imports, 1938-1963
II-b.   Latin American Exports and Imports, 1938-1963 (in percent)
III-a.   Exports of LAFTA Countries and of Bolivia and Venezuela as a Percentage of Total Latin American Exports to Latin American Countries, 1934-1963
III-b.   Exports of LAFTA Countries and of Bolivia and Venezuela as a Percentage of Total Latin American Exports to the World, 1934-1963
IV-a.   Imports of LAFTA Countries and of Bolivia and Venezuela as a Percentage of Total Latin American Imports from Latin American Countries, 1934-1963
IV-b.   Imports of LAFTA Countries and of Bolivia and Venezuela as a Percentage of Total Latin American Imports from the World, 1934-1963

LATIN AMERICAN TRADE BY COUNTRY (Pages 81 to 113)

V-1-a.   Argentina's Exports by Main Trading Areas, 1938-1963
V-1-b.   Argentina's Imports by Main Trading Areas, 1938-1963
V-2-a.   Brazil's Exports by Main Trading Areas, 1938-1963
V-2-b.   Brazil's Imports by Main Trading Areas, 1938-1963
V-3-a.   Chile's Exports by Main Trading Areas, 1938-1963
V-3-b.   Chile's Imports by Main Trading Areas, 1938-1963
V-4-a.   Colombia's Exports by Main Trading Areas, 1938-1963
V-4-b.   Colombia's Imports by Main Trading Areas, 1938-1963
V-5-a.   Ecuador's Exports by Main Trading Areas, 1938-1963
V-5-b.   Ecuador's Imports by Main Trading Areas, 1938-1963

V-6-a.   Mexico's Exports by Main Trading Areas, 1938-1963
V-6-b.   Mexico's Imports by Main Trading Areas, 1938-1963
V-7-a.   Paraguay's Exports by Main Trading Areas, 1938-1963
V-7-b.   Paraguay's Imports by Main Trading Areas, 1938-1963
V-8-a.   Peru's Exports by Main Trading Areas, 1938-1963
V-8-b.   Peru's Imports by Main Trading Areas, 1938-1963
V-9-a.   Uruguay's Exports by Main Trading Areas, 1938-1963
V-9-b.   Uruguay's Imports by Main Trading Areas, 1938-1963
V-10-a.   Bolivia's Exports by Main Trading Areas, 1938-1963
V-10-b.   Bolivia's Imports by Main Trading Areas, 1938-1963
V-11-a.   Venezuela's Exports by Main Trading Areas, 1938-1963
V-11-b.   Venezuela's Imports by Main Trading Areas, 1938-1963
VI-1.   Argentina's Trade with LAFTA Countries, Bolivia and Venezuela, 1948-1963
VI-2.   Brazil's Trade with LAFTA Countries, Bolivia and Venezuela, 1948-1963
VI-3.   Chile's Trade with LAFTA Countries, Bolivia and Venezuela, 1948-1963
VI-4.   Colombia's Trade with LAFTA Countries, Bolivia and Venezuela, 1948-1963
VI-5.   Ecuador's Trade with LAFTA Countries, Bolivia and Venezuela, 1948-1963
VI-6.   Mexico's Trade with LAFTA Countries, Bolivia and Venezuela, 1948-1963
VI-7.   Paraguay's Trade with LAFTA Countries, Bolivia and Venezuela, 1948-1963
VI-8.   Peru's Trade with LAFTA Countries, Bolivia and Venezuela, 1948-1963
VI-9.   Uruguay's Trade with LAFTA Countries, Bolivia and Venezuela, 1948-1963
VI-10.   Bolivia's Trade with LAFTA Countries and Venezuela, 1948-1963
VI-11.   Venezuela's Trade with LAFTA Countries and Bolivia, 1948-1963

*EXPORTS OF LAFTA COUNTRIES AND OF BOLIVIA AND
VENEZUELA TO ONE ANOTHER BY YEAR AND
PRODUCT* (Pages 114 to 275)

ARGENTINA (Pages 114 to 128)

VII-1-1a.   Argentina's Exports to LAFTA Countries, 1959—*Raw Materials*
VII-1-1b.   Argentina's Exports to LAFTA Countries, 1959—*Semi-Processed*
VII-1-1c.   Argentina's Exports to LAFTA Countries, 1959—*Processed or Manufactured*
VII-1-2a.   Argentina's Exports to LAFTA Countries, 1960—*Raw Materials*
VII-1-2b.   Argentina's Exports to LAFTA Countries, 1960—*Semi-Processed*
VII-1-2c.   Argentina's Exports to LAFTA Countries, 1960—*Manufactured or Processed*

VII-1-3a.   Argentina's Exports to LAFTA Countries, 1961—*Raw Materials*
VII-1-3b.   Argentina's Exports to LAFTA Countries, 1961—*Semi-Processed*
VII-1-3c.   Argentina's Exports to LAFTA Countries, 1961—*Processed or Manufactured*
VII-1-4a.   Argentina's Exports to LAFTA Countries, 1962—*Raw Materials*
VII-1-4b.   Argentina's Exports to LAFTA Countries, 1962—*Semi-Processed*
VII-1-4c.   Argentina's Exports to LAFTA Countries, 1962—*Processed or Manufactured*
VII-1-5a.   Argentina's Exports to LAFTA Countries, 1963—*Raw Materials*
VII-1-5b.   Argentina's Exports to LAFTA Countries, 1963—*Semi-Processed*
VII-1-5c.   Argentina's Exports to LAFTA Countries, 1963—*Processed or Manufactured*

BRAZIL   (Pages 129 to 143)

VII-2-1a.   Brazil's Exports to LAFTA Countries, 1959—*Raw Materials*
VII-2-1b.   Brazil's Exports to LAFTA Countries, 1959—*Semi-Processed*
VII-2-1c.   Brazil's Exports to LAFTA Countries, 1959—*Processed or Manufactured*
VII-2-2a.   Brazil's Exports to LAFTA Countries, 1960—*Raw Materials*
VII-2-2b.   Brazil's Exports to LAFTA Countries, 1960—*Semi-Processed*
VII-2-2c.   Brazil's Exports to LAFTA Countries, 1960—*Processed or Manufactured*
VII-2-3a.   Brazil's Exports to LAFTA Countries, 1961—*Raw Materials*
VII-2-3b.   Brazil's Exports to LAFTA Countries, 1961—*Semi-Processed*
VII-2-3c.   Brazil's Exports to LAFTA Countries, 1961—*Processed or Manufactured*
VII-2-4a.   Brazil's Exports to LAFTA Countries, 1962—*Raw Materials*
VII-2-4b.   Brazil's Exports to LAFTA Countries, 1962—*Semi-Processed*
VII-2-4c.   Brazil's Exports to LAFTA Countries, 1962—*Processed or Manufactured*
VII-2-5a.   Brazil's Exports to LAFTA Countries, 1963—*Raw Materials*
VII-2-5b.   Brazil's Exports to LAFTA Countries, 1963—*Semi-Processed*
VII-2-5c.   Brazil's Exports to LAFTA Countries, 1963—*Processed or Manufactured*

CHILE   (Pages 144 to 158)

VII-3-1a.   Chile's Exports to LAFTA Countries, 1959—*Raw Materials*
VII-3-1b.   Chile's Exports to LAFTA Countries, 1959—*Semi-Processed*
VII-3-1c.   Chile's Exports to LAFTA Countries, 1959—*Processed or Manufactured*
VII-3-2a.   Chile's Exports to LAFTA Countries, 1960—*Raw Materials*
VII-3-2b.   Chile's Exports to LAFTA Countries, 1960—*Semi-Processed*
VII-3-2c.   Chile's Exports to LAFTA Countries, 1960—*Processed or Manufactured*
VII-3-3a.   Chile's Exports to LAFTA Countries, 1961—*Raw Materials*
VII-3-3b.   Chile's Exports to LAFTA Countries, 1961—*Semi-Processed*

VII-3-3c.   Chile's Exports to LAFTA Countries, 1961—*Processed or Manufactured*

VII-3-4a.   Chile's Exports to LAFTA Countries, 1962—*Raw Materials*

VII-3-4b.   Chile's Exports to LAFTA Countries, 1962—*Semi-Processed*

VII-3-4c.   Chile's Exports to LAFTA Countries, 1962—*Processed or Manufactured*

VII-3-5a.   Chile's Exports to LAFTA Countries, 1963—*Raw Materials*

VII-3-5b.   Chile's Exports to LAFTA Countries, 1963—*Semi-Processed*

VII-3-5c.   Chile's Exports to LAFTA Countries, 1963—*Processed or Manufactured*

COLOMBIA (Pages 159 to 173)

VII-4-1a.   Colombia's Exports to LAFTA Countries, 1959—*Raw Materials*

VII-4-1b.   Colombia's Exports to LAFTA Countries, 1959—*Semi-Processed*

VII-4-1c.   Colombia's Exports to LAFTA Countries, 1959—*Processed or Manufactured*

VII-4-2a.   Colombia's Exports to LAFTA Countries, 1960—*Raw Materials*

VII-4-2b.   Colombia's Exports to LAFTA Countries, 1960—*Semi-Processed*

VII-4-2c.   Colombia's Exports to LAFTA Countries, 1960—*Processed or Manufactured*

VII-4-3a.   Colombia's Exports to LAFTA Countries, 1961—*Raw Materials*

VII-4-3b.   Colombia's Exports to LAFTA Countries, 1961—*Semi-Processed*

VII-4-3c.   Colombia's Exports to LAFTA Countries, 1961—*Processed or Manufactured*

VII-4-4a.   Colombia's Exports to LAFTA Countries, 1962—*Raw Materials*

VII-4-4b.   Colombia's Exports to LAFTA Countries, 1962—*Semi-Processed*

VII-4-4c.   Colombia's Exports to LAFTA Countries, 1962—*Processed or Manufactured*

VII-4-5a.   Colombia's Exports to LAFTA Countries, 1963—*Raw Materials*

VII-4-5b.   Colombia's Exports to LAFTA Countries, 1963—*Semi-Processed*

VII-4-5c.   Colombia's Exports to LAFTA Countries, 1963—*Processed or Manufactured*

ECUADOR (Pages 174 to 188)

VII-5-1a.   Ecuador's Exports to LAFTA Countries, 1959—*Raw Materials*

VII-5-1b.   Ecuador's Exports to LAFTA Countries, 1959—*Semi-Processed*

VII-5-1c.   Ecuador's Exports to LAFTA Countries, 1959—*Processed or Manufactured*

VII-5-2a.   Ecuador's Exports to LAFTA Countries, 1960—*Raw Materials*

VII-5-2b.   Ecuador's Exports to LAFTA Countries, 1960—*Semi-Processed*

VII-5-2c.   Ecuador's Exports to LAFTA Countries, 1960—*Processed or Manufactured*

VII-5-3a.   Ecuador's Exports to LAFTA Countries, 1961—*Raw Materials*

VII-5-3b.   Ecuador's Exports to LAFTA Countries, 1961—*Semi-Processed*

VII-5-3c.   Ecuador's Exports to LAFTA Countries, 1961—*Processed or Manufactured*

VII-5-4a.   Ecuador's Exports to LAFTA Countries, 1962—*Raw Materials*
VII-5-4b.   Ecuador's Exports to LAFTA Countries, 1962—*Semi-Processed*
VII-5-4c.   Ecuador's Exports to LAFTA Countries, 1962—*Processed or Manufactured*
VII-5-5a.   Ecuador's Exports to LAFTA Countries, 1963—*Raw Materials*
VII-5-5b.   Ecuador's Exports to LAFTA Countries, 1963—*Semi-Processed*
VII-5-5c.   Ecuador's Exports to LAFTA Countries, 1963—*Processed or Manufactured*

MEXICO (Pages 189 to 203)

VII-6-1a.   Mexico's Exports to LAFTA Countries, 1959—*Raw Materials*
VII-6-1b.   Mexico's Exports to LAFTA Countries, 1959—*Semi-Processed*
VII-6-1c.   Mexico's Exports to LAFTA Countries, 1959—*Processed or Manufactured*
VII-6-2a.   Mexico's Exports to LAFTA Countries, 1960—*Raw Materials*
VII-6-2b.   Mexico's Exports to LAFTA Countries, 1960—*Semi-Processed*
VII-6-2c.   Mexico's Exports to LAFTA Countries, 1960—*Processed or Manufactured*
VII-6-3a.   Mexico's Exports to LAFTA Countries, 1961—*Raw Materials*
VII-6-3b.   Mexico's Exports to LAFTA Countries, 1961—*Semi-Processed*
VII-6-3c.   Mexico's Exports to LAFTA Countries, 1961—*Processed or Manufactured*
VII-6-4a.   Mexico's Exports to LAFTA Countries, 1962—*Raw Materials*
VII-6-4b.   Mexico's Exports to LAFTA Countries, 1962—*Semi-Processed*
VII-6-4c.   Mexico's Exports to LAFTA Countries, 1962—*Processed or Manufactured*
VII-6-5a.   Mexico's Exports to LAFTA Countries, 1963—*Raw Materials*
VII-6-5b.   Mexico's Exports to LAFTA Countries, 1963—*Semi-Processed*
VII-6-5c.   Mexico's Exports to LAFTA Countries, 1963—*Processed or Manufactured*

PARAGUAY (Pages 204 to 218)

VII-7-1a.   Paraguay's Exports to LAFTA Countries, 1959—*Raw Materials*
VII-7-1b.   Paraguay's Exports to LAFTA Countries, 1959—*Semi-Processed*
VII-7-1c.   Paraguay's Exports to LAFTA Countries, 1959—*Processed or Manufactured*
VII-7-2a.   Paraguay's Exports to LAFTA Countries, 1960—*Raw Materials*
VII-7-2b.   Paraguay's Exports to LAFTA Countries, 1960—*Semi-Processed*
VII-7-2c.   Paraguay's Exports to LAFTA Countries, 1960—*Processed or Manufactured*
VII-7-3a.   Paraguay's Exports to LAFTA Countries, 1961—*Raw Materials*
VII-7-3b.   Paraguay's Exports to LAFTA Countries, 1961—*Semi-Processed*
VII-7-3c.   Paraguay's Exports to LAFTA Countries, 1961—*Processed or Manufactured*
VII-7-4a.   Paraguay's Exports to LAFTA Countries, 1962—*Raw Materials*
VII-7-4b.   Paraguay's Exports to LAFTA Countries, 1962—*Semi-Processed*

VII-7-4c.   Paraguay's Exports to LAFTA Countries, 1962—*Processed or Manufactured*
VII-7-5a.   Paraguay's Exports to LAFTA Countries, 1963—*Raw Materials*
VII-7-5b.   Paraguay's Exports to LAFTA Countries, 1963—*Semi-Processed*
VII-7-5c.   Paraguay's Exports to LAFTA Countries, 1963—*Processed or Manufactured*

PERU (Pages 219 to 233)
VII-8-1a.   Peru's Exports to LAFTA Countries, 1959—*Raw Materials*
VII-8-1b.   Peru's Exports to LAFTA Countries, 1959—*Semi-Processed*
VII-8-1c.   Peru's Exports to LAFTA Countries, 1959—*Processed or Manufactured*
VII-8-2a.   Peru's Exports to LAFTA Countries, 1960—*Raw Materials*
VII-8-2b.   Peru's Exports to LAFTA Countries, 1960—*Semi-Processed*
VII-8-2c.   Peru's Exports to LAFTA Countries, 1960—*Processed or Manufactured*
VII-8-3a.   Peru's Exports to LAFTA Countries, 1961—*Raw Materials*
VII-8-3b.   Peru's Exports to LAFTA Countries, 1961—*Semi-Processed*
VII-8-3c.   Peru's Exports to LAFTA Countries, 1961—*Processed or Manufactured*
VII-8-4a.   Peru's Exports to LAFTA Countries, 1962—*Raw Materials*
VII-8-4b.   Peru's Exports to LAFTA Countries, 1962—*Semi-Processed*
VII-8-4c.   Peru's Exports to LAFTA Countries, 1962—*Processed or Manufactured*
VII-8-5a.   Peru's Exports to LAFTA Countries, 1963—*Raw Materials*
VII-8-5b.   Peru's Exports to LAFTA Countries, 1963—*Semi-Processed*
VII-8-5c.   Peru's Exports to LAFTA Countries, 1963—*Processed or Manufactured*

URUGUAY (Pages 234 to 248)
VII-9-1a.   Uruguay's Exports to LAFTA Countries, 1959—*Raw Materials*
VII-9-1b.   Uruguay's Exports to LAFTA Countries, 1959—*Semi-Processed*
VII-9-1c.   Uruguay's Exports to LAFTA Countries, 1959—*Processed or Manufactured*
VII-9-2a.   Uruguay's Exports to LAFTA Countries, 1960—*Raw Materials*
VII-9-2b.   Uruguay's Exports to LAFTA Countries, 1960—*Semi-Processed*
VII-9-2c.   Uruguay's Exports to LAFTA Countries, 1960—*Processed or Manufactured*
VII-9-3a.   Uruguay's Exports to LAFTA Countries, 1961—*Raw Materials*
VII-9-3b.   Uruguay's Exports to LAFTA Countries, 1961—*Semi-Processed*
VII-9-3c.   Uruguay's Exports to LAFTA Countries, 1961—*Processed or Manufactured*
VII-9-4a.   Uruguay's Exports to LAFTA Countries, 1962—*Raw Materials*
VII-9-4b.   Uruguay's Exports to LAFTA Countries, 1962—*Semi-Processed*
VII-9-4c.   Uruguay's Exports to LAFTA Countries, 1962—*Processed or Manufactured*
VII-9-5a.   Uruguay's Exports to LAFTA Countries, 1963—*Raw Materials*

VII-9-5b.   Uruguay's Exports to LAFTA Countries, 1963—*Semi-Processed*
VII-9-5c.   Uruguay's Exports to LAFTA Countries, 1963—*Processed or Manufactured*

BOLIVIA (Pages 249 to 260)

VII-10-1a. Bolivia's Exports to LAFTA Countries, 1959—*Raw Materials*
VII-10-1b. Bolivia's Exports to LAFTA Countries, 1959—*Semi-Processed*
VII-10-1c. Bolivia's Exports to LAFTA Countries, 1959—*Processed or Manu-factured*
VII-10-2a. Bolivia's Exports to LAFTA Countries, 1960—*Raw Materials*
VII-10-2b. Bolivia's Exports to LAFTA Countries, 1960—*Semi-Processed*
VII-10-2c. Bolivia's Exports to LAFTA Countries, 1960—*Processed or Manu-factured*
VII-10-3a. Bolivia's Exports to LAFTA Countries, 1961—*Raw Materials*
VII-10-3b. Bolivia's Exports to LAFTA Countries, 1961—*Semi-Processed*
VII-10-3c. Bolivia's Exports to LAFTA Countries, 1961—*Processed or Manu-factured*
VII-10-4a. Bolivia's Exports to LAFTA Countries, 1962—*Raw Materials*
VII-10-4b. Bolivia's Exports to LAFTA Countries, 1962—*Semi-Processed*
VII-10-4c. Bolivia's Exports to LAFTA Countries, 1962—*Processed or Manu-factured*

VENEZUELA (Pages 261 to 275)

VII-11-1a. Venezuela's Exports to LAFTA Countries, 1959—*Raw Materials*
VII-11-1b. Venezuela's Exports to LAFTA Countries, 1959—*Semi-Processed*
VII-11-1c. Venezuela's Exports to LAFTA Countries, 1959—*Processed or Manufactured*
VII-11-2a. Venezuela's Exports to LAFTA Countries, 1960—*Raw Materials*
VII-11-2b. Venezuela's Exports to LAFTA Countries, 1960—*Semi-Processed*
VII-11-2c. Venezuela's Exports to LAFTA Countries, 1960—*Manufactured or Processed*
VII-11-3a. Venezuela's Exports to LAFTA Countries, 1961—*Raw Materials*
VII-11-3b. Venezuela's Exports to LAFTA Countries, 1961—*Semi-Processed*
VII-11-3c. Venezuela's Exports to LAFTA Countries, 1961—*Manufactured or Processed*
VII-11-4a. Venezuela's Exports to LAFTA Countries, 1962—*Raw Materials*
VII-11-4b. Venezuela's Exports to LAFTA Countries, 1962—*Semi-Processed*
VII-11-4c. Venezuela's Exports to LAFTA Countries, 1962—*Processed or Manufactured*
VII-11-5a. Venezuela's Exports to LAFTA Countries, 1963—*Raw Materials*
VII-11-5b. Venezuela's Exports to LAFTA Countries, 1963—*Semi-Processed*
VII-11-5c. Venezuela's Exports to LAFTA Countries, 1963—*Processed or Manufactured*

SUMMARY BASIC TABLES (Pages 276 to 324)

VIII-a.   LAFTA Countries' Share of Intra-LAFTA Exports, 1938-1963
VIII-b.   LAFTA Countries' Share of Intra-LAFTA Imports, 1938-1963

IX-1a. Raw Materials as a Percentage of Exports of Argentina to LAFTA Countries, Bolivia and Venezuela, 1959-1963

IX-1b. Semi-Processed Commodities as a Percentage of Exports of Argentina to LAFTA Countries, Bolivia and Venezuela, 1959-1963

IX-1c. Processed and Manufactured Commodities as a Percentage of Exports of Argentina to LAFTA Countries, Bolivia and Venezuela, 1959-1963

IX-2a. Raw Materials as a Percentage of Exports of Brazil to LAFTA Countries, Bolivia and Venezuela, 1959-1963

IX-2b. Semi-Processed Commodities as a Percentage of Exports of Brazil to LAFTA Countries, Bolivia and Venezuela, 1959-1963

IX-2c. Processed and Manufactured Commodities as a Percentage of Exports of Brazil to LAFTA Countries, Bolivia and Venezuela, 1959-1963

IX-3a. Raw Materials as a Percentage of Exports of Chile to LAFTA Countries, Bolivia and Venezuela, 1959-1963

IX-3b. Semi-Processed Commodities as a Percentage of Exports of Chile to LAFTA Countries, Bolivia and Venezuela, 1959-1963

IX-3c. Processed and Manufactured Commodities as a Percentage of Exports of Chile to LAFTA Countries, Bolivia and Venezuela, 1959-1963

IX-4a. Raw Materials as a Percentage of Exports of Colombia to LAFTA Countries, Bolivia and Venezuela, 1959-1963

IX-4b. Semi-Processed Commodities as a Percentage of Exports of Colombia to LAFTA Countries, Bolivia and Venezuela, 1959-1963

IX-4c. Processed and Manufactured Commodities as a Percentage of Exports of Colombia to LAFTA Countries, Bolivia and Venezuela, 1959-1963

IX-5a. Raw Materials as a Percentage of Exports of Ecuador to LAFTA Countries, Bolivia and Venezuela, 1959-1963

IX-5b. Semi-Processed Commodities as a Percentage of Exports of Ecuador to LAFTA Countries, Bolivia and Venezuela, 1959-1963

IX-5c. Processed and Manufactured Commodities as a Percentage of Exports of Ecuador to LAFTA Countries, Bolivia and Venezuela, 1959-1963

IX-6a. Raw Materials as a Percentage of Exports of Mexico to LAFTA Countries, Bolivia and Venezuela, 1959-1963

IX-6b. Semi-Processed Commodities as a Percentage of Exports of Mexico to LAFTA Countries, Bolivia and Venezuela, 1959-1963

IX-6c. Processed and Manufactured Commodities as a Percentage of Exports of Mexico to LAFTA Countries, Bolivia and Venezuela, 1959-1963

IX-7a. Raw Materials as a Percentage of Exports of Paraguay to LAFTA Countries, Bolivia and Venezuela, 1959-1963

IX-7b. Semi-Processed Commodities as a Percentage of Exports of Paraguay to LAFTA Countries, Bolivia and Venezuela, 1959-1963

IX-7c.   Processed and Manufactured Commodities as a Percentage of Exports of Paraguay to LAFTA Countries, Bolivia and Venezuela, 1959-1963

IX-8a.   Raw Materials as a Percentage of Exports of Peru to LAFTA Countries, Bolivia and Venezuela, 1959-1963

IX-8b.   Semi-Processed Commodities as a Percentage of Exports of Peru to LAFTA Countries, Bolivia and Venezuela, 1959-1963

IX-8c.   Processed and Manufactured Commodities as a Percentage of Exports of Peru to LAFTA Countries, Bolivia and Venezuela, 1959-1963

IX-9a.   Raw Materials as a Percentage of Exports of Uruguay to LAFTA Countries, Bolivia and Venezuela, 1959-1963

IX-9b.   Semi-Processed Commodities as a Percentage of Exports of Uruguay to LAFTA Countries, Bolivia and Venezuela, 1959-1963

IX-9c.   Processed and Manufactured Commodities as a Percentage of Exports of Uruguay to LAFTA Countries, Bolivia and Venezuela, 1959-1963

IX-10a.   Raw Materials as a Percentage of Exports of Bolivia to LAFTA Countries and Venezuela, 1959-1962

IX-10b.   Semi-Processed Commodities as a Percentage of Exports of Bolivia to LAFTA Countries and Venezuela, 1959-1962

IX-10c.   Processed and Manufactured Commodities as a Percentage of Exports of Bolivia to LAFTA Countries and Venezuela, 1959-1962

IX-11a.   Raw Materials as a Percentage of Exports of Venezuela to LAFTA Countries and Bolivia, 1959-1963

IX-11b.   Semi-Processed Commodities as a Percentage of Exports of Venezuela to LAFTA Countries and Bolivia, 1959-1963

IX-11c.   Processed and Manufactured Commodities as a Percentage of Exports of Venezuela to LAFTA Countries and Bolivia, 1959-1963

Xa.   Raw Materials as a Percentage of Total Exports Going to LAFTA Countries, Bolivia and Venezuela, by Country, 1959-1963

Xb.   Semi-Processed Commodities as a Percentage of Total Exports Going to LAFTA Countries, Bolivia and Venezuela, by Country, 1959-1963

Xc.   Processed and Manufactured Commodities as a Percentage of Total Exports Going to LAFTA Countries, Bolivia and Venezuela, by Country, 1959-1963

XI-1.   Percentage of Total Trade to LAFTA Countries, Bolivia and Venezuela, by Country, 1959

XI-2.   Percentage of Total Trade to LAFTA Countries, Bolivia and Venezuela, by Country, 1960

XI-3.   Percentage of Total Trade to LAFTA Countries, Bolivia and Venezuela, by Country, 1961

XI-4.   Percentage of Total Trade to LAFTA Countries, Bolivia and Venezuela, by Country, 1962

XI-5.   Percentage of Total Trade to LAFTA Countries, Bolivia and Venezuela, by Country, 1963

XII.   National Income by LAFTA Countries, Bolivia and Venezuela, 1950-1962

XIII-a.   Total Exports of LAFTA Countries, Bolivia and Venezuela, by Country, 1950-1962

XIII-b.   Total Imports of LAFTA Countries, Bolivia and Venezuela, by Country, 1950-1962

XIV-a.   Total Exports of LAFTA Countries, Bolivia and Venezuela, as a Percentage of National Income, 1950-1962

XIV-b.   Total Imports of LAFTA Countries, Bolivia and Venezuela, as a Percentage of National Income, 1950-1962

XV.   Imports Per Capita of LAFTA Countries, Bolivia and Venezuela, by Country, 1960

PART ONE

Perspective and Analysis

CHAPTER I

Introduction

THE MOST STRIKING ASPECT of Latin America's international trade is that the flow of goods among the countries of the region has been very small. Not that the total foreign trade of these countries has been minor—on an average the sum of exports and imports amounts to over one quarter of national incomes in Latin America—but the direction of trade has not been toward neighbors or other countries in the region but to countries overseas.

On the surface, this trade pattern does not appear "natural" or "normal," and one is led to search for a rationale. A superficial explanation is obvious when one looks only briefly at the structure of production of the region and the composition of Latin American exports. Despite the fairly rapid industrialization of the last two or three decades, the extractive sector (agriculture and mining, including petroleum) is still dominant. Well over 90 percent of exports still consists of primary commodities. With this kind of export base it is not surprising that Latin American countries have not found their markets within their own region but act only as suppliers to industrialized countries.

The economic integration of the region is looked upon by Latin Americans as one of the necessary, but certainly not sufficient, means of breaking out of this pattern and reaching a stage of accelerated and sustained industrialization. As integration proceeds, it is important to determine whether its repercussions on the Latin American economy through increased intraregional trade are consistent with the aims of industrialization and general economic development. If successful, the movement toward regional unity will result in significant changes in the future export base and in the future trade patterns of Latin American countries.

1

Before any studies can be undertaken to evaluate these factors, a basis has to be established on which to build research. It is the objective of this book to provide such a foundation. The study examines existing patterns of trade among countries belonging to the Latin American Free Trade Association (LAFTA) and countries likely to join LAFTA (Bolivia and Venezuela) through an historical background and a systematized collection of data concerning Latin American trade. The presentation is intended as a point of departure for the analysis of the effects which may be traced to LAFTA or other integration attempts and is designed to form the framework for the collection of future trade data.

What emerges from the overview of economic history in Chapter II is an insight into the self-reinforcing nature of the export orientation given to the region in its early stages of colonization. All Latin American colonies—and later nations—have had outlets to the sea,[1] and the infrastructure has been geared to transporting raw material from the production centers in the interior to the ports. Once established, social overhead capital encouraged expansion of overseas-oriented raw material production and the import of processed goods from abroad. This, in turn, led to strengthening the outward-looking infrastructure.[2] There is little doubt that this self-perpetuating and self-reinforcing pattern has been one of the important factors in obstructing internal economic trade and development in Latin America.

About thirty years ago it looked as if a change in export structure would be forced on Latin America by external circumstances. The Great Depression of the 1930's led to the collapse of export earnings of most countries that exported raw materials. It thereby induced the development of import-substituting industries in the more advanced Latin American countries. Because the imports that were replaced by

---

[1] After the War of the Pacific in the early 1880's, Bolivia became landlocked, although formally it maintained an outlet to the sea through the Chilean port, Arica. Paraguay, after formation as a country, also did not border on the sea; but it has been accessible to ocean-going vessels through the La Plata river system.

[2] The term "infrastructure" includes not only physical overhead capital such as transportation but also the institutional apparatus. The export orientation of Latin American countries created paperwork in the government bureaucracies. While this paperwork may be appropriate to safeguard the public interest in overseas trading activities, it has become generalized and has permeated government relations with the industrial sector as well, thus hindering efficient growth.

domestic production were exclusively for local consumption, the export base did not change significantly.

On the other hand, the import-substitution process appreciably reduced the individual economy's dependence on imports at any given level of consumption. Imports of consumer goods declined in importance because of domestic substitution, but the process of industrialization increased the need for imports of capital goods and intermediate goods. What changed was the composition of imports, with the proportion of producer goods increasing at the expense of consumer goods. Latin American countries, therefore, had to keep on earning steadily increasing quantities of foreign exchange in order to maintain growth of national product. Industrialization, if anything, made this dependency more acute because it is more difficult to reduce producer goods imports during a balance-of-payments crisis than consumer goods.

After World War II, Latin American nations engaged in an even more concerted industrialization effort, but this push also failed to bring about a significant modification in trade patterns. In the early 1950's, the United Nations Economic Commission for Latin America, under the leadership of Raúl Prebisch, set forth the rationale for industrialization goals. It was based on the premise that, in the long run, countries exporting raw materials and importing manufactured goods suffer a relative if not absolute deterioration in economic welfare. Tariffs, exchange controls, and other domestic barriers protected domestic industry, and the import-substitution process accelerated. In some countries, manufacturing surpassed agriculture, mining, and other extractive activities in the contribution to the Gross National Product. As before, industrial production remained primarily for domestic consumption and, with rare exceptions, the nationally protected high-cost industries have not been able to reach the export stage. While the structures of Latin American economies have changed and apparently become more diversified, they have on the whole become more rigid than viable.

The condition of a Latin American country's balance of payments has assumed greater importance because the industrial sector now depends upon it. Also, since industrialization has become the primary medium for growth in most of the countries, the focus of economic development has shifted back to the foreign sector. It has been argued in Latin America that economic growth is circumscribed by the rate of expansion of exports plus foreign investment and aid. Because foreign investment and aid can hardly be expected to finance more than a small portion of a nation's imports, the onus falls on export expansion. But raw materials still comprise the bulk of exports, and according to the Latin American thesis, the demand for primary products is generally weak.

Conversely, it is believed in Latin America that the first stages of import-substituting industrialization have come to an end in the major countries of the region. Most consumer goods are now produced domestically, and unless national mass markets are developed, there will be little room for expansion left in this field. The substitution of domestically produced capital goods for imported capital goods, it is said, is much more difficult in markets which are limited in size. Latin American economists, by the end of the 1950's, viewed many of their economies as being in a state of "impasse."

In accord with this viewpoint, pressures mounted in Latin America to arrive at an arrangement for widening markets and integrating the region economically. Such an arrangement, it was hoped, would not only permit another spurt in industrialization but also provide the basis for sustained and sound economic growth.

From the previous discussion it can be seen that the argument for economic integration, as it has evolved in Latin America, has several aspects. First, an increase in the size of the market will set the stage for the second phase of the import-substitution process: the establishment of efficient producer goods industries. These would include both capital goods to provide the machinery and equipment and intermediate goods such as chemicals to supply the raw materials for the industrial plant. The implication is that there are economies of scale in these industries and that unit costs can be minimized only at high levels of production. Second, larger markets will make it possible to expand existing consumer goods industries and, perhaps, to establish new ones in which economies of scale may exist. Hence, manufacturing would not only supply national markets but would be increasingly geared toward exports.

In the earlier stages of Latin American thinking about industrialization and economic integration, exports of primary products were downgraded because of a conviction that relative prices were declining and that, in general, the world demand for raw materials was increasing at a slower pace than it was for manufactured products. More recently, however, there has been a growing awareness that the region must continue to depend on raw material exports for some time to come. Above all, these exports must provide for the rising requirements of foreign exchange to support an industrial acceleration. Furthermore, Latin America's growing industrial plant will consume an increasing share of the region's output of raw materials. For all these reasons it is now generally recognized that the development of natural resources, far from detracting from a country's viability, is an essential part of an industrialization effort, and Latin American countries are now pressing hard for international measures to compensate for losses when world demand fails to keep up with supply.

The economic integration of Latin America is expected eventually to direct more raw material exports to countries within the region. This would be more than mere trade diversion since the demand for raw materials in the industrializing countries of Latin America presumably would grow at a faster rate than in Western Europe and the United States, traditional markets for their primary products.

Of course, the classical thesis of gains from trade through international specialization is also an essential ingredient of Latin American thinking about economic integration. It is sometimes said that a common market arrangement should be easier in a developing region where the level of industrialization is still low than it is in an economically advanced region such as Western Europe. The problem is, however, that countries with incipient industrialization are jealously guarding the few industries which have been established. Most manufacturing industries in Latin American countries are "infant industries" in the classical sense and therefore candidates for protection. Even if the countries agree to accept the rule of comparative advantage in production, they will have difficulty following it because comparative advantage does not obviously manifest itself on an a priori basis in most industries.

A certain amount of production and investment planning on a region-wide scale therefore seems inevitable. Complementarity agreements (see Chapter II) which involve the allocation of product specialization among two or more countries having the same industries, are one step in this direction, although perhaps a highly precarious one.

The efforts toward economic integration resulted first in the Central American Common Market and then in the Montevideo Treaty of 1960, which created the Latin American Free Trade Association (LAFTA). The former consists of five Central American countries (not including Panama), and LAFTA includes Mexico and all the independent South American republics[3] except Bolivia and Venezuela. Venezuela is about to join LAFTA, and Bolivia will probably follow suit in the not too distant future. This study is focused on these eleven countries (the nine LAFTA countries plus Bolivia and Venezuela). They comprise over ninety percent of Latin America's population, gross national product, and trade. The remainder is accounted for by Central America and the Caribbean countries (Dominican Republic, Haiti, and Cuba).

By definition, LAFTA falls far short of being a common market arrangement. It concentrates on tariff reductions and does not concern itself with other trade barriers. Nor are there concrete provisions for harmonizing tax, monetary, and other policies for solving payment and financing problems. There is no machinery for establishing common tariffs against nonmember countries. The internal tariff reduction procedure under LAFTA is tedious and cumbersome. Instead of across-the-board reductions (as in the European Economic Community), concessions must be negotiated individually for each commodity. Yet LAFTA is a beginning; it is more than the proponents of economic integration in Latin America dared to hope for in the immediate postwar years.

---

[3] "Independent South America" excludes British, Dutch, and French Guiana, just as the concept "Latin America" as used here excludes the present and former U.S., British, Dutch, and French overseas territories.

CHAPTER II

Historical Survey

THE PRESENT PATTERN of trade within Latin America results from complex forces which oriented each country to the outside world rather than to its neighbors within the region. The origins of these forces are many and varied. Only the aspects of the past which can shed light on the present trade picture will be discussed here. While Latin America is not homogeneous, its history is not so diverse and so lacking in uniformity as to make generalizations impossible. Certain factors in Latin American economic history have affected the size, composition, and direction of trade: (1) the influence of foreign powers and economies; (2) the conflict among local elites and their control of trade and development; and (3) the effect on trade of natural barriers and transportation costs. To trace the nature and importance of these factors through time, the study of past trade patterns is divided into four periods: Colonialism (1500-1820); Integration into World Markets (1820-1914); World Wars and Depression (1915-1945); Postwar Years and Institutionalized Economic Development (1946-1963).

Colonialism: 1500-1820

Columbus' epic discoveries touched off a great wave of exploration in the New World. In Latin America this exploration was dominated by Spain, the principal exception being Portugal with her activity in Brazil.

During the second half of the fifteenth century there had occurred great improvements in the science of navigation and in the technology of ships. The increased ability to move men and cargo great distances

7

by sea permitted Spain and Portugal to maintain control over their newly acquired lands.

The spearhead of Spanish conquest was formed by men who were recently released from Spain's war of unification and the expulsion of the Moors. Imbued with a spirit of adventure, aggressiveness, and religious zeal, these men sought fame and fortune. They succeeded at first by taking the gold and silver treasures of the Indians and later by mining these precious metals.

(The early trading patterns of Spanish Latin America developed around the transfer of gold and silver to Spain. Inland trails were constructed for the movement of these metals to places where they could be loaded aboard ships and sent to the mother country. Soon the Indian treasures were depleted, and the central activity of the new regions became mining. Port facilities were built and trails improved to expedite the shipment of gold and silver to the ports and of supplies to the mines.) Near the mines land was cultivated to provide food for the miners and other workers at the mine sites. Thus the main internal trade resulted from supplying the local mines. With the exception of this ancillary activity, all trade was directed to or came from Spain.

Except for occasional itinerant traders and government officials, little direct connection existed among the centers of population clustered around the various mine sites. There seemed to be little possibility of trade among these centers because of the difficult terrain which often separated them and because of their parallel activities.

Formalizing administrative control from Spain resulted first in establishment of two Viceroyalties: New Spain, which extended from the Panamanian Isthmus northward; and Peru, which went from the Isthmus southward. Later two additional Viceroyalties were formed: New Granada, which included the territory occupied today by Venezuela, Colombia, and Ecuador; and La Plata, which in general covered present-day Argentina, Bolivia, Paraguay, and Uruguay.

Great power was vested in the viceroys, the royally appointed administrators of the Viceroyalties, who could regulate trade within each of their jurisdictions. Often shipments into and out of a Viceroyalty were required to pass through a specific port. This gave rise to extensive transshipment which inhibited more direct flows of trade but succeeded in maintaining the importance of the specified port and any nearby administrative center, such as Callao-Lima. Thus the former trade routes—from the mines, to the nearest seaport, and on to Spain—were often diverted through a few officially sanctioned ports.

A flagrant example of the inefficiency resulting from such practice is illustrated by the trade route required for moving merchandise between Spain and Buenos Aires. Commodities from Spain were first sent to Panama, where they were transshipped across the Isthmus and then loaded on vessels for Callao-Lima. From Lima the commodities were transported by tortuous trails over the rugged Andes into Argentina, arriving finally at Buenos Aires.[1] This situation, which persisted until 1620, was an extension on a more localized basis of the mercantilist system which was applied with vigor by Spain and Portugal to their New World dependencies.

Initially, Portugal exhibited relatively little interest in exploiting her newly discovered land of Brazil.[2] The first commercial activities involved obtaining dyewood for Europe's expanding textile industry. Later, under threat of French and Spanish incursions into her Latin American possession, Portugal undertook to colonize and consolidate this vast holding. Because of the primacy of sea transportation, settlements were founded along the coast by the Portuguese, who developed an agricultural economy. Trading patterns developed in a fashion similar to those in Spanish America with Portugal attempting to control the flow of goods related to her colonial conquests. Apparently there was greater freedom of movement for commodities among the Brazilian ports than among the ports of Spanish Latin America.

Portugal and Spain tried to exercise full monopolistic control over the trade and other principal economic activities of their Latin American possessions. In keeping with mercantilistic principles of trade, precious metals and raw materials were to flow to the mother countries in exchange for goods such as manufactured products and foodstuffs which were either produced in the mother countries or imported through them before being sent to the colonies.

Local industry in the mother countries was favored by preferential taxes and subsidies.[3] Imports into Spain and Portugal for reshipment

---

[1] Herman G. James and Percy A. Martin, *The Republics of Latin America* (Harper and Brothers, 1923), p. 51.

[2] Hubert Herring, *A History of Latin America*, Second Edition (Alfred A. Knopf, 1962) , p. 219.

[3] William Spence Robertson, *History of Latin American Nations*, Third Edition (D. Appleton-Century Company, 1943), p. 126.

to their American colonies were subject to high taxes and quantitative restrictions in order to encourage the colonists to buy goods produced in their mother countries. Furthermore, colonial production of commodities competing with the products of Spain and Portugal was controlled, restricted, and sometimes prohibited.[4]

Some trade control also took place within Spain. For many years all Spanish trade to Latin America was required to pass through Seville. Later when the Guadalquivir River became too silted to allow passage of large ships, this privileged position was transferred to Cadiz.

The granting of such a special favor to one city is indicative of the philosophy which was associated with control of Latin America by Spain. The king of Spain, not the country of Spain, owned Spanish America. Conquests were made in the name of and for the crown. Thus the king could favor one Spanish city over others by granting privileges associated with his "personal property." Of course, channeling all commerce to Latin America through one city made it easier for the Spanish crown to control the trade.

As the treasure from the west poured into Spain, there was a rapid rise in internal prices which in turn was transferred to the colonists through the goods they purchased from abroad.[5] In addition, Spanish workmanship and output apparently fell so that the quality and quantity of Spanish goods going to Latin America declined.[6] These factors increased the attractiveness of goods from other European countries. Legally, these other goods could be sent to Latin America only through Spain, and they were subject to higher taxes.

It was therefore not surprising that an extensive contraband trade took place between Latin American colonists and aggressive traders from northern Europe. At first, the most important form of contraband trade involved transshipment at sea. Only Spanish ships, registered for the purpose, were permitted to provide transportation between Spanish America and the mother country. It became common practice for outward bound Spanish ships, when sailing alone or in small groups, to be met at sea by merchant ships from England, Holland,

---

[4] Robertson, *op. cit.*, p. 124.

[5] Earl J. Hamilton, *American Treasure and the Price Revolution in Spain* (Harvard University Press, 1934), pp. 189, 215, 271, 390-2. For example, the price of grains increased thirteenfold between 1504 and 1650.

[6] Herring, *op. cit.*, p. 203.

or France. By previous agreement, goods were transferred illegally to the Spanish ships for entry into Latin America. Homeward bound, the Spanish ships would meet the other ships and repay or sell clandestinely gold, silver, and sometimes other products from Latin America. By this method Spanish taxes could be avoided and much profit, otherwise destined for the Spanish crown, went to the merchants instead.

Dutch islands off the coast of Venezuela and English possessions in the Caribbean, notably Jamaica, were used as entrepôts for smuggling commodities to Spanish America on a large scale. The town of Colonia, when controlled by the Portuguese, became an important commercial center solely because of the extensive smuggling from there across the river to Buenos Aires.

Widespread circumvention of laws regulating trade in Spanish and Portuguese America was possible only with the connivance, or at least acquiescence, of most of the colonists and many government administrators. As a result of this long-continued practice public respect for official regulations and authority became severely weakened.[7]

Not only did Spain lose wealth from Latin America through contraband, but she also incurred considerable losses from pirating. She attempted to check these illicit drains on her wealth by organizing a system of convoys and trade fairs.[8] When the system became operative, there were usually two fleets a year. Each fleet was composed of many merchant ships protected and controlled by numerous warships. One fleet stopped first in Havana and then went to Vera Cruz to supply the Viceroyalty of New Spain. The second fleet went first to Cartagena and then to Porto Bello on the Isthmus of Panama. At each stop giant trade fairs were held which formed the basic method of exchange between Spanish America and Europe. Consolidation at a few points of almost all commodities to be traded (legally) between these two areas of the world facilitated government control and collection of taxes. Among these fairs the most important was at Porto Bello, where the exports from almost all of Spanish-controlled South America were assembled for shipment to Spain in exchange for all imports into that region. On their return voyages, the two fleets joined at Havana and sailed for home together.

[7] James and Martin, *op. cit.*, p. 54.
[8] Herring, *op. cit.*, p. 205.

In 1700 the Hapsburgs were replaced by the Bourbon dynasty in Spain, and the new rulers relaxed the monopolistic control over colonial trade. The fleet and fair system was ended, taxation on trade and special privileges for a few ports reduced, and freer trading within the Spanish empire permitted.

Trading regulations for Brazil were never as resolutely administered and enforced by Portugal as were such regulations for Spain's American dependencies. For both sections of Latin America, however, there existed the same philosophy: the colonies were to be used for the enrichment of the mother countries or crowns and trading regulations were to be shaped accordingly. Brazil, to a much greater extent than Spanish America, was exposed to the influences of trading with the major European countries. Portugal, lacking the military might of Spain, had a difficult time maintaining her possession of Brazil.[9] Ostensibly all Brazilian trade was a monopoly of Portugal. However, England, Holland, France, and Spain exercised—through their domination of Portugal or occupation of areas in Brazil—considerable control over Brazil's trade during much of the colonial period.[10] Again, this control was employed in conformance with the mercantilistic notions of that period.

In the early part of the 1800's, Spanish economic oppression gave rise to great political unrest throughout Latin America. At the same time, the machinations of Napoleon on the Iberian Peninsula caused leadership in Spain and Portugal to become confused, vacillating, and diffused. Because the various factions within each of these two countries were preoccupied with the struggle for internal power, the centrally directed administration of the colonies became lax and ineffectual. The time was propitious for the discontented colonists to act. A series of revolutions erupted, and by 1825 the political connections of Spain and Portugal with their possessions in the continental Western Hemisphere had been severed.

[9] Upon regaining independence from Spain in 1640, Portugal, in an extremely weak position, signed treaties with England in 1642, 1654, and 1661 in order to protect her colonies from the Dutch. Thus Portugal retained possession of Brazil; however, British merchants secured freedom of trade with Portuguese colonies and control over customs duties on merchandise imported from England.

[10] For example, the noted Prime Minister of Portugal, the Marques de Pombal, stated that during his time "all the acts of the government were regulated in accordance with the desires of England." Taken from C. Furtado, *The Economic Growth of Brazil* (University of California Press, 1963), p. 37.

Of the several reasons why most of the politically literate population in Latin America sought freedom from the control of Spain or Portugal, one of the most important was economic.[11] Colonial trading regulations were designed to benefit the mother countries, that is, the rulers. Compliance with these regulations usually worked to the economic detriment of the colonists who were frustrated by their inability to utilize legally the many advantageous trading opportunities which the regulations prohibited.

Widespread illegal trading activities persisted through the years. This continuation and extension of contraband trade (with the obvious connivance of many officials) probably reduced the social and political onus attached to persons engaging in such activities. Today smuggling exists on a large scale in many Latin American countries. The customs and mores which were developed in colonial times regarding compliance with official trade control may account for this present circumvention of government restrictions on foreign trade.

The early and persistent focus of Latin American trade on the outside world did much to establish and perpetuate the principal patterns of trade routes and commercial facilities which are to be found today in Latin American countries. These patterns, which in part were formed through administrative prohibitions on intracolonial trade, are still oriented away from intra-Latin American trade. This orientation has been strengthened by the heavy reliance on ships to move cargo and the often arduous task of land transport between countries.

Integration into World Markets: 1820-1914

Freedom from Spain completed the depolarization of trade begun by the Bourbon reforms. Latin America turned to Western Europe and the United States for markets for its mineral and agricultural output and for sources of imports of manufactured goods. As in colonial times, the development of the regions, now nations, depended largely on the possession or production of commodities important in

[11] Samuel Guy Inman, *Latin America—Its Place in World Life,* Revised Edition (Harcourt, Brace and Company, 1942) , p. 73; James and Martin, *op. cit.,* p. 80; Herring, *op. cit.,* p. 244.

the export sector. The combination of foreign interests with those of powerful local groups shaped the pattern of trade and development in this period. In most instances, economic efforts in any direction bore fruit only if they did not conflict with the interests of the "ruling" class.

At the time of independence, this ruling class was made up of *hacendados* (large landowners) and merchants. As the century wore on, new elites emerged who gained political as well as economic control in most countries. This type of national development subordinated national interest to the interest of a single group. In most cases, the relationship of the power elite with foreign economies was extremely significant. These relationships determined trade patterns for the next century, for in no Latin American country did a group in favor of internally oriented markets emerge victorious. As a result, countries came to rely on externally financed investment, and national development was controlled largely by foreign powers whose interests were almost entirely in the foreign trade sector. Transport facilities were designed to bring export goods to market rather than promote internal trade. Except for Paraguay, the markets were chiefly in Europe and the United States; intra-Latin American trade, as a result, was minimal.

Several examples illustrate the way in which trade patterns were formed in Latin America during this period.

In Argentina, the conflict for economic power was represented by the fifty-year struggle between the provinces of the interior and Buenos Aires. With independence, long sought after by Buenos Aires to free itself from the domination of the Lima merchants, the traditional route from the interior industrial centers of Tucumán, Córdoba, and Mendoza to the altiplano of Bolivia and then to Lima disappeared in favor of the cheaper transportation to Buenos Aires. Given the competition of manufactures from northern Europe, these industrial cities could not readily compete in the domestic market without some form of protection.

"Moreover, whatever intercourse developed between the Interior and Buenos Aires, its terms were necessarily more advantageous to the latter. Both as a consumer of the produce and manufactures of the Interior, and as an intermediary in the flow of commerce between the Interior and foreign commerce, Buenos Aires enjoyed a semi-monopolistic position. Far from being dependent on the Interior for the supply of commodities such as wine, coarse textiles, hard leather, sugar, etc., Buenos Aires could easily obtain these goods in European and American markets, and at prices that compared favorably with those demanded by domestic producers. And on the other hand, the Interior had no direct commercial contact with foreign countries, except through the port of Buenos Aires. (Foreign trade, it is true, could be carried on through Chile and Peru, and in fact some provinces [Mendoza, Tucumán] did occasionally use these routes. High costs of transportation, however, seriously hampered the development of trade through these channels.)"[12]

Interior industries were clearly under a serious handicap. Communication over inland routes was costly and difficult; in the 1820's, the cost per ton-league between Salta (Argentina) and Chuquisaca (Bolivia) was 1.2 pesos silver; from Mendoza across the Andes to Chile, 0.3 pesos silver; from Buenos Aires to Salta, the average rate was 0.4 pesos silver. At the same time, the cost of transportation by water between Buenos Aires and European ports averaged 0.006 pesos silver per ton-league.[13] Assuming that the cost between European ports and Buenos Aires per ton-league was equal to the cost to Valparaiso, this means that the total cost per ton between Antwerp and Valparaiso was 17.7 pesos and 24 pesos between Mendoza and Santiago.[14] If industry had flourished in the interior for any extended length of time during this formative period,[15] it is probable that with the advent of the railroad, commerce within Argentina and between Argentina and its neighbors would have become substantial. As it occurred, the development of Argentina was subordinated to the development of the province of Buenos Aires, and that province was under the control of exporters of, first, hides and later beef and hides. The extent of their control was so strong that grain growers even in the province of Buenos Aires found it difficult to secure protection for their products.

[12] Miron Burgin, *The Economic Aspects of Argentine Federalism* (Harvard University Press, 1946), p. 19.

[13] *Ibid.*, p. 117.

[14] In addition, each country had import and export duties. Many provincial governments imposed taxes on goods in transit through their territories. These duties increased the cost of overland trade.

[15] Interior interests did manage to secure a protective tariff in 1835, but the French blockade of the Rio de la Plata in 1838 to protect its trading interests caused that tariff to be replaced by a new revenue tariff law in 1841. Under the protective tariff, Interior industry expanded rapidly, but not rapidly enough to supply national demand during the blockade.

With unification, the second half of the century brought a decline in the influence of the *hacendados* and an expansion of agriculture, meat production (the first refrigerator ship crossed the Atlantic in 1876) and, after 1880, the rise of industry to produce for a greatly increased local demand.[16] By the turn of the century, Argentina had reached a position as one of the most highly "developed" nations of the world, its wealth largely the product of a primary goods export sector.

After a period of isolation in the 1820's and 30's, Paraguay gradually became subordinated to Buenos Aires because that port controlled river traffic. In 1864, Paraguay entered into a war with Argentina, Uruguay, and Brazil. The conflict was disastrous for Paraguay in that she lost almost her entire male population, as well as considerable territory. Argentina completed her domination of the Paraguayan economy: Argentines gained control of landholdings and the commerce to the outside world, especially to Argentina herself. Three-fourths of all foreign investment in Paraguay today is Argentine.[17] As explained in Chapter III, this factor has made Paraguay, relative to her total foreign trade, the largest trader with Latin America; of her exports to Latin America, 75 percent goes to Argentina.[18]

The Pacific west coast countries, Chile and Peru, as well as Bolivia, mountainous and difficult to cultivate, were primarily mineral exporters. Trade boomed for Chile in the 1830's and 40's, and Valparaiso overtook Callao as the principal port of the west coast. Competition among the three countries in mineral exports was strong, and it was one of the factors underlying the two wars between independence and the end of the century: Chile-Peru in 1836 and Chile against Peru and Bolivia in 1879. This second conflict left Chile the victor in the bitter struggle over the control of the nitrate deposits in the provinces of Antofagasta and Tarapacá. Bolivia was left without access to the sea until 1904, when Chile signed a treaty with her to make Arica a free port and to build a railroad from Arica to La Paz. Peru lost Tarapacá and the prosperity which preceded the war. Peru's recovery was slow,

---

[16] The most profound effect was wrought by a flood of immigrants after 1860. Most of these immigrants became farmers.

[17] Hubert Herring, *op. cit.,* p. 710.

[18] See Chapter III, p. 53, and Table VII.

and the finances of the government fell drastically through the curtailment of nitrate revenue.[19]

> "Chile, her territory enlarged, entered upon an era of unequaled prosperity from the sale of nitrates, copper, and other minerals. Nitrates alone furnished the major share of her national budget requirements for forty years—as much as 68 percent in the 1890's."[20]

In the 1880's British and German investors backed nitrate companies in both Chile and Peru. In Chile, the wealth that the mines brought to the country itself took some of the power from the hands of the large landowners and gave it to a new plutocracy, rich from the export of minerals. The influence of this new group did not wane until after World War I, when the invention of synthetics plunged the nitrate industry into a persistent decline.

As Chile became heavily dependent on its minerals and foreign markets for national income and government revenues, Peru lost much of its mineral wealth and became primarily an agricultural exporter. Peru's economy is still controlled mainly by owners of large holdings of agricultural land. The Pacific War (1879-1883) also increased British influence in the economy. A British corporation took over the Peruvian railroad system and the Lake Titicaca steamship line in 1890, in return for the assumption of the entire external debt of Peru.[21]

Brazil's declaration of independence in 1822 merely transferred the seat of Portuguese government from Lisbon to Rio de Janeiro. Stringent international agreements maintained Brazil's commitments to England, however, and Brazil was an economic satellite of the British for almost the entire century. Ultimately the strength to break with England came largely from a shift in trade to the United States through the rapidly expanding production of coffee.[22]

No merchant class grew up in Brazil during the colonial period be-

[19] In addition, the guano deposits, which had been one of Peru's principal exports and a government monopoly, were depleted. See Jonathan V. Levin, *The Export Economies* (Harvard University Press, 1960), pp. 108-12.

[20] Herring, *op. cit.*, p. 586. The nitrate deposits that Peru lost might have turned out to be an important stimulus for diversification, while Chile's efforts in this direction were dampened by the nitrate boom.

[21] Herring, *op. cit.*, p. 543.

[22] Furtado, *op. cit.*, p. 39.

cause of the strict monopoly of the mother country; as a result, the power after independence lay with the great agricultural landlords. After 1831, the landlords prevailed in their desire for freedom of trade. Free trade, of course, was consistent with British interests, but the British policy of actively abolishing the slave trade to Brazil brought about a conflict of interests. Eventually the British imposed their will through their naval strength. Sugar production suffered as a result of both the rise in labor costs and the development of sugar beets in Europe and cane sugar in Cuba. Cotton went into a similarly depressed condition.

At the same time that the production of sugar and cotton was falling, the rise of coffee replaced them. The tremendous increase in coffee production in the fifty years after 1820 created a new elite: the coffee entrepreneurs. These entrepreneurs came to control Brazil's economy and political institutions: by the turn of the century, they were producing 75 percent of the world's coffee. The first voice against the colonial economy and for protective tariffs was heard in this new merchant-entrepreneur class. The Baron de Maua was convinced that Brazil must consume more of its own goods; he advocated the building of farm-to-city railroads and expansion of domestic industry, but he faced continual opposition to his programs from landholders and British merchants.[23]

After 1900, coffee prices began to fall, and an association organized by the coffee planters turned to limiting the size of the crop to maximize revenues. In general, this policy was successful. The other great Brazilian crop, rubber, could not be saved, however. Although Brazil provided 90 percent of the world's rubber by 1900, the first shipments in 1899 of plantation rubber from the Dutch and British East Indies signaled the end of Brazilian domination. By 1921, Brazil had only 10 percent of the market.

The development of trade between the United States and Mexico and the increasing influence of North America in the political and economic affairs of the Caribbean area further illustrate the point that the nineteenth century and first fifteen years of the twentieth century saw an extension of trade into externally oriented patterns whose bases

[23] Herring, *op. cit.*, p. 738.

were developed in the prerevolutionary period. Buenos Aires, Rio de Janeiro, Valparaiso, Callao, and Barranquilla emerged as great centers of trade from which nations prospered or fell into depression. Trade was directed to the manufacturing centers of North America and Europe. In effect, the parallel development of the Latin American countries in supplying raw materials to rapidly expanding industrial economies in other areas precluded trade among themselves, just as such trade had been precluded among the mining centers of the sixteenth century.

Nevertheless, external trade did bring growth and prosperity in the last decades before the First World War, even though such prosperity remained in the hands of a few. The volume of trade increased in this period,[24] further committing most countries to their export sectors. The advent of World War I and the postwar years catalyzed a change in trade that had already begun to take place: the United States replaced Europe as Latin America's primary trading partner.

World Wars and Depression: 1915-1945

World War I found most Latin American nations with the greatest volume of foreign trade in their history. The initial effect of the war was to decrease this trade through an increase in shipping risks. After 1915, however, the rise in demand by the Allies for nitrates, copper, and especially foodstuffs brought about large increases in exports. Although falling prices of rubber and coffee continued to hurt Brazil's trade, prosperity came by the end of the war through a shift to foodstuffs. Mexico was in the midst of a revolution; her trade did not return to normal until 1920. Latin American economies which had depended on European industries for imports were forced to begin producing some import substitutes, and local industry expanded.

The pattern of trade was altered. Great Britain, Germany, and France lost ground to the United States in Latin America which they were never again to recover completely, even during the Depression.[25] Table A shows the percentage distribution of trade from 1910 to 1941.

[24] United Nations, Economic Commission for Latin America (ECLA), *Economic Survey of Latin America, 1949* (1951), pp. 90, 211, 271, 408.
[25] For data on recent years, see Table II-b.

TABLE A. *The Share of Principal Trading Countries in the Imports and Exports of Latin America, Selected Years, 1910–1941*

Percent of the Aggregate Value of Imports into Latin America by Source

Exporting Country	1910	1913	1917	1920	1929	1933	1938	1941
U.S.A............	22.6	25.0	54.0	50.2	38.7	29.2	33.4	62.4
United Kingdom..	25.0	24.4	14.9	16.7	14.9	18.1	12.5	7.8
France...........	8.0	8.3	3.7	4.8	5.1	4.9	3.3	0.1
Germany.........	14.9	16.6	—	3.4	10.8	11.5	16.2	0.5
Italy............	4.9	5.0	—	—	—	—	3.0	0.1
Japan...........	0.1	0.1	—	—	—	1.8	2.6	2.6

Percent of the Aggregate Value of Exports from Latin America by Destination

Importing Country	1910	1913	1917	1920	1929	1933	1938	1941
U.S.A............	33.8	30.8	51.7	47.7	34.0	29.4	33.2	54.0
United Kingdom..	20.5	21.2	21.0	17.9	18.5	22.1	18.6	13.1
France...........	8.4	8.0	8.0	5.3	6.2	6.2	4.1	0.1
Germany.........	10.9	12.4	—	1.8	8.1	6.9	10.4	0.3
Italy............	1.2	2.0	—	—	—	—	1.6	0.02
Japan...........	0.1	0.1	—	—	—	0.3	1.3	2.7

Source: Richard F. Behrendt, *Inter-American Economic Relations* (The Committee on International Economic Policy, 1948), p. 13.

"It is evident how Latin America's trade with the belligerent countries of Europe was affected by two world wars, particularly as far as imports were concerned; and how in both cases the United States made large gains. These gains, however, were largely lost after the First World War, although this is true more with respect to United States purchases from Latin America than with respect to her sales to that region. The latter were, of course, favored by the tremendous development of United States industrial production in the 1920's which placed this country practically beyond the reach of European competition in a number of manufactured articles."[26]

The transition from a warring to a peacetime Europe brought little change in the quantity of exports of most Latin American countries. A notable exception was Chile. The sharp decrease in demand for the

[26] Richard F. Behrendt, *Inter-American Economic Relations* (The Committee on International Economic Policy, 1948), p. 13.

articles of war decreased Chilean sales of copper and nitrates; grave unemployment problems followed the war. During the 1920's, however, Chile recovered from these difficulties despite the fall in nitrate demand, and exports increased steadily to the end of the decade. Some of this increase was due to extensive loans to Chile as part of a general increase in lending to Latin American countries by the United States.

In Brazil, foreign loans served as a basis for expanding the money supply to provide the necessary funds to buy coffee and withhold it from the market.[27] Although Peru was enjoying a substantial export surplus in these years, the loans temporarily relieved exchange difficulties from the servicing of Peru's increased debt. The servicing of this municipal and federal debt, plus the transfer of earnings of foreign capital invested in the country, were offsetting the favorable commodity trade balance.[28]

The period preceding the Great Depression gave little reason for Latin American trade patterns to change. Except for the few years of import difficulties during the war, economies remained dependent on their export sectors for the foreign exchange to fill internal consumer demand with imported goods.

Dependence on the export-import sector decreased after 1929. During the crisis, both the quantity and prices of raw materials exported fell dramatically with the sharp curtailment of aggregate demand in the industrial economies (see Table B). Latin American countries reacted to this situation with measures that they hoped would make them less reliant on external demand in the future. They turned their economies inward in an effort to save foreign exchange. In general, these measures resulted in import-substituting industrialization in many Latin American countries and permitted a recovery to 1929 levels of national income by the end of the 1930's. Yet Latin America remained dependent on raw material exports, now not for consumer goods imports but for capital and intermediate goods for her growing industrial plant. The repercussions on future trade patterns were so important that it would be well to examine in detail some of the specific measures that these countries took to avert the disastrous turn of events in their trade.

[27] Furtado, *op. cit.*, p. 201.
[28] American Bankers Association, *The South American West Coast* (1925).

TABLE B. *Latin America: Population, Exports, and Capacity to Import, 1929–1939*
(1937 = 100)

Year	Population (millions)	Quantum Index of Exports		Price Index		Index of Capacity to Import[a]	
		Total	Per Capita	Export	Import	Total	Per Capita
1929	104.3	108.7	124.1	113.2	117.0	105.1	120.0
1930	105.9	90.4	101.6	90.2	113.0	72.1	81.0
1931	107.4	98.1	108.6	61.6	95.0	63.6	70.4
1932	109.3	82.0	89.3	53.4	76.0	57.6	62.7
1933	111.0	84.7	90.8	57.8	80.0	61.2	65.6
1934	112.8	85.6	90.3	81.5	91.0	76.7	80.9
1935	114.9	93.8	97.1	77.6	92.0	79.1	81.9
1936	117.2	90.3	91.7	87.6	94.0	84.2	85.5
1937	119.0	100.0	100.0	100.0	100.0	100.0	100.0
1938	121.6	91.1	89.1	83.4	99.0	76.7	75.0
1939	124.3	97.0	92.9	81.5	99.0	79.8	76.4

Source: United Nations, Economic Commission for Latin America, *Economic Survey of Latin America, 1949* (1951), p. 17.

[a] Represents the quantum index of exports multiplied by the ratio of the index of export prices to the index of import prices.

Brazil maintained high levels of employment by forsaking the convertibility of the gold standard[29] and through a policy of supporting coffee prices. Total revenue and employment in the coffee export sector was maintained by the Brazilian government's purchasing of all coffee at a given price. Because of Brazil's dominant position she was able to sell part of her production of coffee abroad at the support price. The part of the crop which could not be sold was destroyed.

> "The reduction in monetary income in Brazil between 1929 and the rock-bottom point of the depression was between 25 and 30 percent, hence relatively small compared with that in other countries. In the United States, for instance, the fall exceeded 50 percent, despite the fact that wholesale price indices in that country declined far less than those of coffee prices in international trade. The difference lies in the fact that in the United States price declines entailed an enormous amount of unemployment, whereas in Brazil

[29] In the last quarter of 1929, Brazil's entire metallic reserve disappeared with the foreign capital fleeing the country. Brazil was essentially forced to abandon the gold standard and turn to a floating exchange rate.

employment levels were maintained despite the fact that production had to be destroyed . . . It is therefore quite clear that the recovery of the Brazilian economy which took place from 1933 onward was not unconsciously adopted in Brazil as a by-product of the protection of the coffee interests."[30]

With the fall in coffee prices and outflow of capital in 1929 and 1930, Brazil's foreign exchange situation worsened considerably. The disequilibrium in the trade sector was corrected by abandoning the gold standard and allowing Brazilian currency to drop in value. This raised the prices of imports relative to domestic goods. The rise in import prices coupled with the maintenance of income level increased demand for domestically produced goods, especially import substitutes. Therefore,

". . . the existence of idle capacity in some of the industries serving the domestic market, and the fact that Brazil already had a small nucleus of capital goods industries—accounts for the rapid growth in industrial production. That growing production came to be the main dynamic factor involved in the process of income generation."[31]

At the end of the 1930's the opposite effect occurred and the positive balance of payments raised the value of Brazilian currency. In order to protect domestic industries and because coffee prices to growers were fixed to protect the coffee sector, Brazil fixed the exchange rate of its currency at the level which reflected the relative prices of imports and domestic goods in the earlier years of the decade. The fixing of the exchange rate and exchange controls combined with the effects of World War II to create rapid inflation. The flow of income from exports continued to grow throughout the war; at the same time, imports were cut off, partly by the war and partly by the exchange controls. The government was distributing larger wage and salary payments through war spending and simultaneously reducing part of the national product necessary to meet consumer demand. No measures were taken to curtail private expenditures, such as selling savings certificates, increasing taxation, or rationing scarce goods. Most im-

[30] Furtado, *op. cit.*, pp. 211-12. The high price of coffee drew other producers into the market and increased the amount of coffee Brazil had to destroy. By 1937, she was forced to abandon attempts at price support.

[31] *Ibid.*, p. 222.

portant, however, was that Brazil, unlike many countries, was already at productive capacity when the war broke out in 1939. Her per capita income had increased during the 1930's. In more developed countries the initial years of war provided an opportunity for governments to ready themselves to control an inflationary situation, but Brazil was in it at the outset. Domestic prices rose 98 percent between 1939 and 1944.

In Argentina, the Depression dropped the average prices for exports approximately 4 percent between 1929 and 1933.[32] The value of beef sales on the continent had fallen by one-third between 1924 and 1930, and substituting the U.S. market was not possible. Of course, U.S. demand fell during those years; and, furthermore, the United States raised tariffs in 1930 and prohibited entry of Argentine meat to prevent the possible spread of hoof-and-mouth disease.[33]

In 1930, packers were asked by the Argentine government to maintain prices on "chillers" bought from the cattle raisers. Although this "fixed" price varied over the next several years, it was above the market equilibrium. The effect of this and other price-fixing measures was similar to that in the Brazilian case—they were a form of subsidy which resulted in keeping domestic agricultural incomes from falling. At the same time, of course, it was necessary to invoke exchange controls and to devalue the currency in order to maintain equilibrium in a foreign trade sector marked by rapidly falling prices. Argentina differed from Brazil, however, in that Argentina maintained service on foreign loans; this encouraged foreign investment in the late 1930's, especially by the British.

Argentina was also in a rather special position in that Britain was such a predominant buyer of her exports. When the British decided to encourage commonwealth raw material production in 1932, and therefore to cut the purchase of Argentine beef, Argentina signed a rigid bilateral trade agreement with Britain (the Roca-Runciman Pact) "reminiscent of Spanish colonial mercantilism of the sixteenth century . . . Britain pledged herself not to reduce her purchases of chilled beef below the level of 1932, and Argentina reciprocated by

[32] United Nations, ECLA, *Economic Survey of Latin America, 1949* (1951), p. 98.
[33] Simon G. Hanson, *Argentine Meat and the British Market* (Stanford University Press, 1938), p. 259.

promising that money earned by such sales would be spent on British goods."[34]

The west coast economies of Peru and Chile were among the hardest hit by the Depression. Chile's trade declined relatively more than that of any other nation in the world in the years 1929-1932: mineral production in 1932 was one-half, income from nitrates one-twentieth, and export revenue down 82 percent from the 1927 figures.[35] The government defaulted on its bonds. Chile followed the path of subsidies and tax exemptions to raise domestic employment and controlled imports through restrictions and foreign exchange controls. Although initially the peso fell sharply, it was revalued by the end of the decade. By 1939, the national budget was balanced, but this did not include any provision for the service on foreign debt. About 25 percent of foreign bonds were redeemed, however. With import restrictions, Chile's domestic industry expanded greatly again, especially in import substitutes.

An additional feature of the recovery which was in direct contrast to the Argentine case was the nationalization of several foreign-owned utilities. The government bought the Trans-Andean Railroad from the British, and, without assuming ownership, took control of the American and Foreign Power Corporation and the firms engaged in the export of nitrates. During the Popular Front Administration (1938-41), government intervention was increased by the chartering in 1939 of the Corporación de Fomento for the promotion of industry, mining, fishing, and agriculture. Substantial funds for specific projects came from the Export-Import Bank. Industrial output of chemicals, metals, and textiles increased, as well as the catch of fish and production of agricultural goods. During World War II, Fomento was greatly expanded by further loans from the Bank and the U.S. Government.[36]

Peru's loss of export earnings, though not as great as Chile's, was more disastrous in a sense. It was not followed by a rapid recovery in the late 1930's nor did it prompt a great expansion of internal development in the 1940's and 1950's. This is largely a matter of degree, but an important degree nonetheless. Domestic industry did get an incen-

[34] Herring, *op. cit.*, p. 672.
[35] United Nations, ECLA, *op. cit.*, pp. 272, 287.
[36] *Ibid.*, pp. 595-600.

tive from the developments of the 1930's; however, the capacity to develop in Peru was seriously limited by political control by a small group and lack of trained manpower.

"The 1930-32 depression lent added emphasis to the trend toward stabilization and decline of Peruvian exports since the country suffered one of the heaviest losses in exports of any of the Latin American countries. The total value of exports dropped from 134 million dollars in 1929 to only 38 million in 1932, 28 percent of the 1929 level. This loss was due primarily to a drastic decrease in export prices. Average dollar prices of exports in 1932 were only 46 percent of the 1929 level while the volume of exports dropped to 76 percent.

"Even though imports also decreased, dropping from 76 million dollars in 1929 to only 16 million in 1932 (an 80 percent decrease), the depression created a difficult balance-of-payments situation. Together with the drop in the commercial balance, two other factors also exerted a negative influence on the availability of foreign exchange: a complete stoppage in the flow of foreign credits which in years past had provided an extremely important source of foreign currency, and, on the other hand, the necessity of maintaining the servicing of the foreign debt."[37]

Without going through the experience of all the countries of Latin America in the 1930's and 1940's, it is possible to make certain general conclusions about the crisis and the policies undertaken and their effects on the pattern and quantity of trade.

It is clear that the slump in the external sector, accompanied as it was by net outflows of capital and a great fall in export prices relative to import prices, brought Latin American governments into the market place to attempt to raise severely reduced national incomes. These efforts, in turn, resulted in a stimulation of domestic, import-substituting industries, and, in Mexico and Chile, the nationalization of foreign-owned industries. The measures gave expression to an increased nationalism which was reflected not only in a growing antagonism toward the United States and Great Britain, but in two wars between Latin American nations themselves: the Chaco War (1932-1935) between Bolivia and Paraguay, and an armed dispute

[37] Pan American Union, *The Peruvian Economy* (1950), p. 220. (There seems to be a discrepancy between the percent drop in prices and volume of exports and the percent drop in value of exports in this source: 0.46 times 0.76 equals 0.35 rather than the 0.28 cited.)

(1942) between Peru and Ecuador in which Peru was awarded lands in the Amazon basin.[38]

The inflations now plaguing many of the economies of South America had their origins in the recovery from the Depression of the thirties and the policies pursued during the period. The recovery was largely based on measures fostering industrialization through import substitution. Then came World War II and a large increase in the value of exports to the United States. At the same time imports from the United States and other countries were severely limited because of the demands of war on the output of industrial nations, submarine warfare, and devalued currencies and other import restrictions. The inflation which followed seemed inevitable. Domestic industry, relying on capital imports and increases in the supply of skilled labor for expansion, could neither raise output nor change rapidly enough to meet increased incomes and the changing composition of demand.

European markets were cut off from Latin America by occupation of continental countries and by the diversion of British and other merchant marines to the war effort. This situation gave an increased percentage of Latin American trade to the United States (see Table A). But many groups in Latin America were not at all pleased by the rise in trade during the war. The fall in export earnings after the crash of 1929 and the repercussions in the domestic sector seemed to be indelible in the minds of nationalists. This feeling supplied a paradox: while there was an increase in talk about the necessity of a Latin American common market arrangement which would make Latin America independent of business cycles in the developed countries, there was an even stronger pressure for autonomy on national lines— in other words, the Depression had left its mark so deeply that the turn inward transcended extranational cooperation.

Nevertheless, trade among Latin American countries increased five-fold in current dollars between the average of 1934-38 and the average of 1946-51,[39] and from 9.6 percent of total imports to 11.2 percent and from 5.9 percent of total exports to 9.4 percent[40] (see Table C).

[38] This arbitration result was later not recognized by Ecuador, so that the lands are still disputed.

[39] United Nations, Economic Commission for Latin America, *Study of Inter-Latin American Trade* (1957), p. 122.

[40] *Ibid.*, pp. 19-21.

TABLE C. *Imports from and Exports to Latin America as a Percentage of Imports from and Exports to the World, by Country, 1934–1938 and 1946–1951*

Country	Imports		Exports	
	1934-38	*1946-51*	*1934-38*	*1946-51*
Argentina.........	10.0	15.7	8.7	13.8
Bolivia...........	26.2	38.0	2.5	2.5
Brazil............	15.9	11.3	7.1	11.0
Chile.............	15.2	27.0	4.6	15.1
Colombia.........	2.3	7.0	0.6	1.6
Ecuador..........	7.0	8.7	22.5	27.0
Mexico...........	0.9	1.6	2.3	6.7
Paraguay.........	50.0	42.6	31.0	40.3
Peru.............	11.3	19.9	14.9	33.8
Uruguay..........	17.8	26.3	13.6	7.8
Venezuela........	0.8	5.2	0.7	3.9
Total............	10.7	12.2	6.8	10.4

Source: United Nations, ECLA, *Study of Inter-Latin American Trade* (1957), Tables 7, 10.

The greatest relative increase in the percentage of trade with Latin America in the late thirties and early forties took place in Chile, Mexico, Peru, and Venezuela. Much of the increase in the latter was in petroleum products. The experience of Brazil, Paraguay, and Uruguay was mixed.

Postwar Years and Institutionalized Development: 1946-1963

At the end of World War II, Latin America was considered to be in a relatively strong economic position. The productive processes and manpower of this region had not been ravaged by the war. The products which Latin America had been exporting continued to be in great demand. Foodstuffs were required to feed the millions of people in whose lands normal production had been disrupted. Raw materials were needed for the industries which were being resuscitated.

Aside from facing strong demands for their exports, Latin American countries also had accumulated large reserves of gold and foreign exchange. These reserves were obtained during the war when concentration on production of war materials in industrial centers and lack of shipping deprived Latin Americans of their traditional sources of supply of manufactured imports. Although imports were necessarily reduced in this period, exports flourished (shipping permitting) as the products of Latin America were sought to stoke the industries of war.

The first few years after World War II saw resumption of the prewar orientation of Latin American trade toward North America and Western Europe. During this time there was a wave of importation into Latin America, stemming from the pent-up demand induced by the war. Latin America's gold and foreign exchange reserves were drastically reduced. Many of the foreign exchange reserves still held by Latin American countries were blocked or nonconvertible.[41] As restrictions on the use of these reserves eventually became relaxed, their purchasing power in some instances was reduced through inflation and devaluation. The stock of some capital goods in Latin America which had depreciated during the war had to be replaced at the higher postwar prices.

Fledgling industries in Latin America, which were established during the war and had existed solely through lack of serious competition, soon found that they were incapable of surviving in the competitive markets of the postwar period without government assistance. Latin American governments customarily acceded to the demands of their beleaguered industries for protection. This move toward protectionism coincided with the rise of other areas of the world as major suppliers of products competing with Latin American exports. The spate of intense demand for Latin American exports which immediately followed the end of World War II subsided to a point where world commodity prices could be less controlled by variations in the flow of Latin American exports. Latin America's economic bargaining power weakened considerably.

Upset by this turn of events, the leaders of some Latin American countries sought to recoup the former economic stature of their countries by instigating programs of intensive industrialization, usually predicated on nationalism. Official pronouncements were made proclaiming the need to be "free of foreign economic domination." Through national, controlled industrialization, these countries were to be removed from the "economic rack" on which, supposedly, they

---

[41] Some of these reserves were used at this time by governments in Latin America to purchase foreign-owned enterprises—particularly public utilities—in their own countries.

were being stretched ever tighter by falling prices for their exports and rising prices for their imports.[42]

During the postwar era, waves of social discontent spread over many lands in Latin America. Awareness of rapid economic progress and increased benefits outside the area, gained through new means of mass communication, raised the economic aspirations of Latin Americans and increased their dissatisfaction with existing conditions.

In many Latin American countries the problems of economic development and social unrest were aggravated by rapidly rising populations.[43] Populations were increasing at rates faster than export earnings. In 1946-50, real income per capita in Latin America, on the average, rose by 4.6 percent a year. But from 1955-60 this rate fell to 0.7 percent a year, and in many countries the rates of growth per capita were negative.[44]

Incentives and pressures for economic change increased as the forces, enumerated above, grew in magnitude. Political parties, as never before, became committed to formal programs of economic development, customarily centered on domestic industrialization. Foreign trade, while the mainstay of most economies, was generally held to be inadequate, or at best unreliable, for satisfying the desires for economic progress.

Industrialization was developed on the basis of import substitution. With the introduction of more sophisticated industries, there arose the need for the complex machinery associated with these industries. Thus, not only were there expanding demands for imports of traditional and new consumer commodities (which could only be partly met by the new industrialization) but the process of industrialization itself required large imports. As a result, stricter import and exchange restrictions were applied in an effort to equate uses deemed most essential by the government with export earnings and to promote new industries by restricting competition from abroad.

[42] For a broader expression of this view, see: Hubert Herring, *A History of Latin America, op. cit.,* pp. 388-89, 600, 684.

[43] Death rates in Latin America had dropped sharply through use of new preventive medicines—eliminating or greatly reducing many of the diseases which previously had offset the high birth rates in this area.

[44] United Nations, Economic Commission for Latin America, *The Economic Development of Latin America in the Postwar Period* (1963), Vol. II, Table 6, p. 6.

Many Latin American countries had experienced the conditions and developments just described. Limited international means of payment was a problem common to all of them. To escape such constraints the countries of Latin America endeavored to augment their reserves by banding together under various trading arrangements. Primarily, efforts were made to encourage intra-Latin American trade on bilateral bases.

At first the most common method for stimulating trade between two countries was through use of reciprocal tariff reductions or tariff rebates. However, this method often proved ineffectual because of the necessity for complying with the "most-favored nation" doctrine to which many of the participating countries had subscribed in other trade treaties. For example, eight Latin American countries (Brazil, Chile, Cuba, Dominican Republic, Haiti, Nicaragua, Peru, and Uruguay) were members in 1951 of the General Agreement on Tariffs and Trade (GATT). As members of GATT, these countries generally were required to extend to all GATT countries the same trade privileges they granted to any country.

Given this situation, the same benefits which were devised for promoting trade between two Latin American countries had to be granted to many countries outside of Latin America. In some trade treaties recognition was given to special trading relationships between neighboring countries. According to such a treaty, tariff reductions granted to a neighboring country did not have to be granted to other countries. Under this procedure, some intra-Latin American trade was promoted which otherwise would have been prevented by commitment to the "most-favored nation" doctrine. The foreign exchange resources of Latin American countries were insufficient to withstand the strain of extending freer trade on this broader basis. Therefore, many of the proposed bilateral tariff reductions in Latin America came to nought. Methods were devised for circumventing this impasse through employment of barter agreements, quantitative quotas, special rates of exchange, etc.

Most of the effective bilateral trading arrangements took place among countries of the southern part of Latin America.[45] There are two reasons for this. The countries of southern Latin America apparently

---

[45] Herring, *op. cit.*, p. 119.

possessed less convertible currency than the countries of northern
Latin America (Mexico, Central America, etc.), and trade among the
southern countries had been of relatively greater significance. Although
much of the trade among the countries of the south during the 1950's
was conducted through bilateral agreements, such trade represented
only a small share of the total trade for these countries. This point will
be amplified in Chapter III.

Argentina, in particular, pursued a policy of forming bilateral trading arrangements with a view toward unloading her agricultural
surpluses. For example, in 1953 Argentina agreed to exchange given
quantities of wheat and cattle for given quantities of copper and steel
from Chile. In another instance, Argentina supplied Venezuela with
15,000 tons of frozen meat annually for two years in exchange for two
million barrels of crude petroleum.[46] During the postwar period
Argentina has had bilateral trading agreements of this nature with
most Latin American countries, including all the major ones.[47]

Brazil also has conducted a series of bilateral trading agreements
in Latin America. Of interest is the use by Brazil of bilateral agreements to promote certain long-range trading objectives and to
strengthen trade in manufactured commodities. One such case is the
agreement between Brazil and Bolivia for construction of a railroad
from their common frontier at Corumbá to Santa Cruz, an important
market and distribution center in Bolivia. Construction of this railroad was financed by Brazil with ultimate payment to be made by
Bolivia with exports of petroleum products to Brazil. The railroad
serves as the main link in land transportation between the two countries and permits direct shipment by rail of products from the coast of
Brazil to the heart of Bolivia.

In the years following World War II, many unsuccessful attempts at
forming multilateral trading arrangements within Latin America were
made. Difficulties occurred because of the "most-favored nation" commitments and over use of a clearing mechanism for payments on a
multilateral basis.[48]

[46] United Nations, ECLA, Economic Development of Latin America, *op. cit.*, p. 68.

[47] For a list and brief description of these arrangements, see: United Nations,
ECLA, *Ibid.*, pp. 74-76.

[48] The Havana Charter of 1948, which was to have established the International
Trade Organization, permitted formation of trading regions which could exclude

Efforts were made to form customs unions between Argentina and Chile; between Argentina and Bolivia; and among Venezuela, Panama, Ecuador, and Colombia.

Even before the end of World War II, several attempts had been made at economic integration in South America. In early 1941 a Regional Conference of the La Plata Countries was convened in Montevideo at which a series of agreements were signed by Argentina, Bolivia, Brazil, Paraguay, and Uruguay. These agreements covered the whole gamut of economic relations among the countries, dealing with the fomenting of tourism, international river and road traffic, communications, free trade zones, special tariff treatment for Bolivia and Paraguay, and the study of a customs union.[49] The specific renunciation of the most-favored nation principle was the undoing of the treaty. The United Kingdom and the United States expressed opposition, and the treaty was never ratified by the signatory nations.

Although these movements toward economic integration ended in failure sooner or later, they did succeed in starting a network of communication among the interested leaders and in pointing up the difficulties in such undertakings.

Some efforts to achieve cooperation in specific sectors have met with success. One example which deserves mention is the merchant fleet, Flota Grancolombiana, which is maintained jointly by Colombia and Ecuador.[50] The larger fleet which results from combining the ships of more than one country can provide improved services and increased bargaining power for the owners. Such combinations of shipping lines might afford the financial and political strength needed to promote new trade routes and services within Latin America. Furthermore, this increased strength may also be of importance to Latin America with respect to the international negotiations for setting freight rates in the shipping conferences.

Discussions have been held about the possibility of forming a supra-

---

outside countries from benefit of tariff concessions granted within the region. The Charter was not submitted for ratification in the United States and the United Kingdom.

[49] See "Acta Final de la Conferencia Regional de los Paises de la Plata," Montevideo, February 6, 1941.

[50] Venezuela was also a participant in this enterprise, but withdrew in 1953, six years after the joint fleet was formed.

national airline in Latin America and of establishing common sources and systems for transmitting electricity. Currently there is some likelihood that Chile, Uruguay, and Argentina will join in creating a common power grid to serve sections of their respective countries. The successful outcomes of such cooperative ventures could prove highly beneficial to trade within the region.

In the past most of the many proposals in Latin America to integrate economically in one form or another failed because of indecision and lack of cooperation. Perhaps the pressures toward integration were not strong enough to overcome the rigidities of nationalism and local vested interests. However, as dissonant factions within the countries grew more forceful in their demands for economic improvement and independent solutions proved ineffective, governments apparently became more amenable to cooperation. The practical possibilities for substituting domestic for imported manufactures were largely exhausted. Continued industrialization required a new impetus.

The apparent success of the European Common Market and the widespread publicity attached to it was heeded in Latin America. Economic integration through combining country markets into larger, regional markets became the new nostrum for Latin America's economic ills.

It will be recalled that earlier efforts to reduce tariffs in Latin America among a limited number of countries had been frustrated by the "most-favored nation" doctrine, explicit in the GATT and other important trade treaties. However, the broader objective of mutually reinforcing economic development through increased regional trade stimulated the Latin American countries to seek formal ways of overcoming this doctrine. This was possible within the framework of GATT under its Article XXIV, which permits discriminatory arrangements in the case of bona fide customs unions and free trade areas.[51] The principal nations trading with Latin America had become sympathetic to the concept of using increased intraregional trade to stimulate economic development in Latin America, and they offered no strong objections to this development.

The first of the two major regional groupings was the Central

---

[51] GATT, *Basic Instruments and Selected Documents* (Geneva, May 1952), Vol. I, pp. 52-54.

American Common Market. Composed of the five Central American republics, this group of countries is in the process of freeing all trade among themselves and equalizing tariff barriers against imports from all other countries. In conjunction with the plan, the Central American Bank for Economic Integration has been established to finance industry and to improve methods of trade related to economic integration within this region.[52]

The second major regional grouping is the Latin American Free Trade Association (LAFTA), which officially came into existence on June 1, 1961. Unlike the more unifying association in Central America, LAFTA does not provide for establishing common tariffs against commodities from nonmember countries.

This important distinction necessitates greater administrative control within the LAFTA region in order to make sure that a country with relatively light import restrictions is not used by outside exporters as an inexpensive means of entry into all of LAFTA.

According to the LAFTA plan of economic integration all tariff and similar barriers are to be eliminated on regionally traded commodities which originate in member countries. The process of eliminating these barriers is to take place in no more than twelve years. Each country must reduce annually its LAFTA trade barriers by an amount equivalent to at least 8 percent of its non-LAFTA trade barriers prevailing at the beginning of the period.[53]

More exactly, each participating country is required to reduce annually its LAFTA trade barriers in order that the weighted average of its LAFTA barriers equals or is less than the result of: one hundred minus 8 times the number of years of LAFTA's existence, all multiplied by the weighted average of this country's non-LAFTA barriers.

A "Common Schedule" is formed of commodities for which all trade barriers have been eliminated within LAFTA. Once a commodity is placed on this schedule, it cannot be withdrawn. Furthermore, the

---

[52] For an historical review of the development of the Central American Common Market see: Victor L. Urquidi, *Free Trade and Economic Integration* (University of California Press, 1962), Chapter 7.

[53] For a fuller explanation of the method to be used in calculating required tariff reductions, see: Protocol No. 1, Title I, of the Treaty Establishing a Free-Trade Area and Instituting the Latin American Free Trade Association (commonly referred to as the Treaty of Montevideo).

traded value within LAFTA of commodities appearing on the "Common Schedule" must equal not less than 25, 50, 75, and "substantially" 100 percent of the value of total intra-LAFTA trade in three, six, nine, and twelve years, respectively, from the beginning of LAFTA.

Provisions are made within LAFTA to grant special concessions to countries deemed to be less economically advanced. At present two countries, Ecuador and Paraguay, have been so designated and are allowed to reduce their intraregional trade barriers more slowly than the other countries of LAFTA. Moreover, these other countries assume the collective responsibility for assisting the economically less advanced countries with special privileges and technical assistance.[54]

The postwar changes in Latin American trade patterns have reflected the economic situations of the region and its trading partners. During periods of relatively strong demand in the world export markets, efforts toward conscious promotion of trade within Latin America have been relaxed. During periods of unfavorable international economic conditions, greater urgency has been given to reducing trade barriers within the region. At first these attempts were conducted largely on bilateral bases. Later, when such methods proved ineffective, regional groupings were formed. The principal group of countries is LAFTA, where the policies and development of cooperative measures are closely tied to the programs of industrialization and other forms of economic development in the member countries.

Discussion of a Latin American common market has hinged on this industrialization and its role in the economic development of the region. The arguments in favor of large-scale industrialization have grown out of the experience in the 1930's and the decline in the capacity to import in the early 1940's and again after the Korean War. The crux of these arguments lies in the hypothesis that as per capita incomes rise in the industrial centers which customarily purchase Latin American exports, demand for these exports rises less than proportionally.[55] The assumption is that with increasing income a

---

[54] The complete Montevideo Treaty, which established LAFTA, may be found in United Nations Economic Commission for Latin America, "Economic Bulletin for Latin America" (March 1960), Vol. V, No. 1; and Urquidi, *op. cit.*, Appendix B.

[55] United Nations, Economic Commission for Latin America, *Toward a Dynamic Development Policy for Latin America* (April 14, 1963, mimeographed), pp. 101-134.

higher percentage of this income is spent on manufactured than on the nonmanufactured products which Latin America usually exports. It is argued that the rate of growth in Latin American income obtainable from traditional exports will lag increasingly behind the corresponding rate of growth in the industrial centers of the world. According to this thesis, in order for Latin America to catch up or even maintain a parallel rate of growth with the advanced countries, greater reliance must be placed on industrialization. Large-scale industrialization will need markets larger than most Latin American countries provide individually; therefore, countries should combine economically into regional groupings such as LAFTA.

Also underlying the argument is the experience of the more advanced countries of the region where the import substitution of consumer goods has more or less come to an end. Most of the former imports of consumer goods have already been replaced by domestic products; although in some countries, such as Colombia, Peru, and Venezuela, there is still ample room for further industrialization to produce import-substituting consumer goods. In the more industrial countries expansion in the consumer goods industries is limited to a slow pace, unless there is a considerable rise in the purchasing power of low income groups. The second stage of the industrialization process— domestic production of capital and intermediate goods which were formerly imported—also awaits a widening of the markets.

The argument also implies that an expected effect of larger markets is a fall in unit costs that would enable Latin American producers to compete with United States and European exports. However, even if domestic industries had to be protected from imports by tariffs or import quotas, it is felt by many that the long-run gains to Latin America would overshadow the shorter-run welfare losses from higher prices.

More recently the attempt to promote trade among Latin American countries in conjunction with each country's desire for industrialization has led to consideration of "complementarity agreements." The concept of "complementarity" is a natural outgrowth of both the increased market argument and the desire to protect the existence of already established industries. A complementarity agreement usually allows two or more countries to participate in the same industrial activity, by permitting each country to specialize in the manufacture of one component of a final product. Each component can be produced on a scale greater than the domestic market for the final product in only one country would permit.

The proposed agreement among Brazil, Argentina, and Chile for producing automobiles illustrates the mechanics of complementarity agreements. For a specified type of vehicle it may be decided that Argentina manufactures the engines and electrical systems; Chile furnishes the gear boxes and transmissions; and Brazil supplies the rest of the components.[56] Final assembly could take place in each of the three countries. For Chilean consumption, vehicles would be assembled and sold in Chile, and the revenue derived from this sale would be used to finance the Chilean side of the operation (manufacturing of gear boxes and transmissions, and assembly, distribution, and sale of the vehicles in Chile). The same type of arrangement would apply in Argentina and Brazil.

Through this kind of specialization it is hoped that significant economies of scale can be achieved in Latin America.[57] As a result the unit cost of the product would be lower in each country than if each country produced all of the product only for its own market. Furthermore, cost savings achieved through specialization might make it possible to export components, final products, or both to nations outside the complementarity agreement.[58]

---

[56] Under a proposal which was agreed upon in November 1963, Chile would import the needed parts of the vehicle from Argentina and Brazil up to the value of her exports of gear boxes and transmissions to these countries.

[57] However, gains from economic integration, of which complementarity arrangements are a special form, are not dependent solely upon economies of scale. Even though long-run unit costs do not "decline with increased output rates" (the usual and perhaps too narrow definition of economies of scale), it is still possible for all participating countries to benefit from economic integration.

[58] Complementarity arrangements, however, can cause costly deviations from optimum resource allocation. For example, a certain item may be produced in two or more countries when only one country has a clear advantage in producing and distributing it. To avoid unemployment in the high-cost countries, complementarity agreements might be entered into which would permit the high-cost producers to remain in existence. Each country would specialize in the production of a different part of the item.

While such specialization may be better than no specialization at all, it still does not constitute an optimum allocation of resources. Thus complementarity arrangements can freeze a trade pattern which could represent high social costs to the integration area.

CHAPTER III

Trade Patterns

FOREIGN TRADE is an important factor in the economy of every Latin American country. In 1960, for example, exports as a percentage of national income ranged from a low of 7 percent for Mexico to 42 percent for Venezuela, while the import ratios varied from 11 percent for Brazil and Mexico to 25 percent for Peru and Venezuela (see Table XIV in series of numbered tables beginning on page 74). In most of these economies the ratios of exports and imports to national income have remained rather constant since 1950; it is clear, however, that Argentina's export and import ratios have increased and those of Venezuela decreased since the early 1950's. In Argentina the increase was probably due to the slowing down of internal growth and in Venezuela to accelerated industrialization. Mexico's export and import ratios also fell, but only after 1956.

While the foreign sector plays an influential role in individual economies, it has not made Latin America as a whole a major force in world trade. Nevertheless, the area has been the chief supplier to the world of some basic commodities such as coffee, bananas, natural nitrates, and certain metals, as well as an important supplier of beef, rubber, and recently petroleum.

The participation of Latin America in world trade (from 1938 through 1963) is shown in Table I. Table I shows a rather steady decline in the ratio of Latin American exports to total world exports since World War II. Although Latin American exports between 1948 and 1963 rose about 46 percent, total world exports in this same period rose about 191 percent.

The difference between these two rates of increase results in part from the aftereffects of World War II. In the preceding chapter, it was mentioned that Latin America was one of the few principal sources of supply which was undamaged during the war. During the immediate postwar years foodstuffs exported by Latin America had ready markets because most of the traditional sources of competition had been disrupted and depleted. The export capabilities of the main exporting nations were greatly reduced during the first years following the war. With the rapid economic recovery of the war-ravaged industrial centers of the world, exports from these traditional sources grew rapidly. Therefore, Latin America's share in world exports fell between 1948 and 1963 by 50 percent.

If instead of measuring from 1948, we use the 1934-1938 average as the base, then between those last relatively normal prewar years and 1963 Latin American exports rose over 400 percent while exports for the total world rose more than 600 percent. Comparisons on the basis of the longer time period still indicate that Latin American exports have been declining relative to world exports. Latin America's share in world exports has dropped from the prewar average of 9.4 percent to about 6.4 percent in recent years.

From Table I we find that following World War II, Latin American imports have increased 51 percent while total world imports have increased 184 percent. The fall in Latin America's share of world imports (from 10.1 percent in 1948 to 5.4 percent in 1963) may be related to the corresponding decrease in exports.

When the average for the years 1934-38 is used as the basis for comparison, we see again that the rates of increases in Latin American imports were less than those in total world imports. The differences in these rates are relatively much less than the difference between the 1948 and 1963 rates, which were due in part to war-created distortions of international trade conditions and in part to a greater rate of import-substituting industrialization in Latin America than in the rest of the world.

Observers who have not been exposed to Latin American trade statistics are usually surprised at the small size of intraregional trade. An extensive interchange of goods seems reasonable in a region such as Latin America, given its vast size, great variety of climates, peoples, and natural resources, and its relatively long distance from the important market centers of the rest of the world. But as Table II-b indicates, trade among Latin American countries is relatively unimportant in terms of total foreign trade for Latin America. From 1948 to 1963 the share of total Latin American exports which was absorbed by Latin America never reached 10 percent; while a corresponding share for imports always was below 12 percent.

Of the intra-Latin American trade which did take place, the LAFTA countries were responsible for the greatest part. If the potential members of LAFTA, Bolivia and Venezuela, are included with the present LAFTA countries, then the remaining nations have a very small share in intra-Latin American trade. Collectively, these remaining countries (nine of the twenty republics) have accounted, on an average annual basis, for about 8 percent of the exports and about 11 percent of the imports in intra-Latin American trade from 1952 to 1963.

Argentina and Brazil have been the region's major trading countries for many years. Venezuela became important in the 1950's when its oil accounted for over one-fourth of Latin America's total exports. Argentina and Brazil account for about 60 percent of intra-LAFTA trade. Together with Chile they are the major buyers of LAFTA products, purchasing about three-fourths of all intra-LAFTA imports.

EXPORTS. For the period after World War II, the share of Latin American exports to the United States reached its peak during the Korean conflict and since then has been decreasing steadily. When the fighting in Korea ended, the United States stopped making large-scale purchases for stockpiling and the share of Latin American commodities in United States purchases declined.[1] Meanwhile there was an increase in Latin American exports to Europe which coincided with the period of reconstruction and accelerated economic development there.

Because of Western Europe's economic resurgence in the 1950's, it is surprising that the share of Latin America's exports to that region did not increase at a faster rate. From 1954 to 1963, the share of Latin America's exports to Western Europe rose only 3.3 percentage points.

---

[1] There were other reasons for the decline: (a) a disparate rate of U.S. import growth between primary and manufactured goods; (b) competition from Africa; (c) deterioration of Latin American terms of trade with the United States relative to the world. See David Pollock, "The Development of Commodity Trade Between Latin America and the United States," *Economic Bulletin for Latin America*, Vol. II, No. 2 (October 1961).

One reason for the small increase may be that the countries of Africa, with the commercial advantage of their past and present colonial ties to Europe, are able to supply most of the same types of commodities which Latin America exports, such as coffee, copper, etc.

The data in Table II show a substantial increase in the shares of Latin American exports going to countries which are included in the residual category entitled "others."[2] This export increase (both absolutely and relatively) stems mainly from Japan, where rapid industrial expansion brought about a need to import raw materials and from Russia, where support of the Cuban economy includes purchase of Cuban sugar. The substitution of Russia for the United States as the chief buyer of Cuban sugar also explains to some extent the decline after 1960 in the percentage share of Latin America's exports which have been imported by the United States.

IMPORTS. Since World War II there has been a rather steady rise in the share of Latin American imports coming from Western Europe as a result of the European postwar recovery and the aggressive export drives which have been conducted by the nations of that area. During this period Latin America has substituted imports from Western Europe for imports from the United States, as is indicated by the trends of the data shown in Table II.

Also to be noted is the increase during these years in the share of Latin American imports from the countries grouped in Table II as "others." The increase in this share during the 1950's can be explained to a considerable extent by the re-entry after World War II of Japan as an important international trading power. Many of Japan's traditional markets in the mainland of Asia have been restricted for political reasons. With Africa still primarily oriented toward Western Europe, Japan has turned with increasing interest to Latin America, both as a logical supplier of the raw materials which are required to feed the expanding Japanese industries and as an outlet for some of the products of these industries. The Japanese who immigrated to Brazil and Peru after World War II have prospered, and this situation

[2] The category "others" includes all countries outside Latin America, Western Europe, and the United States, mainly the Soviet bloc countries, India, Australia, Japan, and Canada.

may in time also increase the burgeoning commercial relations between Japan and Latin America.

In addition, the rapid rise since 1960 in the share of Latin American imports from "other" nations reflects the fact that Cuba has changed her trading partners. This change has almost eliminated imports from the United States, which in 1959 supplied about 63 percent of Cuba's imports, in favor of imports from Soviet bloc countries, notably Russia, which increased its share of Cuban imports from nothing in 1959 to over 53 percent in 1963.[3]

General Trade Patterns of LAFTA Countries, Bolivia, and Venezuela

For a more detailed study of the foreign trade of the LAFTA countries and Bolivia and Venezuela, Tables III and IV give a comparison of the importance of each of these countries with respect to intra-Latin American foreign trade and Latin American foreign trade with the world. Foreign trade with the world includes all foreign trade —both within and outside Latin America—for each country considered.

EXPORTS. Among the countries which now constitute LAFTA, Argentina was the most important exporter to other Latin American countries preceding World War II and this situation has in general continued following the war (see Table IIIa). A different pattern of change exists in terms of total Latin American exports to the world (Table IIIb). Although Argentina was the largest total exporter before and immediately after the war, Brazil has since become the most important exporter among the countries of LAFTA.

In the middle of the 1950's, Venezuela became the most important exporting country in Latin America in terms of both exports to the world and exports to Latin America. The increase in Venezuela's share of intra-Latin American exports has been phenomenal: from a 1934-1938 average of only 1.5 percent to 37.3 percent in 1959. This rise is due to the development of Venezuela's petroleum industry and to

[3] International Monetary Fund and International Bank for Reconstruction and Development, *Direction of Trade*, Annual (1958-62), p. 205, and (August 1964), p. 38.

Latin America's greatly increased demand for petroleum products aris-
ing from a growth of industrialization, urbanization, and use of motor
vehicles.

In recent years the success of other nations (notably Chile, Argentina, Brazil, and Peru) in developing their own petroleum industries
has caused a reduction in Venezuela's share of Latin American exports
going to Latin America.

The importance of LAFTA countries as a group in intra-Latin
American exports declined from the average of 94.7 percent before
World War II to the postwar low of 52.7 percent in 1959. Then there
followed a slight increase in the LAFTA share which coincided with
the decrease in Venezuela's share, as described above. If Bolivia and
Venezuela are included with the LAFTA countries, the share of this
larger group of nations in all intra-Latin American exports has been
decreasing only slightly since the end of World War II.

Of the total Latin American exports—going inside as well as outside
Latin America—the LAFTA countries' share has fallen from its prewar level, but since 1952 it has remained fairly constant. When Bolivia
and Venezuela are included with the countries of LAFTA, no significant change from the prewar level can be discerned. This larger group
of countries now accounts for about 86 percent of all Latin American
exports.

The significant differences between the trends in the shares of total
exports and intra-LAFTA exports for the two groups (LAFTA plus
Venezuela and Bolivia, and LAFTA only) rest with Venezuela with
her large-scale exportation of petroleum products. When included with
the LAFTA countries, Venezuela has prevented the total shares of this
group from falling.

IMPORTS. Among the LAFTA countries, Brazil and Argentina together
have generally received over one-half of all intra-Latin American imports. (See Table IV.) Neither of the two appears the more dominant,
and their combined share of intra-Latin American imports has been
falling since the mid-fifties.

Argentina and Brazil are also the main importing countries in
Latin America (Table IVb), although together their shares of total
imports have been less than their corresponding shares of imports
within Latin America. Before World War II, Argentina was the largest

importer in Latin America; after the war Brazil acquired this distinction.

For the LAFTA countries as a group, their postwar shares of intra-Latin American imports have generally remained somewhat lower than their prewar share. The same sort of trend is apparent for the changes in the LAFTA shares of total imports for Latin America, although the levels of these shares are lower than for the corresponding shares of intra-Latin American imports.

Venezuela's shares, both of intra-Latin American imports and of total Latin American imports, have increased considerably since the prewar period. Most of these changes can be attributed to and are parallel to the significant changes in Venezuela's exports which were described earlier in conjunction with Table III.

Individual Analysis of LAFTA Countries

A more concise examination of the trade patterns of the LAFTA countries plus Bolivia and Venezuela—with particular emphasis on the patterns of trade among all of these countries—is afforded by examining the structure of foreign trade for each country separately. In the individual examinations, parallel sets of data will be employed for each country in order to provide a common basis of comparison among all the countries. These data are presented in the following types of tables:

Table V shows each country's exports and imports according to principal trading areas: Latin America, LAFTA, United States, and Western Europe (1938-1963).

Table VI shows each country's exports and imports to and from individual LAFTA countries, Bolivia, and Venezuela (1948-1963).

Table VII is a matrix of the values of classes of commodities exported to each nation in LAFTA, Bolivia and Venezuela by each of these countries (1959-1963). Commodity classes are divided into three groups: (1) raw materials; (2) semi-processed; and (3) processed and manufactured.

In the country-by-country discussions below, the commodity composition of trade within LAFTA (according to the exports of each country) will be presented for the last five years for which statistics are now available. The traded commodities are divided into three general categories, with each category subdivided into more specific product classifications. With this information, the importance of the various commodities in intra-LAFTA trade can be estimated.

ARGENTINA. The ratio of Argentina's LAFTA trade to her total foreign trade grew after World War II, but since 1954 and especially more recently, Argentina's trade with LAFTA has generally been decreasing in relative terms (see Tables V-1-a and V-1-b).[4] Most noticeably, the ratio of Argentine imports from LAFTA to total Argentine imports decreased from 1958 to 1962, increasing only in 1963. During the most recent years, 1958-1963, the share of Argentina's total exports going to LAFTA countries averaged 13 percent, while the comparable share for Argentinian imports from LAFTA averaged 10 percent.

From 1958 through 1963, Argentina's exports to LAFTA countries formed 92 percent of her total exports to Latin America. Over this same period, however, the share of Argentina's imports from LAFTA countries was only 62 percent of her total imports from Latin America. Despite the fact that most of the countries are geographically close, the LAFTA nations have not overwhelmingly dominated Argentina's trade with Latin America.

Within LAFTA, Brazil is Argentina's most important trading partner for both imports and exports (Table VI-1). Venezuela supplies imports to Argentina in much greater value than does any LAFTA country except Brazil.[5]

Chile is Argentina's second most important trading partner within LAFTA. Both Argentina and Chile have relatively well-developed economies, and they share one of the longest common frontiers in the world. However, considering the rugged Andean barrier between the industrial and population centers of both nations, the extent of this trade becomes more impressive.

The share of Argentina's exports to Peru has increased rapidly.

---

[4] Throughout this study, use of the term "LAFTA" refers for all periods of time to the group of countries which comprise the Latin American Free Trade Association, even when this term is applied to periods before formation of LAFTA.

[5] Argentinian imports from Venezuela exceeded those from Brazil in 1959 and 1960.

In general, the direction of Argentinian exports has become slightly more diversified.

Argentina's exports to LAFTA consist primarily of raw materials. Nevertheless, the percentages of manufactured and processed products in relation to total exports to LAFTA have tended to increase in this recent period, particularly in her exports to Brazil.

Unprocessed grains are the chief export of Argentina to LAFTA countries, Bolivia and Venezuela, accounting for between one-fourth to almost two-thirds of total exports to those countries in the years 1959 to 1963. Live animals, meat, and hides have risen in importance during this period from 15 percent of exports in 1959 to 27 percent in 1963 (Table VII-1).

Brazil and Chile are the LAFTA countries which receive the greatest share of Argentina's raw material exports. Chile, Brazil, Uruguay, and Paraguay receive the great majority of Argentina's semi-processed and manufactured exports going to LAFTA.

BRAZIL. Since 1938, there have been large absolute increases in Brazil's trade with the LAFTA countries (Tables V-2-a and V-2-b). However, the ratio of exports to LAFTA to total exports increased immediately after World War II and then gradually returned to the same level as 1938; the corresponding ratio of Brazil's imports from LAFTA has fallen since 1938.

For the six-year period, 1958-1963, Brazilian exports to LAFTA accounted for 7 percent of her total exports, and imports from LAFTA countries represented 8 percent of total Brazilian imports. From 1958 through 1963, the share of Brazil's Latin American exports going to LAFTA was 97 percent, while, by contrast, only one-half of Brazil's Latin American imports came from LAFTA.

Among LAFTA countries, Argentina is by far Brazil's most important trading partner (Table VI-2). Both nations have relatively large populations and advanced economic levels; their industrial and commercial centers are close; therefore, it is not surprising to find that Argentina and Brazil generally dominate each other's trade within LAFTA.

Uruguay and Chile are significant trading partners for Brazil, but with most of the remaining LAFTA countries Brazil has little trade. If Bolivia and Venezuela are included, the data show that Brazil's trade with Bolivia is slight but that Venezuela supplies a large, and recently the largest, share of Brazil's imports from Latin American countries.

Semi-processed goods have been the most important export of Brazil to LAFTA countries, Bolivia, and Venezuela. For the years 1959-1963, this category varied between 68 percent and 82 percent, averaging 74 percent for the period (Table Xb). Processed and manufactured commodities have increased steadily as a percentage of total exports to the area, from 7 percent in 1959 to 20 percent in 1963 (Table Xc).

Vehicles are the most important of the manufactured items exported by Brazil to LAFTA. The last two years have seen a remarkable expansion in this category: in 1963 it accounted for about 5 percent of total exports to LAFTA, Bolivia, and Venezuela; and in 1962, for 7 percent; while in 1960 it represented less than one percent of Brazil's total exports to those countries. Exports of machinery and chemicals to LAFTA have also been increasing (Tables VII-2).

The largest items by far in Brazil's trade with the area, however, have been semi-processed coffee and lumber. Coffee has comprised about 40 percent of exports in the five-year period; lumber, between one-fourth and one-third. Argentina is the main importer of these two products and of vehicles and other manufactured goods as well.

CHILE. Chile has been importing substantially more from LAFTA countries than she has been exporting (Tables V-3-a and V-3-b). The ratios of Chilean imports and exports within LAFTA to total Chilean imports and exports rose (from the 1938 level) after World War II and then declined after 1954, to rise again in 1963. Changes in the value of Chilean LAFTA trade showed a similar pattern, but 1963 imports from LAFTA countries were the highest in history.

From 1958 through 1963, the share of Chile's total exports going to LAFTA countries was 8 percent while the comparable share for Chile's imports from LAFTA was 15 percent. During this same period, Chilean exports to LAFTA comprised 82 percent of total Chilean exports to Latin America, and nearly 90 percent of total Chilean imports from Latin America came from LAFTA countries.

Argentina had been Chile's most important trading partner within LAFTA, but since 1962 Brazil has replaced Argentina as the largest buyer of Chilean products (Table VI-3). Peru also figures prominently in Chile's LAFTA imports. Chile's trade with Venezuela and Bolivia has been rather small in comparison with her total LAFTA trade. Lately, however, there has been a considerable increase in imports of petroleum products from Venezuela.

In 1959 and 1961 Chile exported more manufactured and processed goods to LAFTA than semi-processed and raw materials combined; however, raw materials and processed exports have declined in the last two years to a point where semi-processed goods dominate Chilean exports to these countries. Most of the increase in semi-processed exports consisted of copper sales to Brazil.

The percentage share of manufactured exports to LAFTA, Bolivia, and Venezuela has varied considerably, from a high of 66 percent in 1961 to a low of 32 percent in 1963 (Table Xc). The value of Chile's manufactured exports to LAFTA alone fell from 23 million U.S. dollars in 1961 to 12 million dollars in 1962, rising to 15 million dollars in 1963; while for the same period total Chilean exports to LAFTA increased from 35 to 39 to 49 million dollars. The great decrease in manufactured exports to LAFTA appears to have resulted from a sudden drop in exports of metals, notably sheet steel to Argentina.

Among the manufactured commodities which Chile exports to LAFTA there are several categories which figure prominently: chemicals and drugs, paper, and rolled metals. Argentina receives the main share of Chilean manufactured exports going to LAFTA; Brazil and Peru are also important recipients of these Chilean exports.

For the nonmanufactured commodities, minerals have become most important, particularly in 1962 and 1963, with large increases in copper exports to LAFTA (Table VII-3).

COLOMBIA. Trade with LAFTA countries has been relatively unimportant for Colombia (Tables V-4-a and V-4-b). Colombian exports to the LAFTA region have been rising, although by 1963 these exports were still less than 2 percent of total Colombian exports. There appears to be a large relative rise in the ratio of Colombia's imports from LAFTA in recent years. While Colombian imports have been more significant than exports to LAFTA, they are still small in relation to total imports (about 4 percent in 1963).

Colombia's trade with all of Latin America also has been relatively small. Of this trade, LAFTA has accounted for roughly one-half. From 1958 through 1963 Colombia's exports to LAFTA represented 54 percent of her total exports to Latin America and Colombia's imports from LAFTA were 44 percent of her total imports from Latin America. As may be expected, Colombia's most important trading partners within LAFTA have been Ecuador and Peru (Table VI-4). Since the late 1950's, Ecuador has been Colombia's main LAFTA supplier, although Mexico and Argentina have become significant in the most recent years. Venezuela is also of some trading importance to Colombia.

Apparently there is a considerable amount of contraband flowing between Colombia and Venezuela, and Colombia and Ecuador. If this contraband were included in Colombia's official trade figures, the importance of Venezuela and Ecuador as trading partners with Colombia would be substantially increased.

In considering the composition of Colombia's exports to her LAFTA trading partners, Tables Xa to Xc show that the value of semi-processed products exported by Colombia to LAFTA, Bolivia, and Venezuela has generally been greater than for manufactured products or raw materials. The percentage of manufactured exports to Colombia's total exports to LAFTA has varied considerably in recent years, ranging from 33 to almost 60 percent. Ecuador is the main LAFTA recipient of these exports.

The rise in manufactured exports to the LAFTA area in 1963 may be attributed in good part to the expansion in textile exports, which in 1961 were valued at just 155 thousand dollars, representing about 2 percent of Colombia's exports to LAFTA, and which by 1963 had increased in value to over one million dollars, representing approximately 20 percent of Colombia's exports to LAFTA. Chemicals and drugs and machinery have also figured prominently in Colombia's exportation of manufactured products (Table VII-4).

If the trade data for Venezuela and Bolivia are included with the LAFTA data, then the manufactured share of Colombia's exports to this larger group rises considerably. The main reason for this change is the importance of manufactured goods, notably machinery, which Colombia exports to Venezuela. For the years 1959-1963, the average annual percentage of processed and manufactured commodities of total Colombian exports going to Venezuela was nearly 90 percent.

ECUADOR. The percentage of Ecuador's exports going to LAFTA countries has fallen since the end of World War II, from 18 percent in 1948 to 6 percent in 1963 (Table V-5-a). This decrease in relative importance as an exporter to LAFTA countries has gone along with a decrease in absolute terms (as measured in U.S. dollars) ; Ecuador's export earnings from LAFTA also have fallen, from 8.5 in 1948 to 7.8 million U.S. dollars in 1963. Since World War II, there has been a general decline in the ratio of Ecuador's imports from LAFTA, except for a sudden upsurge in 1962 which was largely maintained in 1963 (Table V-5-b).

For the last six years, 1958-1963, the share of Ecuador's total exports sent to the LAFTA area was 6 percent while the share of Ecuador's total imports received from the LAFTA area was only 3 percent. For the same period, 77 percent of Ecuador's total exports to Latin America went to LAFTA countries while 58 percent of Ecuador's total imports from Latin America came from these countries. Colombia is the LAFTA country of greatest trading significance for Ecuador (Table VI-5). Chile is next in importance. These two countries take about 80 percent of Ecuador's LAFTA exports and supply a much smaller proportion of her LAFTA imports.

Ecuador's manufactured exports have averaged about 14 precent of total exports to LAFTA, Bolivia, and Venezuela. These manufactured exports consist mainly of cosmetics, insecticides, paints, and drugs (Tables VII-5-1c to VII-5-5c). The remaining manufactured exports contribute very little to Ecuador's export earnings from LAFTA. The dominant LAFTA market for Ecuador's manufactured products is Colombia, which for the years between 1959 and 1963 received an average of 85 percent of these products.

Raw material exports are almost entirely consumed by Chile, in the form of bananas, and Colombia, which purchases the largest share of Ecuador's cacao exports to the LAFTA region. Cacao and bananas averaged 35 percent and 31 percent of total exports, respectively, in the five-year period.

When trade data for Venezuela and Bolivia are included with the trade data for LAFTA countries, the commodity composition of Ecuador's exports to LAFTA is altered somewhat for 1959-1960, but for the next two years it remains largely unaffected. This pattern of change coincides with the decrease in Venezuela's influence as a trading partner. Venezuela had been a relatively important purchaser of agricultural products (especially rice) from Ecuador and accounted in

1959 and 1960 for about 39 and 55 percent, respectively, of Ecuador's total exportation of raw materials to LAFTA countries, Bolivia, and Venezuela. In 1961, this percentage fell to zero and in the following years raw material exports to Venezuela remained minimal.

There has been a decline in the value of Ecuador's exports to this group of countries since the late 1950's (Table VI-5), although there was some recovery in 1963. Part of the decline results from the large drop in exports to Venezuela.

MEXICO. Mexico's LAFTA trade as a proportion of her total trade has been smaller than for any other LAFTA country, although recently there have been some significant increases (Tables V-6-a and V-6-b). During the 1950's Mexico's imports from LAFTA constituted less than one-half of 1 percent of her total imports, and the LAFTA proportion of her exports was not much higher. Her LAFTA trade has grown more rapidly than her total trade since 1961, and while the ratio of her LAFTA imports to total imports had hardly reached 1 percent in 1963, the proportion of her LAFTA exports is approaching 3 percent. In 1963 for the first time her LAFTA trade reached more than half of her total Latin American trade.

A large part of the recent rise in Mexico's exports to LAFTA is accounted for by increased sales to Brazil, the country which now receives the greatest amount of Mexican exports within LAFTA (Tables VII-6). Mexico's exports to Brazil between 1961 and 1963 increased more than fivefold. However, Brazil's importance in Mexican trade with LAFTA countries has varied considerably since World War II. This is also true for Mexico's other main trading partners within this region: Argentina, Chile, Colombia, and Peru. For most of the postwar period, Venezuela, of all of these countries, was the prime destination for Mexico's exports, but her share has declined since 1959.

Manufactured products account for the major proportion of Mexico's exports to LAFTA (Tables VII-6-1c to VII-6-5c). Almost two-thirds of Mexican exports going to LAFTA, Bolivia, and Venezuela in recent years has consisted of processed and manufactured commodities (Table Xc). The principal categories of the exported manufactured products have been chemicals, metals and metal products, books, machinery, and textiles. The main LAFTA countries purchasing these exports have been Colombia, Chile, Brazil, and Peru. Venezuela is the largest

Latin American buyer of chemicals from Mexico, but her relatively large purchases have been declining over the period studied, undoubtedly as a result of the development of chemical industries within Venezuela.

Resins and tar extracts have been the most important semi-processed items exported by Mexico to the LAFTA region. Most of these extracts have gone to Argentina, Chile, and Brazil. The last is the only country in the region whose imports from Mexico have been primarily nonmanufactures.

PARAGUAY. The relative importance of LAFTA trade for Paraguay has been greater than for any other LAFTA country although this trade has tended to decline since the mid-1950's (Tables V-7-a and V-7-b). For the period 1958-1963, nearly one-third of Paraguay's total exports went to LAFTA countries and nearly one-fourth of her total imports came from LAFTA.

Paraguay's LAFTA trade is concentrated on Argentina, which absorbs between 80 and 90 percent of her LAFTA exports and provides over 95 percent of her LAFTA imports. There is also some trade with Uruguay and to a lesser extent with Brazil. Occasionally Chile, Peru, and Bolivia (the only non-LAFTA country) show up as minor trading partners (Tables VI-7 and XI-1 to XI-5).

Paraguay's main export to LAFTA countries is lumber which for the five years, 1959-1963, averaged about one-half to two-thirds of Paraguay's total exports to this region. Quebracho extract (a tanning agent) and yerba maté (a kind of tea) are also very important exports to the area; both go, as does lumber, almost entirely to Argentina. The three goods combined have constituted about 80 percent of Paraguay's total exports to LAFTA.

PERU. The percentage of Peruvian exports going to the LAFTA nations decreased between 1948 and 1961, but showed some recovery in the last two years, 1962 and 1963 (Table V-8-a). For imports from LAFTA to Peru from 1948-1961, the percentages change, but no clear trend appears; here, too, however, there is a significant increase in 1962 and 1963 (Table V-8-b). In the most recent five-year period about 10 percent of Peru's total exports went to the countries of LAFTA and a somewhat lower percentage of her total imports came from these countries. LAFTA trade constitutes almost 90 percent of Peru's total Latin American trade.

Within LAFTA, Chile is the largest buyer of Peru's products and Argentina the principal source of her imports (Table VI-8). While Chile's importance as a trading partner has declined since the 1950's, she still receives about one-half of Peru's total exports to the LAFTA region. Approximately two-thirds of Peru's LAFTA imports have come from Argentina in recent years. Argentina is also an important LAFTA purchaser of Peruvian exports. During the period under review, Peru's exports to Brazil have in general increased substantially while those to Colombia have decreased. Peru's trade with Bolivia and Venezuela has moved in opposite directions. Peruvian exports to Bolivia have diminished considerably whereas in general, although sporadically, Peru's trade with Venezuela has increased (Table VI-8).

Raw cotton and sugar have been the two principal products exported to the region between 1959 and 1963 (Tables VII-8-a and VII-8-b). Cotton alone has accounted for between one-third and one-half of Peru's LAFTA exports during this period. Chile is the principal buyer of cotton and sugar. Ores and semi-refined metals along with crude and refined petroleum products—largely to Argentina, Brazil and Chile—form a second group of important exports to LAFTA countries. The largest item in the export category of "processed and manufactured goods" is fish meal, which has increased from zero in 1959 to over 6 percent of Peru's total LAFTA exports in 1963. It is sold primarily to Mexico and represents essentially the only product exported from Peru to Mexico. It is also the largest single item purchased by Venezuela from Peru.

URUGUAY. Although the percentage of Uruguay's exports going to LAFTA countries is now less than in the early 1950's, an upward trend can be noted in the recent years 1959-1963 (Table V-9-a). The importance of LAFTA for imports is substantially greater than for exports, and in 1963 the proportion of imports from LAFTA to Uruguay was greater than in any year since 1958. Over the period 1958-1963, the share of Uruguay's total exports going to LAFTA was approximately 5 percent while 16 percent of Uruguay's total imports came from LAFTA. For this same period Uruguay's exports to LAFTA represented over 90 percent of her total exports to Latin

America, and Uruguay's imports from LAFTA countries were almost 60 percent of her total imports from all of Latin America.

Brazil does the largest volume of trade with Uruguay, in both exports and imports (Table VI-9). In the six-year period 1958-1963, Brazil provided almost two-thirds of Uruguay's imports from LAFTA and purchased nearly half of her LAFTA exports. Argentina is the next most important LAFTA trading partner for Uruguay. Also to be noted is the large share (relative to the LAFTA region) of Uruguayan imports from Venezuela since 1952.

For the five years 1959-1963, there has been a sharp variation in the importance of manufactured products in the composition of Uruguay's exports to LAFTA (Tables VII-9-c and Xa-Xc). The sudden increase in 1960 and 1961 in the percentage of manufactured to total Uruguayan exports going to LAFTA is explained by the reduction in the traditional exports of agricultural commodities.

Within LAFTA, Argentina is the most important recipient of Uruguay's processed and manufactured exports, the largest single item being automobile tires; Brazil is the most important recipient of Uruguay's raw material exports—wheat and, in 1962 and 1963, also cattle and wool.

Individual Analysis of Bolivia and Venezuela

Although Bolivia and Venezuela are not members of LAFTA, their early entry into LAFTA is considered likely. Therefore, it is of interest to present for these two countries the type of description applied to the LAFTA countries. The relevant trade information relating to all these countries can, in this manner, be presented on a parallel basis.

BOLIVIA. The share of Bolivia's total exports going to LAFTA countries was generally rising from 1948 to 1960, and then it decreased abruptly for the next three years (Table V-10-a). On the other hand, there has been a significant decrease since 1948 in the percentage of Bolivia's imports coming from the countries of LAFTA (Table V-10-b).

In the last six years, 1958-1963, about 8 percent of Bolivia's total exports was sent to LAFTA countries while about 17 percent of her total imports came from these countries. For the most recent years, these proportions are smaller. Approximately all Bolivia's exports to Latin America have gone to LAFTA countries, and well above 90 percent of Bolivia's Latin American imports came from LAFTA.

Argentina is Bolivia's main trading partner within Latin America (Table VI-10), supplying about half of her imports from the region. Peru and Chile are also important sources of Bolivia's Latin American imports. After Argentina, Brazil is the largest purchaser of Bolivia's Latin American exports.

While the value of raw material exports to the LAFTA region has declined in recent years, it still comprises more than half of Bolivia's Latin American sales (Tables Xa-Xc). Crude oil is the most important raw material export, nearly all of which goes to Argentina. Metal ore is second in importance, with Brazil as the principal buyer, but in 1962 it practically disappeared as an export item (Table VII-10).

From 1959 to 1962, approximately 30 percent of Bolivia's exports to the region has consisted of semi-processed goods. A major part of these is forestry products, primarily lumber and extracts. The former is exported largely to Argentina, the latter nearly all to Brazil. Bolivia's processed and manufactured exports to Latin America are insignificant.

VENEZUELA. The percentage of Venezuela's exports going to LAFTA countries rose after World War II until 1959 and since then has fallen (Table V-11-a). The share of Venezuela's total imports coming from the countries of LAFTA has risen fivefold since 1954 but nevertheless accounts for relatively little of Venezuela's total imports (Table V-11-b).

For the last six years, 1958-1963, less than 2 percent of Venezuela's total imports was obtained from the LAFTA region; for the same period about 7 percent of Venezuela's total exports went to LAFTA. Most of Venezuela's Latin American trade is with LAFTA countries: approximately 80 percent of her exports and 70 percent of her imports.

Among the countries of LAFTA, Brazil receives the largest share (from 1952 to the present) of Venezuela's exports and Argentina the second largest. Since 1959, the proportion going to Argentina has declined while Brazil's export share has correspondingly increased. Together, Brazil and Argentina have accounted for over 80 percent of Venezuela's total exports to LAFTA.

Argentina customarily supplies the largest portion, approximately one-third, of Venezuela's LAFTA imports. In the late 1950's, Mexico became an important supplier and, in 1963, substantially surpassed Argentina as the chief source of Venezuela's Latin American imports.

The commodity composition of Venezuela's exports to the countries of LAFTA is presented in Tables VII-11-1a through VII-11-5c.

For the years 1959-1963, petroleum products accounted for almost all—more than 95 percent—of Venezuela's exports to the LAFTA region (Table VII-11). During these years total exports declined, principally as a result of Argentina's growing self-sufficiency in oil. Since 1961, refined oil exports declined even more than total exports as the refining capacity in the more industrial Latin American countries increased.

During the period under study, there has been a steady decrease, both absolutely and relatively, in Venezuela's exportation of manufactured products to LAFTA countries. However, for this period the relative importance of these exports was slight—accounting on a yearly average for less than 2 percent of Venezuela's total exports to the countries of LAFTA. A substantial amount of this category consisted of re-exports, particularly of vehicles.

CHAPTER IV

Conclusions

THE DATA IN TABLES I TO XV, beginning on page 74, begin to form the basis for research in the relatively unexplored field of Latin American trade and development. (Such statistics, collected over time, point the way to an analysis of the consistency of economic performance with the general objectives of the Latin American Free Trade Association: to increase trade among member countries and to accelerate their industrialization and growth.)

In several years, when enough data will have been brought together to undertake an evaluation of the movement toward Latin American economic integration, it will be possible to determine the effects of various influences on Latin American trade and, in turn, the effects of changing trade patterns on the welfare of Latin American economies. The text and tables suggest a direction for future research in these areas.

(Before considering variations in LAFTA members' exports and imports, it should be clear that the reduction of tariff barriers is only one of a number of factors affecting trade. Changes in other types of barriers such as quotas and licensing procedures, changes in exchange rates, and alternative taxing schemes are economic variables which will affect a country's imports and exports within LAFTA. There is also a host of noneconomic forces which can affect trade among members. Political factors play a significant role; tradition and habit may be deeply ingrained and thus slow to change; and poor information and knowledge about market conditions and alternative trade possibilities restrain the influence of economic variables. In analyzing changes in Latin American trade patterns, one should bear in mind that reactions to given market stimuli may not conform in degree to the reaction in other regions, in particular those regions from which we have drawn our general conclusions regarding trade.

(Another important restraint of trade in Latin America is transportation costs. As was shown in Chapter II, the influences of historical trading patterns have oriented the flow of trade toward other continents, and coastwise shipping is still expensive compared to overseas transportation.[1] Topographical features (mountain ranges, jungles, and so on), often used to denote political boundaries, sometimes make formidable physical barriers which have limited expansion of land and air transportation within the region.[2] While the framers of the Treaty of Montevideo evidently felt that transport facilities are a function of trade,[3] the causal relationship is by no means clear and the problem of transport policy for LAFTA remains largely an unexplored one.[4] A breakthrough in lowering coastwise maritime transport or in technological advances in highway, rail, and air transportation could, within limits, outweigh tariff reductions as a trade stimulant.)

(In addition to the variables affecting the relative volume of trade among LAFTA members, types of goods traded need examination. Of particular interest is trade in manufactures because of the increased accent on manufactured exports as an indicator of the development of the industrial sector so stressed by Latin American economists in the formation of a free trade area. This accent has emerged from the inability of the export sector in the last decade to provide the stimulus for a higher rate of economic development.)

(The growth of Latin American exports has been sluggish since the mid-1950's. Not only did the region's exports increase at a slower

[1] Inadequate service on some routes, the policies of international shipping conferences, and the high port and handling charges and delays, make for high freight rates. About 60 percent of intra-LAFTA costs for water transportation results from port and handling charges. (Enrique Angulo, "Ante la Reunión de la ALAMAR" in *Comercio Exterior*, Banco Nacional de Comercio Exterior, S.A. [November 1963], p. 806.)

[2] "According to average figures for the three-year period 1950-52, . . . about 92 percent of total inter-South American trade was absorbed by maritime transport. . . ." United Nations, ECLA, *Study of Inter-Latin American Trade* (1957), p. 154.

[3] Miguel Wionczek, *Latin American Free Trade Association* (International Conciliation, January 1965), No. 551, p. 36.

[4] For an important beginning, see Robert Brown, *Transport and the Economic Development of Latin America*, to be published by the Brookings Institution.

pace than world exports (Table I) but also at a lower rate than the exports of the rest of the so-called underdeveloped world. Between 1955 and 1962 the value of Latin America's exports rose by about 17 percent compared to 24 percent for the other developing countries.[5]

Most of this difference has been due to the fact that raw materials constitute a greater share of exports in Latin America (about 90 percent) than in other developing regions (about 82 percent in 1962). World demand for primary products has been rising slowly compared to manufactures. In addition, the export value of manufactures in Latin America increased only by 17 percent between 1955 and 1962, but in the other developing countries the corresponding growth was about 46 percent. While the share of industrial exports in total exports has been increasing in the other developing countries, Latin America's export structure has remained the same.

The region's industrial production accounts for 40 percent of industrial output, but only 20 percent of industrial exports of all the developing countries. This is simply another manifestation of Latin America's greater concentration—compared to the other countries of the underdeveloped world—on the import-substituting industrialization which produces primarily for national markets.

As may be expected, exports to LAFTA are much more diversified than the total exports of LAFTA countries. The relative size of the value of manufactures in the LAFTA trade of some countries is already quite significant: Chile, Colombia, and especially Mexico have a high percentage of their exports to LAFTA in manufactured goods.[6]

---

[5] *Study of the Prospects and Some Problems Facing Latin America in Expanding Its Exports of Manufactures*, Inter-American Economics and Social Council, Pan American Union, Washington, D.C., Table 2.5. "Other developing countries" include total for other regions except for developed areas, Eastern Europe, Continental China, Mongolia, North Korea, and North Viet-Nam.

[6] See Table Xc. As an average for the five-year period, 1959-63, the percentages were 44, 41, and 65 percent, respectively. On the other hand, industrial exports as a percentage of *total* exports was 9 percent for Chile, 1 percent for Colombia, and 13 percent for Mexico during 1959-60. A recent study of Chile's trade suggests that the industrial proportion of exports that goes to LAFTA countries is much higher than the LAFTA proportion of all exports. For instance, Chile's exports of manufactured products to LAFTA countries constituted 55 percent of her total manufactured exports while her total LAFTA exports comprised only 7 percent of her total exports during the five-year period 1957-61. See "Las Exportaciones Chilenas a la Zona Latinoamericana de Libre Comercio en el Quinquenio 1957-1961," Instituto de Economía, Universidad de Chile, Santiago, Chile, 1963, pp. 16 and 18.

At the same time, the percentage of these countries' total exports going to LAFTA is extremely low (see Table V). The ratios of manufactured and processed goods as a percentage of intra-LAFTA trade (Table Xc) show a well-defined change over the five-year period for only two countries: a rapid and consistent rise in Brazil's manufactures, and an equally significant fall in Venezuela's manufactured goods. In global terms, there was a decrease from the 1961 figure in 1962 and a sharp increase in 1963 in the value of manufactured products exported within LAFTA (these exports fell from $70.5 million in 1961 to $61 million in 1962 and rose to $91.5 million in 1963).

In general, the industrial countries stand out as the major processed goods exporters. The combined processed exports to LAFTA from Argentina, Brazil, and Chile have averaged more than 70 percent of total intra-LAFTA manufactured exports between 1959 and 1963.[7] If Mexico, whose manufactured exports to LAFTA increased from 6 to 15 percent of the total between 1959 and 1963, is included in this group, the average climbs to over 80 percent. Because of the great weight of Argentina's, Brazil's, and Chile's exports to LAFTA in total intra-LAFTA exports, however, these three countries combined not only dominate manufactured exports, but also export more than 75 percent of intra-LAFTA semi-processed commodities and raw materials.

(Although industrialization is seen by Latin Americans as the prime means to achieving economic growth in the LAFTA countries, it does not necessarily follow that each country should industrialize to the same extent. Nor is it inconsistent with the final objective of LAFTA (to increase the economic prosperity of each member country) that the manufactured share of some countries' exports to LAFTA fall, since a fall may be more than compensated for by related increases in the exportations to LAFTA of nonmanufactured products and services (shipping, banking, tourism, etc.). For example, some countries may prosper more by supplying the nonmanufactured inputs for the industrialization of the region than by attempting to concentrate on their own industrialization.)

(There are several important issues here. The increased market made available to industries of the zone would tend, through economies of

---

[7] It should be remembered, however, that although Argentina and Brazil are the largest industrial exporters in Latin America, the share of manufactures is still only about one-fifth of total exports of these countries.

scale, to increase the competitiveness of LAFTA-produced manufactures in markets within and outside of LAFTA. There is little concrete research in the comparative costs of production, given various
size markets, of LAFTA-manufactured goods, both among LAFTA
countries and between LAFTA countries and the developed economies.
If LAFTA production costs are higher even at future market levels
than costs in the developed economies, then the problem is one of
weighing the benefits of industrialization with tariff protection against
the costs to the economy that such industrialization would involve. The
possibility that benefits could be increased or costs reduced by a planning approach to the location of new industries leads into yet another
field of investigation, one that has been especially important in the
Central American Common Market and undoubtedly is becoming
of increasing importance for LAFTA.

On the import side, a future evaluation of LAFTA will probably
concentrate on measuring the reduction of the region's dependence
on imports from the developed countries. As was discussed in Chapters
I and II, this dependence has led to persistent balance-of-payments
problems, particularly because of the sluggish growth in exports
noted above. Greater self-sufficiency is therefore looked upon in
Latin America as an important objective of LAFTA. It is based upon
the rationale—still a highly controversial one in economic literature—
that movement in this direction will accelerate economic growth.

In recent years, individual country ratios of LAFTA trade to total
trade have ranged from a high of almost 30 percent for Paraguay to
the low of less than 1 percent for Mexico.[8] LAFTA trade for most
of the countries is small, however, and the average for all LAFTA
countries was only 9 percent between 1958 and 1963. Clearly, one of
the aims of LAFTA is to achieve a sustained increase in this average
by lowering the barriers to trade among member countries.

Trade theory distinguishes between "trade diversion" and "trade
creation" when analyzing the effects of tariff reductions among a given
bloc of countries. Trade diversion or the shifting of trade with
countries outside the bloc to countries within the bloc is generally
not considered as adding to welfare, but any effects which result in the
transfer of resources from high-cost to low-cost activities would increase

---

[8] These percentages are based on annual averages for the period, 1959-1963.

both output and trade and thus raise welfare. This distinction is useful analytically but it cannot be made with great neatness when applied to specific cases. First of all, there is the problem of measurement and of adequately drawing the lines between the two concepts; then there is the more important conceptual question of weighing short-run versus long-run consequences. It is most likely that the establishment of a free trade area will have primarily diversionary effects on trade in the short run, but it is not at all clear that these may not be welfare-producing in the long run.

A simple measure of the effectiveness of LAFTA in the movement toward greater self-sufficiency (or in diverting trade) is the change in the value of a LAFTA country's imports from other LAFTA countries as a percentage of its total imports. Such a measure, when applied over several years, will tend to pick up most of the increase in imports from LAFTA due to tariff change. It is primarily an indicator of trade diversion. While the trade-creating effects of tariff changes cannot be directly reflected in such an index, in the short run these effects will tend to be minor in any case, particularly because the share of most member countries' LAFTA trade is small.

This index can be used in a global fashion as in Table D, which shows the changes in the percentage of imports coming from LAFTA

TABLE D: *LAFTA Import Index*[a] *for All LAFTA Countries, 1960–1961 and 1962–1963*

Country	1960-61 Average	1962-63 Average
Argentina.................	8.6	9.0
Brazil....................	5.2	10.0
Chile....................	16.1	17.3
Colombia................	1.6	3.3
Ecuador.................	2.0	4.4
Mexico..................	0.4	0.7
Paraguay................	26.7	19.8
Peru....................	7.0	9.8
Uruguay.................	14.2	16.5
Total LAFTA............	6.2	8.1

Source: Tables V-1-b to V-11-b.

[a] Imports from LAFTA as a percentage of total imports for each country listed and for the whole region.

by country between the two years immediately preceding the Montevideo Treaty and the two years immediately following it.

Imports from LAFTA as a percentage of imports from the world increased in these years for every LAFTA country except Paraguay. This exception might be explained by Paraguay's special treatment in lowering tariffs.[9] At any rate, however, inferences drawn from a study at only a few points in time must be used with extreme caution.[10]

The LAFTA import index will yield more information when applied on the basis of commodity groups such as those which are presented in Table E. For each product group listed in Table E the changes in the proportion of total imports which consists of imports from LAFTA countries can be followed over a number of years in order to estimate some of the effects of LAFTA tariff reductions.

The problems discussed above are all indications of the research that is necessary in the study of LAFTA before the effects of such an association are begun to be understood. An important task will be to estimate the welfare gains and losses for each country from increased trade with the zone. It is clear that the data presented in the tables of this particular study form only a foundation for future statistical work which will lead to analyses of trends of trade patterns within LAFTA and between LAFTA and the rest of the world. By continuing the series on trade by commodities and by country, both in an absolute and relative framework, the influence of LAFTA on exports can be established. Further studies, delving deeper into the commodity categories, should yield the effect of the reduction of trade barriers on the composition and quantity of exports and imports by member countries.

[9] Less developed economies such as Paraguay and Ecuador are permitted by the Treaty (Article 32) to add products to both the National and Common Schedules at a slower rate than other countries to protect these two countries against the possibility of large losses incurred in joining LAFTA.

[10] Table V shows the degree of fluctuation which intra-LAFTA imports into each LAFTA member have been subject to since 1948; given this variation, the changes indicated in Table D could well have been spurious for our purposes, influenced by a combination of non-price variables or accidental factors such as weather conditions and special economic policies. Other factors determining import demand, such as national income changes, for example, would be reflected in the LAFTA import index if the income elasticity of the goods from the world differs from the income elasticity of LAFTA goods. (Income elasticity measures the relationship of relative changes in demand for particular commodities with relative changes in per capita incomes.) For instance, as per capita income grows, preference for U.S. or European over Latin American goods may also increase.

PART TWO

Trade Statistics

Note on Sources

The primary objective of this study is to provide a systematized collection of data concerning Latin American trade, particularly intra-LAFTA trade. These data, which are presented on the following pages, have been compiled from the sources judged to be most accurate. Use has been made of statistics presented in the official documents on foreign trade which are published by each country included in this study. In addition, statistics have been obtained from publications of the United Nations, International Monetary Fund, International Bank for Reconstruction and Development, and from special studies of the Department of Commerce of the United States, the United Nations Economic Commission for Latin America, and the Latin American Free Trade Association.

Exports by product and by country of destination are presented in detail in the foreign trade statistics of each LAFTA country. In order to summarize the value of the products traded, they are categorized as shown in Tables E and F. Products are divided into five classifications, each of which is in turn divided into three levels of production: raw materials, semi-processed, and processed (manufactured). Under the production levels, the values of goods traded are aggregated into general groupings. These groupings are described by number in Table VII, the numbers corresponding to the key in Table E. It is particularly important to note that for reasons of space only one product name follows the group numbers in Table VII. Thus, there may be more than the one indicated product represented in the group. Table E, which follows below, should be consulted in conjunction with Table VII in order to get the complete representation of products included in each category.

It is felt that the manufactured products category should be restricted to the processed goods level of production; while this rigid definition tends to underestimate the industrialized sector of the economy, the alternative of overestimation effected by including semi-

TABLE E. *Categories of Latin American Exports*

	Raw Materials	Semi-Processed	Processed or Manufactured
Animal	1a. Live animals 1b. Wool and other fibers of animal origin 1c. Fresh seafood 1d. Other	2a. Hides 2b. Animal fat, edible, inedible 2c. Meat: fresh, frozen or chilled 2d. Pelts and plumes 2e. Other	3a. Leather 3b. Canned meat 3c. Dairy products 3d. Fish meal 3e. Canned and frozen sea products including salted fish 3f. Other
Agricultural	1a. Grains 1b. Raw and baled fibers (other than wool) 1c. Fresh fruits and vegetables 1d. Seeds and nuts 1e. Other (includes sugar cane)	2a. Flour 2b. Other milled, rolled or flattened grains 2c. Semi-refined sugar 2d. Dried fruits and vegetables 2e. Coffee, cocoa, yerba mate, tea 2f. Other	3a. Food (bottled or canned) 3b. Tobacco 3c. Beverages 3d. Vegetable oils, waxes, greases 3e. Textiles (includes wool textiles) 3f. Refined sugar 3g. Other
Forestry	1a. Live plants	2a. Logs, lumber, boards, blocks, posts, stakes, beams 2b. Extracts, rubber, cork, quebracho, resins	3a. Furniture and wood manufactures 3b. Cellulose pulp, paper, paper products, plywood, fiber board

TABLE E. (*continued*)

Mineral

1a. Ores or semi-refined metals	2a. Refined metals (ingots and bars)
1b. Oil (crude)	2b. Refined oil products
1c. Stone, clay, granite, sand	3a. Rolled metal products (wire, tubes, etc.)
1d. Nonmetallic ores	3b. Machinery and machinery parts
1e. Other (includes natural gas)	3c. Vehicles and vehicle parts
	3d. Cement, bricks, cinder blocks
	3e. Chemicals, drugs, plastics, paints, varnishes, fertilizers
	3f. Glass, crystal

Miscellaneous Manufactures

a. Metal consumer products
b. Textile consumer products
c. Stone, porcelain products, glass products
d. Rubber products
e. Books
f. Other

TABLE F. *SITC Code Corresponding to Categories of Table E*

TABLE E Code	SITC Code	TABLE E Code	SITC Code
ANIMAL		**FORESTRY**	
1a.	001, 921	1a.	292-01, 292-03, 292-04, 292-06, 292-07
1b.	262	2a.	241, 242, 243
1c.	031	2b.	231-01, 244, 292-02, 292-09, 633
1d.	271-01, 291		
2a.	211	3a.	632, 821
2b.	091, 411, 413-04	3b.	251, 631, 641, 642
2c.	011		
2d.	212, 613	**MINERAL**	
2e.	411-01		
3a.	211-05, 611, 612	1a.	272-15, 272-16, 281 - 283, 285
3b.	012, 013		
3c.	021-025, 029	1b.	312
3d.	081-04	1c.	272-02 - 272-04, 272-07, 272-08, 272-11, 272-13
3e.	032		
3f.	026, 081-04	1d.	271, 272-01, 272-05, 272-06, 272-12, 272-14, 311, 672-01
AGRICULTURAL		1e.	272-19, 314, 315
1a.	041, 042-01, 043 - 045	2a.	284, 681-01, 681-02, 681-03, 682-01, 683-01, 684-01, 685-01, 686-01, 688-01, 689-01
1b.	261, 263 - 265		
1c.	051-01 - 051-06, 054-01, 054-03, 054-09		
1d.	051-07, 221, 292-05	2b.	313, 521
1e.	061-01, 081-01	3a.	681-04 - 681-15, 682-02, 683-02, 684-02, 685-02, 686-02, 687-02, 688-02, 689-02, 699-01 - 699-07
2a.	046 - 047		
2b.	042-02, 046 - 047		
2c.	061-01		
2d.	052-01, 054-02, 055-01	3b.	711 - 713, 715, 716, 721
2e.	071, 072, 074	3c.	731 - 735
2f.	048-02, 48-09, 055-04, 061-03, 075, 081-02	3d.	661, 662
3a.	048-01, 048-03, 048-04, 053, 055-02, 055-03	3e.	266, 511, 512, 531 - 533, 541, 551, 552, 561, 591, 599
3b.	111, 112	3f.	664
3c.	121, 122		
3d.	081-03, 412, 413		
3e.	267, 651 - 655		
3f.	061-02		
3g.	061-04, 061-09, 073-01, 081-09, 099		

TABLE F. *SITC Code Corresponding to Categories of Table E (continued)*

TABLE E Code	SITC Code	TABLE E Code	SITC Code
MISCELLANEOUS MANUFAC-TURES		MISCELLANEOUS MANUFAC-TURES (continued)	
a.	671, 673, 691, 699-08 - 699-29, 714, 721-12, 861	d.	231-02 - 231-04, 621, 629, 841-07, 851-04
b.	656, 657, 841-01 - 841-05, 841-08, 841-12, 841-19	e.	892
c.	663, 665, 666, 672	f.	657-04, 811, 812, 831, 841-06, 841-11, 851, 862, 863, 891, 864, 899, 911, 931

Source: United Nations, *Commodity Indexes for the Standard International Trade Classifications*, Statistical Papers, Series M, No. 10 (April 1953).

processed goods under manufacturing might be much more misleading in the description of trade patterns of LAFTA countries. In any case, the rather detailed breakdown of Table E enables the reader to make alternative assumptions in defining the manufacturing sector.

The country totals for each year, presented in the "c" part of Table VII,[1] should agree with the export figures by country and by year shown in Table VI. Although the totals of Table VII are the result of adding the product breakdowns within the table and the data of Table VI originate in IMF publications (in the period 1959-1963), IMF data are taken from totals provided by country sources similar or equal to those we have used. Where figures do not coincide it is the result of one of four possible factors: (1) In the cases of Colombia and Peru, in which the sources give data in local currency, discrepancies may appear because of exchange rates used to convert to dollars. This study employs the method of equating the LAFTA total and the total for LAFTA, Bolivia, and Venezuela (in local currency times an implicit exchange rate) to the LAFTA total and the total of LAFTA, Bolivia, and Venezuela given in dollars by the IMF for exports in that year (Table VI). The average of the two implicit exchange rates found was

[1] Table VII includes data for all the countries under consideration in the period 1959-1962. The year 1963 is complete except in the case of Bolivia, for which breakdowns of exports into product categories and countries of destination are not available at the writing of this study.

applied to all the figures for each year in Table VII to get the dollar figures shown. The method was used not only for Colombia and Peru, but also for Venezuela (for which, however, no discrepancies occur). Chilean figures appearing in "pesos de oro" were converted by a constant factor (4.8546 pesos/dollar) to dollars; Mexican data were converted for all years at 12.5 pesos to the dollar. (2) In several instances export figures were omitted by the IMF although these figures were larger than 50 thousand dollars. Chile's exports to Colombia in 1959, 1960, and 1961; Paraguay's exports to Brazil in 1960, 1961, and 1963; and Paraguay's exports to Chile in 1963 are examples of this error. (3) Apparently there are some cases in which Table VII totals check with source totals, but IMF totals (Table VI) do not. This is true for all discrepancies in Ecuador's exports between Tables VI and VII. The same type of error is evident in the totals for Mexican exports as exports to Ecuador in 1960 and 1961, and Mexican exports to Bolivia in 1960. (4) Most difficult to reconcile is the rather large difference found in six places due to the disagreement between the totals in Table VII and those of the original sources. (It is assumed that these sources were also used by IMF.) Unless figures have been omitted or included in the product breakdown in the sources which were then accounted for in the final total, it is felt that there are adding errors in the original sources and that the figures of Table VII are the correct ones. Such errors have been found in the exports to the following countries for the cited years: Brazil to Uruguay, 1959; Brazil to Chile, 1963; Brazil to Paraguay, 1963; and Mexico to Colombia in 1961, 1962, and 1963.

In spite of the effort expended on collecting Latin American trade statistics, errors are likely to occur. The accuracy of the data provided by some countries is greater than for others. This is made evident in cross-checking exports and imports in Table VI. It might well be expected that for a given year the exports of country A to country B would equal country B's imports from country A, allowing for shipping, insurance, and other charges. Because of differences in recording dates extending from one year to another and different accounting procedures, however, such statistics are not always comparable. Some of these inconsistencies result from faulty data at collection points: estimates are frequently incomplete or certain administrative procedures become lax.

In some cases re-exports play an important role and, not being separately shown in a country's trade data, will tend to bias the export figures. And, of course, contraband is still significant in Latin America, but can never be adequately reflected in official data. (There may even exist a combination of the re-export and contraband problems, as when, for instance, Brazilian drugs are smuggled into Venezuela and then exported to Ecuador.)

The limitations and the possibility of inaccuracies in the trade data presented in this study do not preclude their use in analyzing general patterns of Latin American and intra-LAFTA trade. These data are the best available. Although one might be wary of attaching too much importance to and credence in a specific datum, one should be able to discern with confidence the broader trends in the flows of commodities among the countries of LAFTA. It is to this purpose that the data in the study are applied.

Basic Tables

General Latin American Trade

Table I. *World and Latin American Foreign Trade, 1934-1963*
(Dollar items in millions of U.S. dollars)

Year	Exports [a]			Imports [a]		
	Total World	Total Latin American Countries	Ratio of Latin America to World (percent)	Total World	Total Latin American Countries	Ratio of Latin America to World (percent)
Average 1934-38	20,358	1,923	9.4	22,477	1,358	6.3
1938	20,946	1,856	8.9	22,615	1,472	6.5
1948	53,302	6,666	12.5	56,910	5,746	10.1
1952	73,365	7,000	9.5	76,440	7,011	9.2
1954	76,712	7,736	10.1	76,389	6,874	9.0
1956	92,870	8,395	9.0	94,687	7,581	8.0
1958	109,748	8,155	7.4	114,705	8,171	7.1
1959	117,446	8,243	7.0	121,473	7,650	6.3
1960	131,492	8,660	6.6	134,897	8,014	5.9
1961	136,710	8,552	6.3	140,626	8,383	6.0
1962	142,471	9,114	6.4	148,997	8,351	5.6
1963	154,978 [b]	9,740 [c]	6.3	161,593 [d]	8,696 [c]	5.4

Sources: United Nations, International Monetary Fund, International Bank for Reconstruction and Development, Direction of International Trade, Series T, Vol. 7, No. 6; Series T, Vol. 8, No. 7; Series T, Vol. 9, No. 10; Series T, Vol. 6, No. 9, Washington, D.C. International Monetary Fund, International Bank for Reconstruction and Development, Direction of Trade, Annual 1958-62, Washington, D.C.

[a] Exports FOB; imports CIF.

[b] International Monetary Fund, International Financial Statistics, September, 1964. This figure is generally about 1.5 percent lower than the DIT total would be for 1963, based on 1959-1962 differences.

[c] Ibid. Difference in DIT and IFS totals is less than 0.5 percent.

[d] Ibid. Difference in DIT and IFS totals is less than 0.5 percent.

Table II-a. Latin American Exports and Imports, 1938-1963ᵃ

(Millions of U.S. Dollars)

Year	LAFTA	LAFTA, Bolivia and Venezuela	All Latin America	United States	Western Europe	Others	World Total
Latin American Exports to:							
1938	102	107	114	537	925	280	1856
1948	491	548	609	2505	2431	1121	6666
1952	515	552	601	3533	1728	1138	7000
1954	671	701	750	3243	2371	1372	7736
1956	557	589	653	3867	2539	1336	8395
1958	582	618	737	3594	2335	1489	8155
1959	546	588	718	3602	2442	1481	8243
1960	555	583	689	3675	2663	1633	8660
1961	472	498	580	3213	2718	2041	8552
1962	558	591	694	3244	3021	2155	9114
1963	564	595	718	3340	3276	2323	9657
Latin American Imports from:							
1938	114	116	122	508	696	146	1472
1948	555	614	655	3261	1324	506	5746
1952	453	620	681	3713	1929	688	7011
1954	563	720	770	3348	1956	800	6874
1956	463	696	749	3812	2086	934	7581
1958	457	815	877	4064	2358	872	8171
1959	410	718	808	3667	2337	838	7650
1960	422	710	791	3628	2551	1044	8014
1961	407	610	690	3494	2775	1424	8383
1962	475	683	786	3402	2729	1434	8351
1963	583	788	882	3348	2548	1772	8550

Sources: United Nations, International Monetary Fund, International Bank for Reconstruction and Development, Direction of International Trade, Series T, Vol. 7, No. 6; Series T, Vol. 8, No. 7; Series T, Vol. 9, No. 10; Series T, Vol. 6, No. 9, Washington, D.C. International Monetary Fund, International Bank for Reconstruction and Development, Direction of Trade, Annual 1958-62, and May-September, 1964, Washington, D.C.

aᐟ Exports FOB; imports CIF.

Table II-b. *Latin American Exports and Imports, 1938-1963*[a]

(Percent)

Year	LAFTA	LAFTA, Bolivia and Venezuela	All Latin America	United States	Western Europe	Others	World Total
Latin American Exports to:							
1938	5.5	5.8	6.1	28.9	49.8	15.1	100.0
1948	7.4	8.2	9.1	37.6	36.5	16.8	100.0
1952	7.4	7.9	8.6	50.5	24.7	16.3	100.0
1954	8.7	9.1	9.7	41.9	30.6	17.7	100.0
1956	6.6	7.0	7.8	46.1	30.2	15.9	100.0
1958	7.1	7.6	9.0	44.1	28.6	18.3	100.0
1959	6.6	7.1	8.7	43.7	29.6	18.0	100.0
1960	6.4	6.7	8.0	42.4	30.8	18.9	100.0
1961	5.5	5.8	6.8	37.6	31.8	23.9	100.0
1962	6.1	6.5	7.6	35.6	33.1	23.6	100.0
1963	5.8	6.2	7.4	34.6	33.9	24.0	100.0
Latin American Imports from:							
1938	7.7	7.9	8.3	34.5	47.3	9.9	100.0
1948	9.7	10.7	11.4	56.8	23.0	8.8	100.0
1952	6.5	8.8	9.7	53.0	27.5	9.8	100.0
1954	8.2	10.5	11.2	48.7	28.5	11.6	100.0
1956	6.1	9.2	9.9	50.3	27.5	12.3	100.0
1958	5.6	10.0	10.7	49.7	28.9	10.7	100.0
1959	5.4	9.4	10.6	47.9	30.5	11.0	100.0
1960	5.3	8.9	9.9	45.3	31.8	13.0	100.0
1961	4.9	7.3	8.2	41.7	33.1	17.0	100.0
1962	5.7	8.2	9.4	40.7	32.7	17.2	100.0
1963	6.8	9.2	10.3	39.2	29.8	20.7	100.0

Sources: United Nations, International Monetary Fund, International Bank for Reconstruction and Development, Direction of International Trade, Series T, Vol. 7, No. 6; Series T, Vol. 8, No. 7; Series T, Vol. 9, No. 10; Series T, Vol. 6, No. 9, Washington, D.C. International Monetary Fund, International Bank for Reconstruction and Development, Direction of Trade, Annual 1958-62, and May-September, 1964, Washington, D.C.

[a] Exports FOB; imports CIF.

Table III-a. *Exports of LAFTA Countries and of Bolivia and Venezuela as a Percentage of Total Latin American Exports to Latin American Countries, 1934-1963*

Country	Average 1934-38	Average 1946-51	1952	1954	1956	1959	1960	1961	1962	1963
Argentina	41.7	31.3	15.0	33.0	19.1	20.8	24.8	19.4	22.6	27.8
Brazil	19.2	23.5	21.0	19.4	15.7	10.7	12.9	16.9	11.3	11.7
Chile	5.3	7.9	11.7	8.0	7.1	6.4	5.5	7.8	7.4	7.5
Colombia	0.4	0.9	0.7	1.2	1.5	1.0	1.3	1.6	1.6	1.7
Ecuador	2.6	2.2	1.3	1.7	1.4	1.5	1.3	1.4	0.9	1.2
Mexico	4.3	5.1	3.7	3.2	3.9	3.5	3.5	5.2	5.5	7.4
Paraguay	2.3	2.0	1.8	2.4	2.3	1.1	1.3	1.7	1.6	1.4
Peru	10.6	10.4	12.3	6.1	8.1	7.2	6.3	6.6	7.7	7.5
Uruguay	8.3	2.6	5.1	5.3	4.3	0.5	0.6	1.0	1.3	2.2
Totals	94.7	85.9	72.6	80.3	63.8	52.7	57.5	61.6	59.9	68.4
Bolivia	1.0	0.4	0.6	0.4	1.1	1.0	1.2	0.9	0.4	0.4
Venezuela	1.5	6.7	17.4	16.1	28.8	37.3	33.6	28.9	26.7	23.2
Total LAFTA, Bolivia and Venezuela	97.2	93.0	90.6	96.8	93.7	91.0	92.3	91.4	87.0	92.1
Total Exports (FOB) from Latin American Countries to Latin American Countries (Millions of U.S. dollars)	113	581	601	750	653	718	689	580	694	718

Sources: United Nations, Study of Inter-Latin American Trade, Economic Commission for Latin America, 1957, p. 22. United Nations, International Monetary Fund, International Bank for Reconstruction and Development, Direction of International Trade, Series T, Vol. 7, No. 6; Series T, Vol. 8, No. 7; Series T, Vol. 9, No. 10; Series T, Vol. 6, No. 9, Washington, D.C. International Monetary Fund, International Bank for Reconstruction and Development, Direction of Trade, Annual 1958-62, and May-September, 1964, Washington, D.C.

Table III-b. *Exports of LAFTA Countries and of Bolivia and Venezuela as a Percentage of Total Latin American Exports to the World, 1934-1963*

Country	Average 1934-38	Average 1946-51	1952	1954	1956	1959	1960	1961	1962	1963
Argentina	28.1	21.4	9.9	14.0	11.2	12.2	12.5	11.3	13.3	14.1
Brazil	15.8	20.2	20.1	20.2	17.7	15.5	14.8	16.4	13.3	14.6
Chile	6.7	4.9	6.6	5.2	6.5	6.0	5.7	5.9	5.8	5.6
Colombia	4.1	5.2	6.8	8.5	7.1	5.7	5.4	5.1	5.1	4.6
Ecuador	0.7	0.8	1.1	1.3	1.1	1.2	1.1	1.1	1.3	1.4
Mexico	10.8	7.1	8.5	6.5	7.9	9.1	8.8	9.6	10.2	10.0
Paraguay	0.4	0.4	0.4	0.4	0.4	0.4	0.3	0.4	0.4	0.4
Peru	4.2	2.9	3.4	3.2	3.7	3.8	5.0	5.8	5.9	5.6
Uruguay	3.6	3.2	3.0	3.2	2.5	1.2	1.5	2.0	1.7	1.7
Totals	74.4	66.1	59.8	62.5	58.1	55.1	55.2	57.6	57.0	58.1
Bolivia	2.4	1.7	2.0	1.4	1.3	0.9	0.8	0.9	0.8	0.9
Venezuela	11.6	16.3	20.7	22.0	25.2	28.7	29.1	28.2	28.5	27.2
Total LAFTA, Bolivia and Venezuela	88.4	84.1	82.5	85.9	84.6	84.7	85.1	86.7	86.3	86.2
Total Exports (FOB) from Latin American Countries to the World (Millions of U.S. dollars)	1923	6147	7000	7736	8395	8243	8660	8552	9114	9657

Sources: United Nations, Study of Inter-Latin American Trade, Economic Commission for Latin America, 1957, p. 22. United Nations, International Monetary Fund, International Bank for Reconstruction and Development, Direction of International Trade, Series T, Vol. 7, No. 6; Series T, Vol. 8, No. 7; Series T, Vol. 9, No. 10; Series T, Vol. 6, No. 9, Washington, D.C. International Monetary Fund, International Bank for Reconstruction and Development, Direction of Trade, Annual 1958-62, and May-September, 1964, Washington, D.C.

Table IV-a. *Imports of LAFTA Countries and of Bolivia and Venezuela as a Percentage of Total Latin American Imports from Latin American Countries, 1934-1963*

Country	Average 1934-38	Average 1946-51	1952	1954	1956	1959	1960	1961	1962	1963
Argentina	28.9	28.3	32.2	29.9	29.1	27.5	25.6	28.5	19.9	14.6
Brazil	31.9	21.3	25.5	30.5	31.7	28.9	28.9	21.1	30.3	29.8
Chile	8.8	11.3	11.4	13.7	8.7	7.0	10.8	15.3	12.7	15.9
Colombia	1.4	4.0	2.6	3.2	2.7	2.5	2.6	3.6	3.3	4.1
Ecuador	0.6	0.7	0.4	0.7	0.7	0.7	0.4	0.4	0.7	2.0
Mexico	0.9	1.6	0.8	0.6	1.6	1.5	1.6	1.6	1.6	2.2
Paraguay	3.8	1.9	0.8	1.6	1.3	0.9	1.0	1.2	0.7	0.9
Peru	4.4	3.8	2.9	3.0	3.4	2.9	3.9	5.6	6.7	7.6
Uruguay	8.4	8.5	9.5	9.2	8.3	5.5	8.6	6.9	6.0	5.2
Totals	89.1	81.4	86.1	92.4	87.5	77.4	83.4	84.2	81.9	82.2
Bolivia	5.6	4.6	3.9	2.5	2.8	2.1	1.5	2.1	1.5	1.1
Venezuela	0.5	5.5	2.5	1.0	1.3	4.9	3.0	3.3	3.3	3.0
Total LAFTA, Bolivia and Venezuela	95.2	91.5	92.5	95.9	91.6	84.4	87.9	89.6	86.7	86.3
Total Imports (CIF) of Latin American Countries from Latin America (Millions of U.S. dollars)	130	645	681	770	749	808	791	690	786	882

Sources: United Nations, Study of Inter-Latin American Trade, Economic Commission for Latin America, 1957, p. 22. United Nations, International Monetary Fund, International Bank for Reconstruction and Development, Direction of International Trade, Series T, Vol. 7, No. 6; Series T, Vol. 8, No. 7; Series T, Vol. 9, No. 10; Series T, Vol. 6, No. 9, Washington, D.C. International Monetary Fund, International Bank for Reconstruction and Development, Direction of Trade, Annual 1958-62, and May-September, 1964, Washington, D.C.

Table IV-b. *Imports of LAFTA Countries and of Bolivia and Venezuela as a Percentage of Total Latin American Imports from the World, 1934-1963*

Country	Average 1934-38	Average 1946-51	1952	1954	1956	1959	1960	1961	1962	1963
Argentina	27.8	20.2	17.1	13.9	14.9	13.0	15.6	17.4	16.2	11.5
Brazil	19.2	21.1	28.7	23.8	16.3	18.0	18.2	17.4	17.7	17.4
Chile	5.5	4.7	5.3	5.0	4.7	5.4	6.2	7.0	6.1	7.4
Colombia	5.7	6.4	5.9	9.8	8.7	5.4	6.4	6.4	6.4	5.8
Ecuador	0.9	0.8	0.8	1.3	1.1	1.2	1.3	1.2	1.1	1.5
Mexico	9.3	10.6	10.5	11.6	14.1	13.1	14.8	13.6	13.7	14.5
Paraguay	0.8	0.5	0.3	0.5	0.3	0.3	0.4	0.4	0.4	0.4
Peru	3.7	3.1	4.1	3.6	4.8	3.8	4.7	5.6	6.4	6.5
Uruguay	4.5	3.6	3.7	4.0	2.8	2.1	3.0	2.5	2.8	2.1
Totals	77.4	71.0	76.4	73.5	67.7	62.3	70.6	71.5	70.8	67.2
Bolivia	2.0	1.3	1.3	1.0	1.1	0.8	0.9	0.9	1.0	1.2
Venezuela	5.8	12.0	10.8	13.2	13.5	18.4	13.3	12.7	11.9	10.2
Total LAFTA, Bolivia and Venezuela	85.2	84.3	88.5	87.7	82.3	81.5	84.8	85.1	83.7	78.6
Total Imports (CIF) of Latin American Countries from the World (Millions of U.S. dollars)	1358	5755	7011	6874	7581	7650	8014	8383	8351	8550

Sources: United Nations, Study of Inter-Latin American Trade, Economic Commission for Latin America, 1957, p. 22. United Nations, International Monetary Fund, International Bank for Reconstruction and Development, Direction of International Trade, Series T, Vol. 7, No. 6; Series T, Vol. 8, No. 7; Series T, Vol. 9, No. 10; Series T, Vol. 6, No. 9, Washington, D.C. International Monetary Fund, International Bank for Reconstruction and Development, Direction of Trade, Annual 1958-62, and May-September, 1964, Washington, D.C.

Latin American Trade by Country

Table V-1-a. *Argentina's Exports by Main Trading Areas, 1938-1963*

(Dollar items in millions of U.S. dollars)

Year	To LAFTA Value ($)	To LAFTA Percent	To all Latin America Value ($)	To all Latin America Percent	To United States Value ($)	To United States Percent	To Western Europe Value ($)	To Western Europe Percent	Total Exports Value ($)	Total Exports Percent
1938	40.6	8.8	43.7	9.5	46.1	10.0	341.3	74.0	461.0	100
1948	148.2	9.1	171.6	10.5	159.1	9.8	1,131.9	69.6	1,626.7	100
1952	84.1	11.9	90.3	12.7	161.5	22.8	373.3	52.6	709.4	100
1954	175.6	16.3	247.8	22.9	122.4	11.3	586.4	54.3	1,079.9	100
1956	112.5	11.9	124.8	13.2	117.5	12.4	603.1	63.9	943.8	100
1958	118.7	11.9	132.2	13.3	128.4	12.9	621.4	62.5	994.1	100
1959	137.6	13.6	149.3	14.8	107.8	10.7	655.0	64.9	1,009.0	100
1960	162.5	15.1	171.1	15.8	91.9	8.5	693.0	64.2	1,079.5	100
1961	100.0	10.4	112.8	11.7	83.8	8.7	475.8	49.3	964.2	100
1962	141.5	11.6	156.5	12.9	90.9	7.5	835.5	68.7	1,215.8	100
1963	185.0	13.6	200.0	14.6	153.6	11.2	884.1	64.8	1,364.6	100

Sources: United Nations, International Monetary Fund, International Bank for Reconstruction and Development, Direction of International Trade, Series T, Vol. 7, No. 6; Series T, Vol. 8, No. 7; Series T, Vol. 9, No. 10; Series T, Vol. 6, No. 9, Washington, D.C. International Monetary Fund, International Bank for Reconstruction and Development, Direction of Trade, Annual 1958-62, and July, 1964, Washington, D.C.

Table V-1-b. *Argentina's Imports by Main Trading Areas, 1938-1963*
(Dollar items in millions of U.S. dollars)

Year	From LAFTA Value ($)	From LAFTA Percent	From all Latin America Value ($)	From all Latin America Percent	From United States Value ($)	From United States Percent	From Western Europe Value ($)	From Western Europe Percent	Total Imports Value ($)	Total Imports Percent
1938	26.6	5.4	27.7	5.6	100.0	20.4	292.4	59.6	490.8	100
1948	187.5	11.8	230.0	14.5	604.0	38.0	589.8	37.1	1,590.4	100
1952	155.2	13.0	220.0	18.4	229.9	19.2	471.9	39.5	1,195.8	100
1954	182.3	19.1	230.6	24.2	141.2	14.8	321.7	33.7	954.8	100
1956	140.9	12.5	217.9	19.3	230.4	20.4	403.2	35.8	1,127.6	100
1958	175.6	14.3	284.8	23.1	202.7	16.5	512.2	41.6	1,232.1	100
1959	107.3	10.8	222.0	22.4	191.1	19.3	409.8	41.3	992.2	100
1960	106.5	8.5	202.4	16.2	327.4	26.2	437.1	35.0	1,247.4	100
1961	126.0	8.6	196.9	13.5	383.2	26.2	695.5	47.6	1,460.4	100
1962	103.2	7.6	156.7	11.6	389.9	29.4	617.8	45.6	1,355.8	100
1963	101.0	10.3	129.0	13.2	241.7	24.6	457.7	46.7	980.9	100

Sources: United Nations, International Monetary Fund, International Bank for Reconstruction and Development, Direction of International Trade, Series T, Vol. 7, No. 6; Series T, Vol. 8, No. 7; Series T, Vol. 9, No. 10; Series T, Vol. 6, No. 9, Washington, D.C. International Monetary Fund, International Bank for Reconstruction and Development, Direction of Trade, Annual 1958-62, and July, 1964, Washington, D.C.

Table V-2a. *Brazil's Exports by Main Trading Areas, 1938-1963*

(Dollar items in millions of U.S. dollars)

Year	To LAFTA Value ($)	To LAFTA Percent	To all Latin America Value ($)	To all Latin America Percent	To United States Value ($)	To United States Percent	To Western Europe Value ($)	To Western Europe Percent	Total Exports Value ($)	Total Exports Percent
1938	17.9	6.2	18.1	6.3	99.3	34.3	146.5	50.7	289.2	100
1948	147.9	12.6	158.9	13.5	507.4	43.3	372.7	31.8	1,172.7	100
1952	125.5	8.9	126.2	9.0	726.5	51.6	455.4	32.3	1,408.8	100
1954	144.4	9.2	145.3	9.3	578.6	37.0	694.3	44.5	1,561.8	100
1956	99.8	6.7	102.5	6.9	734.6	49.5	518.9	35.0	1,482.6	100
1958	143.1	11.5	146.3	11.8	534.4	43.0	414.0	33.3	1,242.9	100
1959	75.1	5.9	76.9	6.0	592.2	46.2	540.4	35.1	1,281.9	100
1960	86.4	6.8	89.0	7.0	563.7	44.1	455.7	35.6	1,270.9	100
1961	95.2	6.8	97.8	7.0	562.8	40.1	537.3	38.3	1,402.3	100
1962	75.7	6.2	78.7	6.5	484.8	39.9	482.8	39.8	1,213.8	100
1963	76.0	5.4	83.8	6.0	530.9	37.7	584.4	41.5	1,407.0	100

Sources: United Nations, International Monetary Fund, International Bank for Reconstruction and Development,
Direction of International Trade, Series T, Vol. 7, No. 6; Series T, Vol. 8, No. 7; Series T, Vol. 9,
No. 10; Series T, Vol. 6, No. 9, Washington, D.C. International Monetary Fund, International Bank
for Reconstruction and Development, Direction of Trade, Annual 1958-62, and May, 1964, Washington,
D.C.

Table V-2-b. *Brazil's Imports by Main Trading Areas, 1938-1963*
(Dollar items in millions of U.S. dollars)

Year	From LAFTA Value ($)	From LAFTA Percent	From all Latin America Value ($)	From all Latin America Percent	From United States Value ($)	From United States Percent	From Western Europe Value ($)	From Western Europe Percent	Total Imports Value ($)	Total Imports Percent
1938	40.9	13.9	40.9	13.9	71.3	24.2	154.4	52.4	294.8	100
1948	102.9	9.1	114.6	10.1	587.8	51.8	290.3	25.6	1,134.2	100
1952	87.2	4.3	173.6	8.6	837.0	41.7	765.4	37.9	2,009.5	100
1954	153.1	9.5	235.4	14.6	537.0	33.3	573.2	35.5	1,633.5	100
1956	117.1	9.5	237.1	19.2	355.1	28.8	406.4	32.9	1,233.9	100
1958	106.5	7.9	247.4	18.3	482.7	35.7	409.8	30.3	1,352.8	100
1959	116.9	8.5	233.8	17.0	461.3	33.6	451.2	32.8	1,374.4	100
1960	108.7	7.4	228.9	15.5	443.2	30.3	510.2	34.9	1,463.1	100
1961	44.9	3.1	146.0	10.0	514.8	35.2	476.9	32.6	1,461.6	100
1962	128.7	8.7	238.2	16.1	457.1	31.0	503.6	34.1	1,475.5	100
1963	164.0	11.3	262.4	17.6	456.5	30.7	475.8	32.0	1,487.4	100

Sources: United Nations, International Monetary Fund, International Bank for Reconstruction and Development, Direction of International Trade, Series T, Vol. 7, No. 6; Series T, Vol. 8, No. 7; Series T, Vol. 9, No. 10; Series T, Vol. 6, No. 9, Washington, D.C. International Monetary Fund, International Bank for Reconstruction and Development, Direction of Trade, Annual 1958-62, and May, 1964, Washington, D.C.

Table V-3-a. *Chile's Exports by Main Trading Areas, 1938-1963*
(Dollar items in millions of U.S. dollars)

Year	To LAFTA Value ($)	To LAFTA Percent	To all Latin America Value ($)	To all Latin America Percent	To United States Value ($)	To United States Percent	To Western Europe Value ($)	To Western Europe Percent	Total Exports Value ($)	Total Exports Percent
1938	4.5	3.2	6.4	4.5	22.2	15.7	74.1	52.6	141.0	100
1948	27.3	8.3	36.6	11.1	174.4	52.9	92.1	27.9	329.8	100
1952	63.6	13.8	70.5	15.3	264.0	57.2	109.9	23.8	461.7	100
1954	56.6	14.0	59.7	14.8	187.1	46.4	145.6	36.1	403.2	100
1956	41.8	7.7	46.6	8.6	243.5	44.7	242.9	44.6	544.3	100
1958	32.7	8.4	37.8	9.7	157.4	40.5	187.8	48.3	388.8	100
1959	38.7	7.8	45.6	9.2	193.5	39.0	245.7	49.5	496.6	100
1960	29.3	6.0	38.2	7.8	182.1	37.1	256.6	52.4	489.7	100
1961	34.8	6.8	45.1	8.9	185.7	36.5	246.8	48.5	508.6	100
1962	39.5	7.4	51.5	9.7	193.9	36.5	248.3	46.7	531.2	100
1963	49.4	9.1	54.0	10.0	185.0	34.2	257.6	47.6	541.6	100

Sources: United Nations, International Monetary Fund, International Bank for Reconstruction and Development, Direction of International Trade, Series T, Vol. 7, No. 6; Series T, Vol. 8, No. 7; Series T, Vol. 9, No. 10; Series T, Vol. 6, No. 9, Washington, D.C. International Monetary Fund, International Bank for Reconstruction and Development, Direction of Trade, Annual 1958-62, and September, 1964, Washington, D.C.

Table V-3-b. *Chile's Imports by Main Trading Areas, 1938-1963*
(Dollar items in millions of U.S. dollars)

Year	From LAFTA Value ($)	From LAFTA Percent	From all Latin America Value ($)	From all Latin America Percent	From United States Value ($)	From United States Percent	From Western Europe Value ($)	From Western Europe Percent	Total Imports Value ($)	Total Imports Percent
1938	12.4	12.0	14.2	13.8	28.6	27.8	51.9	50.4	103.0	100
1948	75.1	28.1	80.3	29.8	114.3	42.5	47.8	17.8	269.1	100
1952	67.9	18.3	77.4	20.9	191.4	51.6	86.4	23.3	370.9	100
1954	96.1	28.0	105.8	30.8	139.8	40.4	85.0	24.8	343.1	100
1956	60.9	17.2	65.2	18.4	161.5	45.7	105.0	29.7	353.6	100
1958	46.3	11.2	54.6	13.2	213.3	51.7	124.0	30.0	412.7	100
1959	54.6	13.2	56.9	13.8	218.9	53.1	119.4	30.0	411.9	100
1960	81.4	16.3	85.4	17.1	239.0	47.8	151.2	33.0	499.4	100
1961	93.6	15.9	105.6	17.9	237.7	40.4	195.6	33.2	589.0	100
1962	80.5	15.8	99.7	19.6	195.0	38.3	172.4	33.9	509.1	100
1963	120.0	18.8	140.1	22.0	223.9	35.1	221.3	34.7	637.5	100

Sources: United Nations, International Monetary Fund, International Bank for Reconstruction and Development, Direction of International Trade, Series T, Vol. 7, No. 6; Series T. Vol. 8, No. 7; Series T, Vol. 9, No. 10; Series T, Vol. 6, No. 9, Washington, D.C. International Monetary Fund, International Bank for Reconstruction and Development, Direction of Trade, Annual 1958-62, and September, 1964, Washington, D.C.

Table V-4-a. *Colombia's Exports by Main Trading Areas, 1938-1963*
(Dollar items in millions of U.S. dollars)

Year	To LAFTA Value ($)	To LAFTA Percent	To all Latin America Value ($)	To all Latin America Percent	To United States Value ($)	To United States Percent	To Western Europe Value ($)	To Western Europe Percent	Total Exports Value ($)	Total Exports Percent
1938	.2	.2	.7	.9	42.6	52.8	19.0	23.5	80.7	100
1948	2.3	.9	4.6	1.6	239.7	83.1	14.0	4.9	288.5	100
1952	2.9	.6	4.4	.9	380.9	80.5	43.9	7.3	473.2	100
1954	3.6	.5	9.3	1.4	518.4	78.9	77.7	11.8	657.1	100
1956	3.2	.5	9.5	1.6	435.2	72.6	97.6	16.3	599.1	100
1958	3.0	.7	7.1	1.5	318.8	69.2	93.6	20.3	460.7	100
1959	2.8	.6	7.3	1.6	321.4	69.0	117.1	25.1	466.0	100
1960	4.8	1.0	8.9	1.9	298.4	64.0	128.8	27.6	465.1	100
1961	6.1	1.4	9.4	2.2	260.0	59.8	137.4	31.6	434.8	100
1962	7.4	1.6	11.2	2.4	266.7	57.5	149.7	32.3	463.6	100
1963	6.0	1.3	12.4	2.8	233.7	52.3	150.0	33.6	446.6	100

Sources: United Nations, International Monetary Fund, International Bank for Reconstruction and Development, *Direction of International Trade*, Series T, Vol. 7, No. 6; Series T, Vol. 8, No. 7; Series T, Vol. 9, No. 10; Series T, Vol. 6, No. 9, Washington, D.C. International Monetary Fund, International Bank for Reconstruction and Development, *Direction of Trade*, Annual 1958-62, and June, 1964, Washington, D.C.

Table V-4.b. *Colombia's Imports by Main Trading Areas, 1938-1963*

(Dollar items in millions of U.S. dollars)

Year	From LAFTA Value ($)	From LAFTA Percent	From all Latin America Value ($)	From all Latin America Percent	From United States Value ($)	From United States Percent	From Western Europe Value ($)	From Western Europe Percent	Total Imports Value ($)	Total Imports Percent
1938	.8	.9	1.5	1.7	44.4	49.9	36.5	41.0	89.0	100
1948	27.2	8.2	32.1	9.5	235.0	69.8	56.0	16.6	336.6	100
1952	13.1	3.2	17.9	4.3	278.8	67.1	90.3	21.7	415.3	100
1954	15.6	2.3	24.6	3.7	420.9	62.7	15.6	2.3	671.8	100
1956	14.7	2.2	20.4	3.1	405.9	61.8	186.9	28.4	657.2	100
1958	7.1	1.8	17.8	4.5	237.7	59.5	121.4	30.4	399.6	100
1959	9.0	2.2	20.3	4.9	245.4	59.2	112.6	27.2	414.2	100
1960	6.7	1.3	20.9	4.1	293.6	57.1	160.7	31.2	513.1	100
1961	10.2	1.9	25.2	4.7	278.8	51.7	189.0	35.0	539.3	100
1962	13.0	2.4	26.3	4.9	277.7	51.8	186.8	34.8	536.2	100
1963	21.3	4.2	36.5	7.3	259.9	51.9	161.8	32.3	500.7	100

Sources: United Nations, International Monetary Fund, International Bank for Reconstruction and Development, Direction of International Trade, Series T, Vol. 7, No. 6; Series T, Vol. 8, No. 7; Series T, Vol. 9, No. 10; Series T, Vol. 6, No. 9, Washington, D.C. International Monetary Fund, International Bank for Reconstruction and Development, Direction of Trade, Annual 1958-62, and June, 1964, Washington, D.C.

Table V-5-a. *Ecuador's Exports by Main Trading Areas, 1938-1963*
(Dollar items in millions of U.S. dollars)

Year	To LAFTA Value ($)	To LAFTA Percent	To all Latin America Value ($)	To all Latin America Percent	To United States Value ($)	To United States Percent	To Western Europe Value ($)	To Western Europe Percent	Total Exports Value ($)	Total Exports Percent
1938	2.5	21.0	2.7	22.7	4.5	37.8	4.1	34.5	11.9	100
1948	8.5	17.5	14.5	29.8	21.0	43.2	5.8	11.9	48.6	100
1952	6.9	8.6	8.4	10.5	43.6	54.5	16.0	20.0	80.0	100
1954	12.0	12.0	12.7	12.7	64.6	64.6	20.4	20.4	100.2	100
1956	7.1	7.5	9.6	10.2	56.2	59.5	27.0	28.6	94.4	100
1958	7.4	7.8	11.1	11.7	55.2	58.2	25.9	27.3	94.8	100
1959	7.8	8.1	10.4	10.8	58.1	60.1	24.7	25.5	96.7	100
1960	5.2	5.0	9.1	8.7	65.4	62.6	27.3	26.1	104.6	100
1961	6.8	7.1	8.3	8.6	58.9	61.1	27.6	28.6	96.4	100
1962	5.6	4.9	6.2	5.3	75.7	64.9	30.1	25.8	116.6	100
1963	7.8	5.9	8.3	6.3	74.0	56.4	31.6	24.1	131.2	100

Sources: United Nations, International Monetary Fund, International Bank for Reconstruction and Development, Direction of International Trade, Series T, Vol. 7, No. 6; Series T, Vol. 8, No. 7; Series T, Vol. 9, No. 10; Series T, Vol. 6, No. 9, Washington, D.C. International Monetary Fund, International Bank for Reconstruction and Development, Direction of Trade, Annual 1958-62, and September, 1964, Washington, D.C.

Table V-5-b. *Ecuador's Imports by Main Trading Areas, 1938-1963*

(Dollar items in millions of U.S. dollars)

Year	From LAFTA Value ($)	From LAFTA Percent	From all Latin America Value ($)	From all Latin America Percent	From United States Value ($)	From United States Percent	From Western Europe Value ($)	From Western Europe Percent	Total Imports Value ($)	Total Imports Percent
1938	.3	2.9	.6	5.7	3.6	34.3	4.8	45.7	10.5	100
1948	3.3	6.6	4.0	8.0	34.2	68.8	8.8	17.7	49.7	100
1952	2.8	4.8	3.0	5.2	35.9	61.9	15.0	25.9	58.0	100
1954	3.9	4.5	5.6	6.5	45.9	53.3	26.7	31.0	86.1	100
1956	4.6	5.7	5.5	6.9	41.7	52.0	28.5	35.5	80.2	100
1958	2.2	2.4	3.4	3.8	46.0	50.8	34.2	37.8	90.5	100
1959	2.5	2.8	5.4	5.9	47.2	51.8	32.0	35.1	91.2	100
1960	2.7	2.6	3.4	3.3	49.4	48.2	40.9	39.9	102.3	100
1961	1.3	1.3	2.8	2.8	48.3	47.9	39.9	39.5	100.8	100
1962	4.6	4.8	5.4	5.6	42.5	44.1	37.0	38.4	96.3	100
1963	5.3	4.1	17.5	13.5	49.9	38.6	45.1	34.8	129.4	100

Sources: United Nations, International Monetary Fund, International Bank for Reconstruction and Development, Direction of International Trade, Series T, Vol. 7, No. 6; Series T, Vol. 8, No. 7; Series T, Vol. 9, No. 10; Series T, Vol. 6, No. 9, Washington, D.C. International Monetary Fund, International Bank for Reconstruction and Development, Direction of Trade, Annual 1958-62, and September, 1964, Washington, D.C.

Table V-6-a. *Mexico's Exports by Main Trading Areas, 1938-1963*
(Dollar items in millions of U.S. dollars)

Year	To LAFTA Value ($)	To LAFTA Percent	To all Latin America Value ($)	To all Latin America Percent	To United States Value ($)	To United States Percent	To Western Europe Value ($)	To Western Europe Percent	Total Exports Value ($)	Total Exports Percent
1938	.6	.3	1.4	.8	125.1	67.7	53.5	28.9	185.6	100
1948	6.4	1.4	31.0	6.5	359.6	75.4	54.2	11.4	477.1	100
1952	5.1	.9	22.7	3.8	466.0	78.6	54.8	9.2	592.5	100
1954	6.6	1.3	23.8	4.7	365.2	72.7	73.9	14.7	502.2	100
1956	5.4	.8	25.4	3.9	480.7	72.9	100.4	15.2	659.6	100
1958	3.3	.4	27.4	3.7	439.3	59.7	62.9	8.6	735.5	100
1959	4.9	.7	25.4	3.4	439.6	58.6	66.0	8.8	749.8	100
1960	5.2	.7	24.2	3.2	455.3	59.6	84.4	11.1	764.4	100
1961	7.2	.9	30.2	3.7	502.0	60.8	69.3	8.4	825.2	100
1962	16.8	1.8	38.2	4.1	553.3	59.6	74.2	8.0	929.1	100
1963	25.9	2.7	52.8	5.4	597.5	61.5	80.4	8.3	971.2	100

Sources: United Nations, International Monetary Fund, International Bank for Reconstruction and Development, Direction of International Trade, Series T, Vol. 7, No. 6; Series T, Vol. 8, No. 7; Series T, Vol. 9, No. 10; Series T, Vol. 6, No. 9, Washington, D.C. International Monetary Fund, International Bank for Reconstruction and Development, Direction of Trade, Annual 1958-62, and May, 1964, Washington, D.C.

Table V-6-b. *Mexico's Imports by Main Trading Areas, 1938-1963*
(Dollar items in millions of U.S. dollars)

Year	To LAFTA Value ($)	Percent	To all Latin America Value ($)	Percent	To United States Value ($)	Percent	To Western Europe Value ($)	Percent	Total Exports Value ($)	Percent
1938	1.5	21.7	1.5	21.7	.8	11.6	2.5	36.2	6.9	100
1948	11.3	40.2	11.4	40.6	.3	1.1	2.0	7.1	28.1	100
1952	10.8	34.6	10.9	34.9	10.4	33.3	8.7	27.9	31.2	100
1954	17.9	52.6	17.9	52.6	6.3	18.5	3.8	11.2	34.0	100
1956	14.7	40.1	14.7	40.1	6.5	17.7	12.0	32.7	36.7	100
1958	13.7	40.1	13.7	40.1	8.3	24.3	9.6	28.1	34.2	100
1959	7.5	24.0	7.8	25.0	10.3	33.0	9.0	28.8	31.2	100
1960	8.9	32.9	8.9	32.9	7.2	26.7	7.6	28.2	27.0	100
1961	9.9	32.2	9.9	32.2	7.2	23.5	8.2	26.7	30.7	100
1962	10.9	32.6	10.9	32.6	7.0	21.0	9.3	27.8	33.4	100
1963	10.1	25.1	10.1	25.1	9.1	22.6	13.1	32.5	40.3	100

Sources: United Nations, International Monetary Fund, International Bank for Reconstruction and Development, Direction of International Trade, Series T, Vol. 7, No. 6; Series T, Vol. 8, No. 7; Series T, Vol. 9, No. 10; Series T, Vol. 6, No. 9, Washington, D.C. International Monetary Fund, International Bank for Reconstruction and Development, Direction of Trade, Annual 1958-62, and May, 1964, Washington, D.C.

Table V-7-a. *Paraguay's Exports by Main Trading Areas, 1938-1963*
(Dollar items in millions of U.S. dollars)

Year	From LAFTA Value ($)	From LAFTA Percent	From all Latin America Value ($)	From all Latin America Percent	From United States Value ($)	From United States Percent	From Western Europe Value ($)	From Western Europe Percent	Total Imports Value ($)	Total Imports Percent
1938	.5	.5	.7	.6	63.1	57.7	40.0	36.6	109.4	100
1948	3.0	.6	4.4	.8	458.6	86.8	47.4	9.0	528.6	100
1952	1.6	.2	5.7	.8	611.9	82.8	93.5	12.7	739.1	100
1954	2.3	.3	4.7	.6	646.6	80.9	108.1	13.5	798.9	100
1956	2.7	.3	11.8	1.1	838.5	78.2	165.1	15.4	1,071.6	100
1958	3.4	.3	10.1	.9	869.0	77.0	195.8	17.4	1,128.4	100
1959	3.9	.4	12.4	1.2	733.9	73.0	202.0	20.1	1,005.3	100
1960	3.6	.3	12.4	1.0	856.4	72.2	245.5	20.7	1,186.3	100
1961	4.1	.4	11.4	1.0	797.9	70.1	255.9	22.5	1,138.4	100
1962	6.2	.5	12.8	1.1	782.5	68.5	269.8	23.6	1,142.2	100
1963	10.8	.9	19.2	1.5	850.2	68.6	269.0	21.7	1,239.5	100

Sources: United Nations, International Monetary Fund, International Bank for Reconstruction and Development, Direction of International Trade, Series T, Vol. 7, No. 6; Series T, Vol. 8, No. 7; Series T, Vol. 9, No. 10; Series T, Vol. 6, No. 9, Washington, D.C. International Monetary Fund, International Bank for Reconstruction and Development, Direction of Trade, Annual 1958-62, and May, 1964, Washington, D.C.

Table V-7-b. *Paraguay's Imports by Main Trading Areas, 1938-1963*

(Dollar items in millions of U.S. dollars)

Year	From LAFTA		From all Latin America		From United States		From Western Europe		Total Imports	
	Value ($)	Percent	Value ($)	Percent	Value ($)	Percent	Value ($)	Percent	Value ($)	Percent
1938	3.1	41.3	3.1	41.3	.7	9.3	2.3	30.7	7.5	100
1948	9.9	40.7	9.9	40.7	6.6	27.2	4.3	17.7	24.3	100
1952	5.7*	24.3	5.7*	24.3	7.0*	29.8	9.6*	40.9	23.5*	100
1954	12.3	37.4	12.3	37.4	6.5	19.8	11.8	35.9	32.9	100
1956	9.9	40.2	9.9	40.2	3.3	13.4	5.7	23.2	24.6	100
1958	8.0	24.5	8.0	24.5	8.9	27.2	9.2	28.1	32.7	100
1959	7.6	28.9	7.6	28.9	5.3	20.2	7.9	30.0	26.3	100
1960	7.6	25.2	7.6	25.2	7.6	25.2	8.4	27.9	30.1	100
1961	8.6	28.2	8.6	28.2	5.3	17.4	9.4	30.8	30.5	100
1962	5.3	15.5	5.3	15.5	10.8	31.6	10.5	30.7	34.2	100
1963	7.9	24.2	7.9	24.2	9.6	29.4	8.4	25.8	32.6	100

Sources: United Nations, International Monetary Fund, International Bank for Reconstruction and Development, Direction of International Trade, Series T, Vol. 7, No. 6; Series T, Vol. 8, No. 7; Series T, Vol. 9, No. 10; Series T, Vol. 6, No. 9, Washington, D.C. International Monetary Fund, International Bank for Reconstruction and Development, Direction of Trade, Annual 1958-62, and May, 1964, Washington, D.C.

*Based on data which are derived from statistics of trading partners.

Table V-8a. *Peru's Exports by Main Trading Areas, 1938-1963*
(Dollar items in millions of U.S. dollars)

Year	To LAFTA Value ($)	Percent	To all Latin America Value ($)	Percent	To United States Value ($)	Percent	To Western Europe Value ($)	Percent	Total Exports Value ($)	Percent
1938	13.7	17.9	15.3	20.0	20.5	26.8	33.4	43.6	76.6	100
1948	55.4	34.1	63.2	38.9	39.9	24.6	45.3	27.9	162.4	100
1952	66.3	27.8	74.1	31.0	66.7	27.9	82.8	34.7	238.7	100
1954	39.9	16.1	46.0	18.6	88.1	35.6	84.9	34.3	247.5	100
1956	46.8	15.0	52.9	17.0	114.9	36.9	107.2	34.4	311.4	100
1958	38.1	13.1	43.0	14.8	110.8	38.0	106.2	36.5	291.3	100
1959	46.6	14.9	51.8	16.5	98.4	31.4	123.6	39.4	313.7	100
1960	33.4	7.8	43.6	10.1	156.2	36.2	177.0	40.9	431.5	100
1961	31.5	6.4	38.4	7.7	178.3	36.0	209.7	42.3	495.9	100
1962	48.8	9.1	53.7	10.0	188.2	34.9	237.2	44.0	539.0	100
1963	49.1	9.1	54.2	10.0	190.9	35.3	230.8	42.6	541.1	100

Sources: United Nations, International Monetary Fund, International Bank for Reconstruction and Development, Direction of International Trade, Series T, Vol. 7, No. 6; Series T, Vol. 8, No. 7; Series T, Vol. 9, No. 10; Series T, Vol. 6, No. 9, Washington, D.C. International Monetary Fund, International Bank for Reconstruction and Development, Direction of Trade, Annual 1958-62, and September, 1964, Washington, D.C.

Table V-8-b. *Peru's Imports by Main Trading Areas, 1938-1963*

(Dollar items in millions of U.S. dollars)

Year	From LAFTA Value ($)	Percent	From all Latin America Value ($)	Percent	From United States Value ($)	Percent	From Western Europe Value ($)	Percent	Total Imports Value ($)	Percent
1938	5.9	10.1	6.2	10.7	19.9	34.2	25.8	44.3	58.2	100
1948	38.7	23.2	40.3	24.0	90.8	54.1	24.1	14.4	167.7	100
1952	17.4	6.0	19.9	6.9	161.4	56.1	74.6	25.9	287.5	100
1954	21.1	8.5	23.3	9.3	129.5	51.9	80.9	32.4	249.7	100
1956	20.3	5.6	25.7	7.1	179.2	49.6	128.6	35.6	361.1	100
1958	20.6	6.2	25.9	7.7	157.8	47.1	121.9	36.4	334.9	100
1959	20.8	7.1	23.7	8.1	132.6	45.1	106.8	36.3	294.1	100
1960	27.4	7.3	31.1	8.3	164.2	43.8	135.5	36.2	373.5	100
1961	31.7	6.8	39.0	8.3	207.0	44.1	173.8	37.0	469.2	100
1962	45.3	8.4	53.0	9.9	212.9	39.6	209.4	39.0	537.4	100
1963	62.0	11.1	66.8	12.0	207.6	37.3	210.2	37.7	557.1	100

Sources: United Nations, International Monetary Fund, International Bank for Reconstruction and Development, Direction of International Trade, Series T, Vol. 7, No. 6; Series T, Vol. 8, No. 7; Series T, Vol. 9, No. 10; Series T, Vol. 6, No. 9, Washington, D.C. International Monetary Fund, International Bank for Reconstruction and Development, Direction of Trade, Annual 1958-62, and September, 1964, Washington, D.C.

Table V-9-a. *Uruguay's Exports by Main Trading Areas, 1938-1963*
(Dollar items in millions of U.S. dollars)

Year	To LAFTA Value ($)	Percent	To all Latin America Value ($)	Percent	To United States Value ($)	Percent	To Western Europe Value ($)	Percent	Total Exports Value ($)	Percent
1938	8.2	13.3	8.6	14.0	2.4	3.9	44.5	72.2	61.6	100
1948	14.8	8.3	20.4	11.4	51.4	28.7	95.7	53.5	178.9	100
1952	29.0	13.9	30.6	14.6	51.0	24.4	115.5	55.3	208.9	100
1954	38.9	15.6	39.9	16.0	32.6	13.1	136.6	54.9	249.0	100
1956	27.0	12.8	27.8	13.2	24.6	11.7	144.3	68.4	211.1	100
1958	12.9	9.3	13.9	10.0	10.7	7.7	82.1	59.1	138.8	100
1959	2.7	2.7	3.4	3.4	11.6	11.7	53.2	53.8	98.8	100
1960	3.4	2.6	4.0	3.1	19.8	15.6	88.9	68.7	129.5	100
1961	5.8	3.3	6.0	3.4	24.6	14.1	119.9	68.8	174.3	100
1962	8.0	5.2	8.9	5.8	24.3	15.9	90.7	59.2	153.1	100
1963	15.1	9.1	15.8	9.6	19.2	11.6	108.7	65.8	165.3	100

Sources: United Nations, International Monetary Fund, International Bank for Reconstruction and Development, Direction of International Trade, Series T, Vol. 7, No. 6; Series T, Vol. 8, No. 7; Series T, Vol. 9, No. 10; Series T, Vol. 6, No. 9, Washington, D.C. International Monetary Fund, International Bank for Reconstruction and Development, Direction of Trade, Annual 1958-62, and June, 1964, Washington, D.C.

97

Table V-9.b. *Uruguay's Imports by Main Trading Areas, 1938-1963*
(Dollar items in millions of U.S. dollars)

Year	From LAFTA Value ($)	Percent	From all Latin America Value ($)	Percent	From United States Value ($)	Percent	From Western Europe Value ($)	Percent	Total Imports Value ($)	Percent
1938	11.7	19.0	11.8	19.2	7.2	11.7	32.6	52.9	61.6	100
1948	49.5	24.6	54.7	27.2	67.4	33.5	61.3	30.4	201.4	100
1952	45.3	17.7	64.5	25.1	60.8	23.6	110.8	43.1	257.2	100
1954	52.5	19.1	70.9	25.8	45.3	16.5	135.7	49.4	274.5	100
1956	36.8	17.5	62.1	29.2	32.8	15.4	76.2	35.8	212.6	100
1958	30.9	20.4	61.5	40.5	16.5	10.9	51.5	33.9	151.8	100
1959	28.7	17.9	44.3	27.7	32.0	20.0	62.6	39.1	159.9	100
1960	29.0	11.9	68.2	27.1	65.2	26.8	77.3	31.8	243.1	100
1961	34.4	16.5	47.5	22.7	47.0	22.5	89.3	42.7	209.0	100
1962	34.0	14.8	46.8	20.3	43.9	19.1	106.8	46.4	230.2	100
1963	32.2	18.2	45.5	25.7	27.3	15.4	77.0	43.4	177.2	100

Sources: United Nations, International Monetary Fund, International Bank for Reconstruction and Development, Direction of International Trade, Series T, Vol. 7, No. 6; Series T, Vol. 8, No. 7; Series T, Vol. 9, No. 10; Series T, Vol. 6, No. 9, Washington, D.C. International Monetary Fund, International Bank for Reconstruction and Development, Direction of Trade, Annual 1958-62, and June, 1964, Washington, D.C.

Table V-10-a. *Bolivia's Exports by Main Trading Areas, 1938-1963*

(Dollar items in millions of U.S. dollars)

Year	To LAFTA Value ($)	To LAFTA Percent	To all Latin America Value ($)	To all Latin America Percent	To United States Value ($)	To United States Percent	To Western Europe Value ($)	To Western Europe Percent	Total Exports Value ($)	Total Exports Percent a/
1938	1.3	3.7	1.3	3.7	1.6	4.6	31.6	91.1	34.7	100
1948	2.0	1.8	2.0	1.8	70.6	62.6	40.1	35.5	112.8	100
1952	3.6	2.5	3.7	2.6	92.5	65.1	45.7	32.2	142.1	100
1954	3.3	3.0	3.3	3.0	65.3	58.7	42.5	38.2	111.2	100
1956	7.1	6.6	7.1	6.6	57.3	53.4	43.1	40.1	107.4	100
1958	7.6	11.7	7.6	11.7	21.2	32.7	35.5	54.8	64.8	100
1959	7.4	9.6	7.4	9.6	27.0	34.9	40.2	52.0	77.3	100
1960	8.4	12.4	8.4	12.4	15.8	23.1	41.2	60.8	67.9	100
1961	5.5	7.2	5.5	7.2	24.6	32.3	42.0	55.1	76.2	100
1962	3.1	4.1	3.1	4.1	23.0	30.3	48.2	63.4	76.0	100
1963	3.0	3.5	3.0	3.5	27.9	32.3	53.9	62.5	86.3	100

Sources: United Nations, International Monetary Fund, International Bank for Reconstruction and Development, Direction of International Trade, Series T, Vol. 6; Series T, No. 6; Series T, Vol. 8, No. 7; Series T, Vol. 9, No. 10; Series T, Vol. 6, No. 9, Washington, D.C. International Monetary Fund, International Bank for Reconstruction and Development, Direction of Trade, Annual 1958-62, and July, 1964, Washington, D.C.

a/ Represent market valuations abroad, thus including freight, and for metals, which constitute about 90 percent of exports, including also the costs of smelting abroad.

Table V-10-b. *Bolivia's Imports by Main Trading Areas, 1938-1963*
(Dollar items in millions of U.S. dollars)

Year	From LAFTA		From all Latin America		From United States		From Western Europe		Total Imports	
	Value ($)	Percent	Value ($)	Percent	Value ($)	Percent	Value ($)	Percent	Value ($)	Percent
1938	7.0	28.1	7.0	28.1	6.5	26.1	8.9	35.7	24.9	100
1948	23.8	34.6	23.8	34.6	33.7	49.1	7.7	11.2	68.7	100
1952	25.8	27.8	26.4	28.4	37.9	40.9	21.1	22.8	92.6	100
1954	18.8	28.7	19.0	29.0	24.9	38.0	16.0	24.4	65.5	100
1956	20.8	24.8	21.1	25.1	38.5	45.8	22.6	26.9	84.0	100
1958	12.5	17.8	13.4	19.2	36.9	52.8	16.1	23.0	69.9	100
1959	15.2	26.0	16.7	28.6	28.8	49.3	10.0	17.1	58.4	100
1960	10.2	14.4	12.0	16.8	30.8	43.3	21.2	29.8	71.1	100
1961	13.5	17.4	14.6	18.8	32.8	42.3	23.2	29.9	77.6	100
1962	15.0	15.3	16.0	16.3	39.0	39.8	32.0	32.7	97.9	100
1963	9.4	9.1	10.0	9.6	49.5	47.7	33.7	32.5	103.8	100

Sources: United Nations, International Monetary Fund, International Bank for Reconstruction and Development, Direction of International Trade, Series T, Vol. 7, No. 6; Series T, Vol. 8, No. 7; Series T, Vol. 9, No. 10; Series T, Vol. 6, No. 9, Washington, D.C. International Monetary Fund, International Bank for Reconstruction and Development, Direction of Trade, Annual 1958-62, and July, 1964, Washington, D.C.

Table V-11-a. *Venezuela's Exports by Main Trading Areas, 1938-1963*

(Dollar items in millions of U.S. dollars)

Year	To LAFTA Value ($)	To LAFTA Percent	To all Latin America Value ($)	To all Latin America Percent	To United States Value ($)	To United States Percent	To Western Europe Value ($)	To Western Europe Percent	Total Exports [a]/ Value ($)	Total Exports [a]/ Percent
1938	.9	.5	1.0	.6	23.9	13.2	15.1	8.3	180.9	100
1948	39.9	3.9	40.2	3.9	277.7	26.7	70.7	6.8	1,040.1	100
1952	102.8	7.1	104.5	7.2	496.1	34.2	105.2	7.3	1,450.2	100
1954	114.0	6.8	120.8	7.2	623.3	36.9	158.7	9.4	1,689.8	100
1956	172.9	8.2	188.3	8.9	835.2	39.4	313.6	14.8	2,118.4	100
1958	189.2	8.2	251.5	10.8	975.6	42.1	358.5	15.5	2,319.4	100
1959	202.1	8.5	268.0	11.3	988.2	41.8	369.5	15.6	2,366.6	100
1960	195.7	7.8	231.8	9.2	1,097.1	43.6	402.8	16.1	2,517.7	100
1961	160.7	6.7	167.4	6.9	940.5	39.0	467.0	19.4	2,411.2	100
1962	165.0	6.4	185.4	7.1	894.8	34.5	523.9	20.2	2,594.3	100
1963	125.6	4.8	166.9	6.3	882.5	33.5	573.0	21.8	2,629.0	100

Sources: United Nations, International Monetary Fund, International Bank for Reconstruction and Development, Direction of International Trade, Series T, Vol. 7, No. 6; Series T, Vol. 8, No. 7; Series T, Vol. 9, No. 10; Series T, Vol. 6, No. 9, Washington, D.C. International Monetary Fund, International Bank for Reconstruction and Development, Direction of Trade, Annual 1958-62, and September, 1964, Washington, D.C.

Table V-11-b. *Venezuela's Imports by Main Trading Areas, 1938-1963*
(Dollar items in millions of U.S. dollars)

Year	From LAFTA Value ($)	From LAFTA Percent	From all Latin America Value ($)	From all Latin America Percent	From United States Value ($)	From United States Percent	From Western Europe Value ($)	From Western Europe Percent	Total Imports Value ($)	Total Imports Percent
1938	.7	.7	.8	.8	54.1	56.5	37.3	38.9	95.8	100
1948	29.8	4.1	40.6	5.6	544.0	74.8	113.5	15.6	727.1	100
1952	5.9	.8	16.8	2.2	523.5	69.0	167.8	22.1	758.8	100
1954	4.6	.5	7.7	.7	563.5	62.3	259.1	28.6	904.9	100
1956	8.0	.8	9.9	1.0	606.9	59.1	334.6	32.6	1,026.4	100
1958	15.1	1.1	18.6	1.3	819.2	57.4	479.7	33.6	1,427.5	100
1959	21.4	1.5	39.8	2.8	750.2	53.2	511.1	36.2	1,410.6	100
1960	16.8	1.6	23.6	2.2	551.5	51.7	379.6	35.6	1,062.6	100
1961	16.6	1.6	22.6	2.1	577.5	54.1	358.6	33.6	1,067.9	100
1962	15.9	1.6	26.3	2.6	519.7	52.3	338.2	34.1	992.9	100
1963	24.5	2.8	26.2	3.0	470.3	54.0	274.1	31.5	870.6	100

Sources: United Nations, International Monetary Fund, International Bank for Reconstruction and Development, Direction of International Trade, Series T, Vol. 7, No. 6; Series T, Vol. 8, No. 7; Series T, Vol. 9, No. 10; Series T, Vol. 6, No. 9, Washington, D.C. International Monetary Fund, International Bank for Reconstruction and Development, Direction of Trade, Annual 1958-62, and September, 1964, Washington, D.C.

Table VI-1. *Argentina's Trade with LAFTA Countries, Bolivia and Venezuela, 1948-1963*[a]

(Millions of U.S. Dollars)

Country	1948	1952	1954	1956	1958	1959	1960	1961	1962	1963
EXPORTS										
Brazil	75.7	37.9	92.6	65.4	76.1	88.8	82.8	26.8	68.5	77.5
Chile	19.1	31.2	53.2	20.4	20.9	25.1	41.7	43.0	31.8	41.5
Colombia	4.8	.4	.4	.2	.3	.2	.3	.3	2.3	8.2
Ecuador	.1	.1	.1	--	--	--	.1	.1	.1	.3
Mexico	1.7	.9	.5	1.0	1.4	.7	.8	1.2	1.0	2.7
Paraguay	10.3	3.0	9.9	6.2	7.9	8.4	8.5	8.7	5.5	9.6
Peru	24.1	8.7	17.2	14.6	11.2	8.3	15.5	14.2	25.6	35.5
Uruguay	12.4	.5	1.7	4.7	.9	6.1	12.9	5.8	6.7	9.7
Total LAFTA	148.2	82.7	175.6	112.5	118.7	137.6	162.5	100.0	141.5	185.0
Bolivia	8.9	12.7	3.1	8.0	6.7	5.3	2.3	7.5	7.6	4.5
Venezuela	9.6	1.7	3.0	3.7	5.8	5.6	5.4	4.7	5.6	8.2
Total	166.7	97.1	181.7	124.2	131.2	148.5	170.2	112.2	154.7	197.7
IMPORTS										
Brazil	133.5	95.5	120.0	84.8	127.9	57.6	63.4	77.6	62.6	57.9
Chile	19.0	39.0	22.6	25.3	25.3	28.5	19.3	24.1	15.1	17.2
Colombia	2.7	2.1	2.0	1.1	--	--	.1	.1	.8	--
Ecuador	2.9	.2	3.0	4.1	1.4	1.3	--	.1	.4	1.3
Mexico	3.8	.5	.3	1.3	.5	.3	.8	.9	1.7	3.7
Paraguay	8.2	6.7	15.4	14.6	14.6	9.3	9.1	10.6	9.5	9.4
Peru	9.3	10.7	19.0	9.7	4.2	9.8	11.9	10.4	10.6	9.2
Uruguay	8.1	.5	--	--	1.7	.5	1.9	2.2	2.5	2.3
Total LAFTA	187.5	155.2	182.3	140.9	175.6	107.3	106.5	126.0	103.2	101.0
Bolivia	1.3	1.1	1.8	2.5	7.5	5.5	4.6	4.4	2.0	3.0
Venezuela	40.7	63.1	46.0	74.4	101.6	107.5	90.5	66.0	48.0	21.3
Total	229.5	219.4	230.1	217.8	284.7	220.3	201.6	196.4	153.2	125.3

Sources: United Nations, International Monetary Fund, International Bank for Reconstruction and Development, Direction of International Trade, Series T, Vol. 7, No. 6; Series T, Vol. 8, No. 7; Series T, Vol. 9, No. 10; Series T, Vol. 6, No. 9, Washington, D.C. International Monetary Fund, International Bank for Reconstruction and Development, Direction of Trade, Annual 1958-62, and July, 1964, Washington, D.C.

[a]/ Exports, FOB, Imports, CIF.

Table VI-2. *Brazil's Trade with LAFTA Countries, Bolivia and Venezuela, 1948-1963*[a]

(Millions of U.S. Dollars)

Country	1948	1952	1954	1956	1958	1959	1960	1961	1962	1963
					EXPORTS					
Argentina	111.0	95.5	100.0	65.5	107.0	42.9	56.4	67.5	48.4	46.2
Chile	12.7	11.6	11.9	10.3	12.0	9.8	11.6	8.8	9.4	10.4
Colombia	4.2	.1	.4	--	--	.2	.3	1.1	.2	.6
Ecuador	.6	--	.1	--	--	--	--	.1	--	--
Mexico	.5	--	.1	.1	.1	.1	.2	.2	.3	1.4
Paraguay	1.1	.2	.2	.1	1.3	.8	1.0	.6	2.1	2.9
Peru	.2	.1	--	.1	.2	.2	.4	1.2	1.2	1.0
Uruguay	17.6	16.9	30.8	23.7	22.5	21.0	16.6	15.7	14.1	13.5
Total LAFTA	147.9	124.4	143.5	99.8	143.1	75.1	86.4	95.2	75.7	76.0
Bolivia	6.7	.5	.5	2.0	.4	.2	.6	.4	.9	1.1
Venezuela	6.5	.6	.4	.6	2.1	1.2	1.3	1.6	.4	3.4
Total	155.1	125.5	144.4	102.4	145.6	76.5	88.2	97.2	77.0	80.5
					IMPORTS					
Argentina	80.8	37.9	104.9	76.8	88.1	104.5	94.9	29.8	85.6	88.0
Chile	10.9	16.4	10.3	6.9	6.1	8.7	8.7	7.8	15.6	31.3
Colombia	.1	.1	--	.4	--	--	--	--	--	.2
Ecuador	.1	--	--	--	--	--	--	--	--	--
Mexico	.8	.1	.5	.3	1.5	.7	1.4	1.6	10.4	17.9
Paraguay	.1	--	--	.1	--	.1	.5	.5	1.0	.9
Peru	.5	.9	.8	3.0	1.7	1.5	2.6	3.7	13.5	15.4
Uruguay	9.6	29.9	36.6	29.6	9.1	1.4	.6	1.5	2.6	10.3
Total LAFTA	102.9	85.4	153.1	117.1	106.5	116.9	108.7	44.9	128.7	164.0
Bolivia	.1	.3	.5	1.6	.3	.5	2.6	.9	.5	.1
Venezuela	11.1	85.9	80.0	118.0	139.9	110.5	114.5	99.4	107.7	97.5
Total	114.1	171.6	233.6	236.7	246.7	227.9	225.8	145.2	236.9	261.6

Sources: United Nations, International Monetary Fund, International Bank for Reconstruction and Development, Direction of International Trade, Series T, Vol. 7, No. 6; Series T, Vol. 8, No. 7; Series T, Vol. 9, No. 10; Series T, Vol. 6, No. 9, Washington, D.C. International Monetary Fund, International Bank for Reconstruction and Development, Direction of Trade, Annual 1958-62, and May, 1964, Washington, D.C.

a/ Exports, FOB; Imports, CIF.

Table VI-3. Chile's Trade with LAFTA Countries, Bolivia and Venezuela, 1948-1963a

(Millions of U.S. dollars)

Country	1948	1952	1954	1956	1958	1959	1960	1961	1962	1963
EXPORTS										
Argentina	13.8	39.0	36.4	30.5	23.3	24.0	17.9	23.2	14.9	14.5
Brazil	7.4	8.6	8.5	5.0	4.3	8.2	5.8	6.3	18.5	27.0
Colombia	.9	1.0	.8	1.4	--	--	--	--	.7	.9
Ecuador	.8	1.1	1.1	.9	1.1	1.0	.7	.5	.5	.7
Mexico	.2	.1	.5	.2	.4	1.3	.4	.3	.7	1.2
Paraguay	.2	.1	--	--	--	--	--	--	--	--
Peru	3.0	4.4	2.2	2.7	2.7	3.0	3.4	2.9	3.1	3.7
Uruguay	1.0	9.3	7.1	1.1	.9	1.2	1.1	1.4	1.1	1.4
Total LAFTA	27.3	63.6	56.6	41.8	32.7	38.7	29.3	34.8	39.4	49.4
Bolivia	2.4	2.0	1.2	1.8	.9	1.7	1.8	1.9	1.7	.5
Venezuela	.6	.5	.5	.6	1.3	.9	.9	1.1	1.4	1.4
Total	30.3	66.1	58.3	44.2	34.9	41.3	32.0	37.8	42.4	51.3
IMPORTS										
Argentina	25.8	31.2	52.8	24.5	18.2	26.6	39.6	55.1	42.8	52.5
Brazil	11.0	10.9	13.3	11.4	13.5	7.2	13.5	9.8	7.1	18.8
Colombia	.2	--	--	.4	.1	.1	--	--	.3	1.4
Ecuador	1.7	1.3	2.5	1.6	1.6	3.1	4.1	2.4	2.5	7.3
Mexico	.9	.4	.7	.9	.9	1.3	1.7	2.0	2.8	11.0
Paraguay	--	.1	.1	.1	.1	.1	--	--	.1	.5
Peru	35.5	23.5	26.3	22.0	11.9	16.2	22.2	24.0	24.0	26.5
Uruguay	--	.5	.4	.1	.2	--	.3	.6	.9	2.0
Total LAFTA	75.1	67.9	96.1	60.9	46.3	54.6	81.4	93.9	80.5	120.0
Bolivia	.2	.2	.2	.6	.8	.3	.2	.4	.2	.3
Venezuela	.4	.1	.1	--	--	.1	.3	7.0	10.4	7.4
Total	75.7	68.2	96.4	61.5	47.1	55.0	81.9	101.3	91.1	127.7

Sources: United Nations, International Monetary Fund, International Bank for Reconstruction and Development, Direction of International Trade, Series T, Vol. 7, No. 6; Series T, Vol. 8, No. 7; Series T, Vol. 9, No. 10; Series T, Vol. 6, No. 9, Washington, D.C. International Monetary Fund, International Bank for Reconstruction and Development, Direction of Trade, Annual 1958-62, and September, 1964, Washington, D.C.

a/
  Exports, FOB, Imports, CIF.

Table VI-4. *Colombia's Trade with LAFTA Countries, Bolivia and Venezuela, 1948-1963*[a]

(Millions of U.S. dollars)

Country	1948	1952	1954	1956	1958	1959	1960	1961	1962	1963
					EXPORTS					
Argentina	1.7	2.1	1.6	1.0	--	.1	.1	.2	.7	.6
Brazil	.1	.1	--	.3	--	--	--	.2	--	.1
Chile	.2	--	.1	.9	1.2	1.2	1.0	.3	1.0	.3
Ecuador	.1	.3	.5	.3	.2	.3	.4	1.2	1.5	2.7
Mexico	--	.2	.1	.2	.1	--	.1	.2	.1	.2
Paraguay	--	--	--	--	--	--	--	--	--	--
Peru	.2	--	.9	.1	1.5	1.2	3.2	3.9	3.8	1.8
Uruguay	--	--	.4	.4	--	--	--	.1	.3	.3
Total LAFTA	2.3	2.9	3.6	3.2	3.0	2.8	4.8	6.1	7.4	6.0
Bolivia	--	--	--	.9	--	--	--	--	--	--
Venezuela	.9	.4	3.8	2.3	1.2	1.5	1.4	1.3	1.0	.9
Total	3.2	3.3	7.4	6.4	4.2	4.3	6.2	7.4	8.4	6.9
					IMPORTS					
Argentina	6.3	.4	.4	.2	.2	.2	.3	.4	2.3	8.7
Brazil	4.9	.1	--	--	--	.1	.2	1.2	.1	.5
Chile	1.0	.8	1.2	1.7	.8	.5	1.4	.3	.2	1.0
Ecuador	3.6	5.9	8.1	4.9	4.0	4.4	2.4	6.3	4.9	4.4
Mexico	1.0	.5	1.2	.8	.4	1.8	1.0	1.0	2.2	3.1
Paraguay	.3	--	--	--	--	--	--	--	--	--
Peru	9.6	9.6	3.1	6.4	1.2	1.6	1.1	.5	.9	1.9
Uruguay	.5	.5	1.6	.7	.5	.4	.3	.5	2.4	1.7
Total LAFTA	27.2	17.8	15.6	14.7	7.1	9.0	6.7	10.2	13.0	21.3
Bolivia	--	--	--	--	--	--	--	--	--	--
Venezuela	1.7	.7	1.8	.6	3.4	1.5	1.7	1.9	1.6	1.1
Total	28.9	18.5	17.4	15.3	10.5	10.5	8.4	12.1	14.6	22.4

Sources: United Nations, International Monetary Fund, International Bank for Reconstruction and Development, *Direction of International Trade*, Series T, Vol. 7, No. 6; Series T, Vol. 8, No. 7; Series T, Vol. 9, No. 10; Series T, Vol. 6, No. 9, Washington, D.C. International Monetary Fund, International Bank for Reconstruction and Development, *Direction of Trade*, Annual 1958-62, and June, 1964, Washington, D.C.

[b]
Exports, FOB, Imports, CIF.

Table VI-5. *Ecuador's Trade with LAFTA Countries, Bolivia and Venezuela, 1948-1963*[a]

(Millions of U.S. dollars)

Country	1948	1952	1954	1956	1958	1959	1960	1961	1962	1963
					EXPORTS					
Argentina	1.0	.2	1.6	.7	.5	.3	--	.1	.2	.4
Brazil	--	.2	--	--	--	--	--	--	--	--
Chile	1.3	1.0	2.1	1.2	2.2	2.2	2.4	2.4	2.3	2.4
Colombia	3.3	4.7	7.8	4.9	4.4	5.2	2.7	4.2	3.0	4.2
Mexico	--	--	--	--	--	--	--	--	--	--
Paraguay	--	--	.1	--	--	--	--	--	--	--
Peru	1.8	.2	.1	.3	.3	.1	.1	.1	.1	.8
Uruguay	1.1	.6	.3	--	--	--	--	--	--	--
Total LAFTA	8.5	6.9	12.0	7.1	7.4	7.8	5.2	6.8	5.6	7.8
Bolivia	.2	.1	.2	.1	--	--	--	--	--	--
Venezuela	1.3	.1	.3	.1	3.3	1.9	2.9	.6	--	--
Total	10.0	7.1	12.5	7.3	10.7	9.7	8.1	7.4	5.6	7.8
					IMPORTS					
Argentina	.2	.1	--	--	--	--	--	.1	1.8	.2
Brazil	.6	.1	--	--	--	--	--	--	--	--
Chile	.9	1.1	1.7	1.0	1.1	.8	.7	.4	.4	.8
Colombia	.3	.1	.2	.2	.4	.3	.4	.3	.6	2.3
Mexico	.3	.1	.1	.2	--	--	--	--	.4	.9
Paraguay	--	--	--	--	--	--	--	--	--	--
Peru	.7	1.4	1.8	3.1	.7	1.4	1.6	.5	1.3	.9
Uruguay	.3	--	.1	.1	--	--	--	--	.1	.2
Total LAFTA	3.3	2.8	3.9	4.6	2.2	2.5	2.7	1.3	4.6	5.3
Bolivia	--	--	--	--	--	--	--	--	--	--
Venezuela	--	--	.1	--	.5	2.4	.1	1.1	.6	11.9
Total	3.3	2.8	4.0	4.6	2.7	4.9	2.8	2.4	5.2	17.2

Sources: United Nations, International Monetary Fund, International Bank for Reconstruction and Development, *Direction of International Trade*, Series T, Vol. 7, No. 6; Series T, Vol. 8, No. 7; Series T, Vol. 9, No. 10; Series T, Vol. 6, No. 9, Washington, D.C. International Monetary Fund, International Bank for Reconstruction and Development, *Direction of Trade*, Annual 1958-62, and September, 1964, Washington, D.C.

a/ Exports, FOB, Imports, CIF.

Table VI-6. *Mexico's Trade with LAFTA Countries, Bolivia and Venezuela, 1948-1963*[a]

(Millions of U.S. dollars)

Country	1948	1952	1954	1956	1958	1959	1960	1961	1962	1963
EXPORTS										
Argentina	2.5	.5	.8	1.4	.4	.5	.6	1.1	2.3	2.5
Brazil	2.0	1.3	2.0	.3	.9	.3	1.2	1.8	7.6	10.1
Chile	.3	.8	.6	.9	.3	1.4	1.4	1.5	2.3	5.0
Colombia	.9	.5	1.6	1.2	.9	1.3	1.2	1.8	1.7	3.9
Ecuador	.2	.1	.6	.5	--	.4	--	--	.7	.9
Paraguay	--	--	--	.1	--	.1	--	--	--	--
Peru	.2	1.8	.8	.7	.6	.8	.7	.8	1.7	3.0
Uruguay	.3	.1	.2	.3	.2	.1	.1	.2	.5	.5
Total LAFTA	6.4	5.1	6.6	5.4	3.3	4.9	5.2	7.2	16.8	25.9
Bolivia	.2	.1	1.0	--	--	--	--	--	.1	.2
Venezuela	3.9	1.5	1.3	3.2	4.5	4.7	2.9	3.1	4.4	5.8
Total	10.5	6.7	8.9	8.6	7.8	9.6	8.1	10.3	21.3	31.9
IMPORTS										
Argentina	1.7	.9	.6	1.0	1.9	1.2	1.2	1.3	1.6	3.0
Brazil	.3	.1	--	.4	.1	.1	.1	.2	.3	1.0
Chile	.6	.2	1.3	.2	.4	1.5	.9	.4	.6	1.5
Colombia	--	.1	--	--	.1	.1	.2	.2	.2	.2
Ecuador	--	.1	--	--	--	--	--	--	--	--
Paraguay	--	--	--	--	--	.2	--	--	--	--
Peru	.1	--	.1	.2	.3	.7	.9	1.2	2.0	3.7
Uruguay	.3	.2	.3	.9	.6	.2	.3	.8	1.5	1.4
Total LAFTA	3.0	1.6	2.3	2.7	3.4	3.9	3.6	4.1	6.2	10.8
Bolivia	--	--	--	.1	--	.1	--	--	--	--
Venezuela	--	.1	--	.3	.2	.2	.2	.4	.2	.6
Total	3.0	1.7	2.3	3.0	3.6	4.2	3.8	4.5	6.4	11.4

Sources: United Nations, International Monetary Fund, International Bank for Reconstruction and Development, Direction of International Trade, Series T, Vol. 7, No. 6; Series T, Vol. 8, No. 7; Series T, Vol. 9, No. 10; Series T, Vol. 6, No. 9, Washington, D.C. International Monetary Fund, International Bank for Reconstruction and Development, Direction of Trade, Annual 1958-62, and May, 1964, Washington, D.C.

[a] Exports, FOB, Imports, CIF.

Table VI-7. *Paraguay's Trade with LAFTA Countries, Bolivia and Venezuela, 1948-1963*[a]

(Millions of U.S. dollars)

Country	1948	1952	1954	1956	1958	1959	1960	1961	1962	1963
EXPORTS										
Argentina	9.2	6.7	14.7	12.8	13.2	6.4	7.7	8.7	9.6	8.6
Brazil	--	--	--	--	--	--	--	--	.1	--
Chile	--	--	--	--	--	.2	--	--	--	--
Colombia	--	--	--	--	--	--	--	--	--	--
Ecuador	--	--	--	--	--	--	--	--	--	--
Mexico	--	--	--	--	--	--	--	--	--	--
Peru	--	--	--	--	--	--	--	--	--	--
Uruguay	2.1	4.1	3.2	1.9	.5	.9	1.2	1.1	1.1	1.5
Total LAFTA	11.3	10.8	17.9	14.7	13.7	7.5	8.9	9.8	10.8	10.1
Bolivia	--	--	--	--	--	.3	--	--	--	--
Venezuela	--	--	--	--	--	--	--	--	--	--
Total	11.3	10.8	17.9	14.7	13.7	7.8	8.9	9.8	10.8	10.1
IMPORTS										
Argentina	8.2	3.0	9.2	7.1	7.2	7.4	7.5	8.3	5.0	7.6
Brazil	1.4	.2	.2	.1	--	--	--	--	--	--
Chile	--	.1	--	--	--	--	--	--	--	--
Colombia	--	--	--	--	--	--	--	--	--	--
Ecuador	--	--	--	--	--	--	--	--	--	--
Mexico	--	--	--	--	--	--	--	--	--	--
Peru	--	--	--	.9	.8	.2	.1	.3	.3	.3
Uruguay	.3	2.4	2.9	1.8	--	--	--	--	--	--
Total LAFTA	9.9	5.7	12.3	9.9	8.0	7.6	7.6	8.6	5.3	7.9
Bolivia	--	--	--	--	--	--	--	--	--	--
Venezuela	--	--	--	--	--	--	--	--	--	--
Total	9.9	5.7	12.3	9.9	8.0	7.6	7.6	8.6	5.3	7.9

Sources: United Nations, International Monetary Fund, International Bank for Reconstruction and Development, Direction of International Trade, Series T, Vol. 7, No. 6; Series T, Vol. 8, No. 7; Series T, Vol. 9, No. 10; Series T, Vol. 6, No. 9, Washington, D.C. International Monetary Fund, International Bank for Reconstruction and Development, Direction of Trade, Annual 1958-62, and May, 1964, Washington, D.C.

a/ Exports, FOB, Imports, CIF.

Table VI-8. *Peru's Trade with LAFTA Countries, Bolivia and Venezuela, 1948-1963*[a]

(Millions of U.S. dollars)

Country	1948	1952	1954	1956	1958	1959	1960	1961	1962	1963
EXPORTS										
Argentina	6.6	10.7	6.0	5.3	2.6	10.0	9.4	8.2	8.3	6.3
Brazil	.3	.5	.6	1.9	1.5	1.4	2.1	3.8	11.1	9.9
Chile	30.7	42.0	26.2	27.4	29.5	29.7	16.5	14.4	23.7	24.8
Colombia	9.5	5.1	3.0	5.9	1.1	1.4	.8	.9	1.0	1.7
Ecuador	1.4	2.1	2.3	3.9	2.7	2.8	3.1	1.9	1.8	1.6
Mexico	.1	--	.1	--	.2	.6	.8	.9	--	2.4
Paraguay	--	--	--	.5	--	--	--	--	--	--
Uruguay	6.8	5.9	1.7	1.8	.5	.7	.7	1.4	1.4	2.4
Total LAFTA	55.4	66.3	39.9	46.8	38.1	46.6	33.4	31.5	48.8	49.1
Bolivia	6.0	7.0	4.8	4.7	3.5	3.2	2.9	1.4	1.6	1.8
Venezuela	.2	.1	1.0	.5	.4	.5	.5	.8	1.7	3.0
Total	61.6	73.4	45.7	52.0	42.0	50.3	36.8	33.7	52.1	53.9
IMPORTS										
Argentina	29.5	8.7	17.5	15.1	11.7	13.7	17.7	21.0	30.0	49.0
Brazil	1.1	2.5	.1	--	.2	.2	.5	1.0	1.9	1.0
Chile	5.3	5.2	2.5	3.6	3.1	3.2	3.3	3.3	3.5	4.4
Colombia	--	.1	.1	.1	1.7	2.5	3.5	4.3	4.7	2.3
Ecuador	2.4	.2	.2	.4	.3	.3	1.5	1.1	3.2	2.3
Mexico	.3	.5	.7	.7	.7	.8	.8	.8	1.7	2.3
Paraguay	--	--	--	--	--	.1	--	--	.2	.1
Uruguay	.1	.2	--	.4	2.9	--	.1	.2	.1	.6
Total LAFTA	38.7	17.4	21.1	20.3	20.6	20.8	27.4	31.7	45.3	62.0
Bolivia	.1	.1	.1	.2	.4	.2	.2	.3	.2	.1
Venezuela	--	--	.1	2.4	.1	.3	1.3	2.8	3.3	3.6
Total	38.8	17.5	21.3	22.9	21.1	21.3	28.9	34.8	48.8	65.7

Sources: United Nations, International Monetary Fund, International Bank for Reconstruction and Development, Direction of International Trade, Series T, Vol. 7, No. 6; Series T, Vol. 8, No. 7; Series T, Vol. 9, No. 10; Series T, Vol. 6, No. 9, Washington, D.C. International Monetary Fund, International Bank for Reconstruction and Development, Direction of Trade, Annual 1958-62, and September, 1964, Washington, D.C.

a/ Exports, FOB, Imports, CIF.

Table VI-9. Uruguay's Trade with LAFTA Countries, Bolivia and Venezuela, 1948-1963ᵃ

(Millions of U.S. dollars)

Country	1948	1952	1954	1956	1958	1959	1960	1961	1962	1963
EXPORTS										
Argentina	4.0	.5	--	.3	1.3	.4	2.4	1.8	1.6	.9
Brazil	10.0	24.9	34.3	23.7	9.0	1.4	.3	1.8	3.0	9.7
Chile	--	.2	.2	.4	--	--	.3	.8	.9	1.5
Colombia	.4	.5	1.4	.5	.3	.2	.3	.5	2.0	1.7
Ecuador	.1	.1	--	.1	--	.1	.1	.1	.1	.2
Mexico	.1	--	.1	.1	--	--	--	--	--	.4
Paraguay	.2	2.4	2.6	1.6	.5	.1	.1	.5	.2	.6
Peru	--	.4	.3	.3	1.8	.6	.1	.1	.1	
Total LAFTA	14.8	29.0	38.9	27.0	12.9	2.7	3.4	5.8	8.0	15.1
Bolivia	.3	.4	.5	.3	--	--	.2	.2	.1	.1
Venezuela	1.3	.3	.2	.4	.5	.2	--	--	--	--
Total	16.4	29.7	39.8	27.7	13.4	2.9	3.6	6.0	8.1	15.2
IMPORTS										
Argentina	16.5	.5	1.0	4.1	2.7	2.7	9.8	11.9	8.6	9.6
Brazil	19.5	18.6	33.6	24.7	24.7	22.8	15.3	17.5	20.5	13.9
Chile	1.2	8.2	5.8	1.2	1.0	1.3	1.8	1.8	1.1	1.4
Colombia	--	--	--	1.7	.6	--	.1	.1	.1	.6
Ecuador	1.6	3.8	3.8	.5	--	--	--	--	--	--
Mexico	.8	1.4	--	.2	--	.1	--	--	.7	1.3
Paraguay	3.0	6.6	4.0	2.2	1.3	1.0	1.4	1.7	1.8	2.4
Peru	6.9	6.2	4.3	2.2	.6	.8	.6	1.4	1.2	3.0
Total LAFTA	49.5	45.3	52.5	36.8	30.9	28.7	29.0	34.4	34.0	32.2
Bolivia	--	--	--	--	--	--	--	--	--	--
Venezuela	4.2	14.3	17.0	13.3	30.3	15.1	37.5	12.0	10.6	8.7
Total	53.7	59.6	69.5	50.1	61.2	43.8	66.5	46.4	44.6	40.9

Sources: United Nations, International Monetary Fund, International Bank for Reconstruction and Development, Direction of International Trade, Series T, Vol. 7, No. 6; Series T, Vol. 8, No. 7; Series T, Vol. 9, No. 10; Series T, Vol. 6, No. 9, Washington, D.C. International Monetary Fund, International Bank for Reconstruction and Development, Direction of Trade, Annual 1958-62, and June, 1964, Washington, D.C.

a/ Exports, FOB, Imports, CIF.

Table VI-10. *Bolivia's Trade with LAFTA Countries and Venezuela, 1948-1963*[a]

(Millions of U.S. dollars)

Country	1948	1952	1954	1956	1958	1959	1960	1961	1962	1963
EXPORTS										
Argentina	22.5	31.7	33.8	51.7	74.2	86.2	68.3	53.0	34.7	15.5
Brazil	8.4	58.7	67.8	91.8	97.1	85.1	84.8	82.0	98.4	85.0
Chile	.1	.5	--	10.0	--	8.4	9.4	6.8	11.1	6.3
Colombia	.7	1.1	--	.5	--	3.2	1.6	2.7	1.5	1.2
Ecuador	.2	--	--	--	--	3.9	3.0	2.7	3.3	2.7
Mexico	--	.1	--	--	--	.4	.1	.1	.5	.2
Paraguay	--	--	--	--	--	.1	3.5	.6	.3	.4
Peru	.1	.3	--	1.6	--	.3	1.8	1.8	2.7	4.2
Uruguay	7.9	10.4	12.4	17.3	17.9	14.5	23.2	11.0	12.7	10.1
Total LAFTA	39.9	102.8	114.0	172.9	189.2	202.1	195.7	160.7	165.0	125.6
Bolivia	--	--	--	--	--	--	--	--	--	--
Total	39.9	102.8	114.0	172.9	189.2	202.1	195.7	160.7	165.0	125.6
IMPORTS										
Argentina	10.3	1.7	2.4	3.5	6.2	6.4	5.6	6.5	6.2	7.1
Brazil	7.0	.9	.4	.4	2.4	2.7	1.3	2.0	.4	.9
Chile	.8	.4	--	.6	1.4	.7	.7	.9	1.2	1.1
Colombia	2.6	.5	--	.5	1.1	1.9	1.5	1.6	.9	.8
Ecuador	1.5	.1	--	--	--	2.1	3.3	.4	--	.8
Mexico	5.8	1.8	1.8	2.6	3.5	6.7	3.6	3.9	5.3	11.2
Paraguay	--	--	--	--	--	--	--	--	.3	--
Peru	.2	.2	--	.4	.5	.6	.7	1.1	1.6	2.5
Uruguay	1.6	.3	--	--	--	.3	.1	.2	--	.1
Total LAFTA	29.8	5.9	4.6	8.0	15.1	21.4	16.8	16.6	15.9	24.5
Bolivia	--	--	--	--	--	--	--	--	--	--
Total	29.8	5.9	4.6	8.0	15.1	21.4	16.8	16.6	15.9	24.5

Sources: United Nations, International Monetary Fund, International Bank for Reconstruction and Development, Direction of International Trade, Series T, Vol. 7, No. 6; Series T, Vol. 8, No. 7; Series T, Vol. 9, No. 10; Series T, Vol. 6, No. 9, Washington, D.C. International Monetary Fund, International Bank for Reconstruction and Development, Direction of Trade, Annual 1958-62, and September, 1964, Washington, D.C.

a/ Exports, FOB, Imports, CIF.

Table VI-11. *Venezuela's Trade with LAFTA Countries and Bolivia, 1948-1963*[a]

(Millions of U.S. dollars)

Country	1948	1952	1954	1956	1958	1959	1960	1961	1962	1963
					EXPORTS					
Argentina	1.5	1.1	1.3	2.7	6.0	4.6	3.9	2.6	1.9	2.1
Brazil	.1	1.6	.9	2.8	.5	1.5	4.0	2.3	.8	.7
Chile	.3	.6	1.1	1.4	.6	.1	.3	.5	.3	.1
Colombia	--	--	--	--	--	--	--	--	--	--
Ecuador	--	--	--	--	--	--	--	--	--	--
Mexico	--	--	--	--	--	.4	.1	--	--	--
Paraguay	--	--	--	--	--	.5	--	--	--	--
Peru	.1	.2	--	.1	.5	.1	.1	.1	.1	.1
Uruguay	--	.1	--	.1	--	--	--	--	--	--
Total LAFTA	2.0	3.6	3.3	7.1	7.6	7.4	8.4	5.5	3.1	3.0
Venezuela	--	--	--	--	--	--	--	--	--	--
Total	2.0	3.6	3.3	7.1	7.6	7.4	8.4	5.5	3.1	3.0
					IMPORTS					
Argentina	11.1	12.7	7.7	12.3	6.5	8.1	4.2	7.0	8.0	4.1
Brazil	2.0	2.5	.6	1.4	.2	.4	.7	1.0	.6	1.6
Chile	3.7	3.0	1.3	1.5	2.1	2.5	2.6	2.5	4.3	1.6
Colombia	--	--	--	.1	--	--	--	--	--	--
Ecuador	--	.1	.7	.1	--	--	--	--	--	.3
Mexico	--	--	1.0	--	--	--	--	--	.2	--
Paraguay	--	--	--	--	--	--	--	--	--	--
Peru	7.0	6.5	7.4	5.3	3.7	4.2	2.7	3.0	1.6	1.7
Uruguay	--	.9	.1	.1	--	--	--	--	.3	.1
Total LAFTA	23.8	25.8	18.8	20.8	12.5	15.2	10.2	13.5	15.0	9.4
Venezuela	--	--	--	--	--	--	--	--	.2	--
Total	23.8	25.8	18.8	20.8	12.5	15.2	10.2	13.5	15.2	9.4

Sources: United Nations, International Monetary Fund, International Bank for Reconstruction and Development, Direction of International Trade, Series T, Vol. 7, No. 6; Series T, Vol. 8, No. 7; Series T, Vol. 9, No. 10; Series T, Vol. 6, No. 9, Washington, D.C. International Monetary Fund, International Bank for Reconstruction and Development, *Direction of Trade*, Annual 1958-62, and July, 1964, Washington, D.C.

a/ Exports, FOB, Imports, CIF.

Exports of LAFTA Countries and of Bolivia and Venezuela to One Another by Year and Product

Table VII-1-1a. *Argentina's Exports to LAFTA Countries, 1959—Raw Materials*

(Thousands of U.S. Dollars)

	Brazil	Chile	Colombia	Ecuador	Mexico	Paraguay	Peru	Uruguay	Total LAFTA	Bolivia	Venezuela	TOTAL
ANIMAL												
1a. Live	47.0	10,697.1	33.9	2.5	0.2	36.9	144.8	58.3	11,020.7	0.8	160.9	11,182.4
1b. Fibers	5.0	352.3	88.6		75.3	16.6			538.3		0.5	538.8
1c. Fish												
1d. Other										21.6		21.6
AGRICULTURAL												
1a. Grains	75,400.7	2,530.1				4,855.4	3,736.6	2,228.9	88,751.7	1,070.8		89,822.5
1b. Fibers	46.8								46.8		16.6	63.4
1c. Fruits	6,200.3	73.5				276.4	164.0	933.8	7,647.8	80.5	1,614.5	9,342.8
1d. Seeds	345.7					14.8	7.0	1,159.3	1,526.8		32.2	1,559.0
1e. Other	102.0					4.0			106.0	0.1		106.1
FORESTRY												
1a. Plants	123.9								123.9			123.9
MINERAL												
1a. Metals												
1b. Oil												
1c. Stone	2.0	67.2				42.0			111.2	48.6		159.8
1d. Non-metals		6.6			17.6	19.5		3.1	46.8	0.3		47.1
1e. Other	16.7								16.7			16.7
TOTAL RAW MATERIALS	82,290.1	13,727.1	122.5	2.5	93.1	5,265.6	4,052.4	4,383.4	109,936.7	1,222.7	1,824.7	112,984.1

Source: Secretaría de Estado de Hacienda, Dirección Nacional de Estadística y Censo, *Comercio Exterior, 1959*, Buenos Aires, 1960.

Table VII-1-1b. *Argentina's Exports to LAFTA Countries, 1959—Semi-Processed*
(Thousands of U.S. Dollars)

	Brazil	Chile	Colom-bia	Ecuador	Mexico	Para-guay	Peru	Uruguay	Total LAFTA	Bolivia	Vene-zuela	TOTAL
ANIMAL												
2a. Hides		2,160.3						0.1	2,160.4		55.2	2,215.6
2b. Fat		4,037.4				24.3	30.4		4,092.1	558.1	1.0	4,651.2
2c. Meat	640.2	962.9					2,165.1	920.9	4,689.1	20.6		4,709.7
2d. Pelts	27.7								27.7			27.7
2e. Other												
AGRICULTURAL												
2a. Flour		20.1				56.1			76.2	1,516.5		1,592.7
2b. Grains	1,719.5	99.2				72.8			1,891.5	500.5		2,392.0
2c. Sugar		0.3							0.3	0.2		0.5
2d. Fruits	1,130.4	0.8			0.3	30.0	27.0	39.4	1,227.9	1.1	1.8	1,230.8
2e. Coffee		148.4		0.8	0.7		0.9	3.0	153.8	7.8	0.4	162.0
2f. Other	1,451.5	7.5				4.3	0.4	3.4	1,467.1	1.2		1,468.3
FORESTRY												
2a. Lumber						4.4		32.0	36.4			36.4
2b. Extracts	211.2	1,049.0	30.6	1.2	292.6		580.4	127.0	2,292.0	77.6	620.0	2,989.6
MINERAL												
2a. Metals						1.6			1.6			1.6
2b. Oil						7.3		280.6	287.9	60.6		348.5
TOTAL SEMI-PROCESSED	5,180.5	8,485.9	30.6	2.0	293.6	200.8	2,804.2	1,406.4	18,404.0	2,744.2	678.4	21,826.6

Table VII-1-1c. *Argentina's Exports to LAFTA Countries, 1959—Processed or Manufactured*
(Thousands of U.S. Dollars)

	Brazil	Chile	Colombia	Ecuador	Mexico	Paraguay	Peru	Uruguay	Total LAFTA	Bolivia	Venezuela	TOTAL
ANIMAL												
3a. Leather	21.0	23.0				0.5	257.1	10.3	301.6		80.7	382.3
3b. Canned	121.1	0.7	1.4		64.9		68.3	5.5	266.7	12.5	436.0	715.2
3c. Dairy	9.9	291.0		2.3	125.8	411.4	647.4		1,496.3	105.3	1,136.6	2,738.2
3d. Meal												
3e. Seafood						0.9	0.4		1.3	9.5		10.8
3f. Other	62.2	42.2	0.7		7.3	0.4	27.3		140.1	2.8	652.6	795.5
AGRICULTURAL												
3a. Food	345.5	2.6				28.4	3.4	14.0	393.9	108.6	243.1	745.6
3b. Tobacco		2.1				7.8		0.6	10.5			10.5
3c. Beverage	2.0					58.7		0.6	61.3	2.2		63.5
3d. Oils	347.4	1,199.3			4.6	4.8	398.2	17.5	1,971.8	432.8	3.1	2,407.7
3e. Textiles												
3f. Sugar												
3g. Other		3.3				65.0			68.3	31.4	1.2	100.9
FORESTRY												
3a. Wood												
3b. Paper												
MINERAL												
3a. Metals	40.7					26.5		51.7	67.2	65.6	0.3	133.1
3b. Machinery	32.2	1,125.3	4.1		2.0	433.3	18.3	0.1	1,664.9	26.2	4.3	1,695.4
3c. Vehicles		4.8				6.6	9.1		20.6			20.6
3d. Cement	15.3	1.1				42.7		3.9	63.0	0.3		63.3
3e. Chemicals	179.4	43.6	46.5	1.4	51.7	685.7	20.6	117.1	1,146.0	84.7	204.8	1,435.5
3f. Glass												
MISCELLANEOUS MANUFACTURES	130.1	181.9	28.2	7.1	45.2	1,111.9	45.4	42.2	1,592.0	417.0	307.3	2,316.3
TOTAL PROCESSED	1,306.8	2,921.9	80.9	10.8	301.5	2,884.6	1,495.5	263.5	9,265.5	1,298.9	3,070.0	13,634.4
TOTAL EXPORTS	88,777.4	25,134.9	234.0	15.3	688.2	8,351.0	8,352.1	6,053.3	137,606.2	5,265.8	5,573.1	148,445.1

116

Table VII-1-2a. *Argentina's Exports to LAFTA Countries, 1960—Raw Materials*

(Thousands of U.S. Dollars)

	Brazil	Chile	Colombia	Ecuador	Mexico	Paraguay	Peru	Uruguay	Total LAFTA	Bolivia	Venezuela	TOTAL
ANIMAL												
1a. Live	80.1	20,205.2	93.9	12.5	64.1	51.7	163.2	174.9	20,781.5	0.7	67.6	20,849.8
1b. Fibers	806.9	1,055.0	40.3	28.7			129.1		2,124.1	19.6		2,143.7
1c. Fish	0.4								0.4			0.4
1d. Other						9.7			9.7			9.7
AGRICULTURAL												
1a. Grains	65,894.4	7,481.0				4,692.3	11,904.6	2,412.4	92,384.7	45.3	284.8	92,714.8
1b. Fibers	8.4								8.4		48.3	56.7
1c. Fruits	6,769.4	731.7				283.5	113.7	2,732.3	10,630.6	109.7	1,538.2	12,278.5
1d. Seeds	1,023.1	71.2				8.7	15.7	674.5	1,793.2	2.7	52.5	1,848.4
1e. Other												
FORESTRY												
1a. Plants	2.0	2.4							4.4	0.1		4.5
MINERAL												
1a. Metals	48.7	24.6				2.4			83.3			83.3
1b. Oil								7.6				
1c. Stone	25.7	1.8				107.3			139.0	44.1		183.1
1d. Non-metals	90.5	16.5			4.2	204.6		75.3	386.9	17.3		404.2
1e. Other		14.4							14.4			14.4
TOTAL RAW MATERIALS	74,749.6	29,603.8	134.2	41.2	68.3	5,360.2	12,326.3	6,077.0	128,360.6	239.5	1,991.4	130,591.5

Source: Secretaría de Estado de Hacienda, Dirección Nacional de Estadística y Censo, *Comercio Exterior, 1960*, Buenos Aires, 1961.

117

Table VII-1-2b. *Argentina's Exports to LAFTA Countries, 1960—Semi-Processed*
(Thousands of U.S. Dollars)

	Brazil	Chile	Colombia	Ecuador	Mexico	Paraguay	Peru	Uruguay	Total LAFTA	Bolivia	Venezuela	TOTAL
ANIMAL												
2a. Hides	1.0	1,595.5					412.2		2,008.7		43.8	2,052.5
2b. Fat	103.7	2,116.0				183.8	50.2	101.9	2,555.6			2,555.6
2c. Meat	134.9	2,880.1					382.5	800.6	4,198.1	3.1	1.7	4,202.9
2d. Pelts	1.9							1.5	3.4		0.3	3.7
2e. Other	1.5	314.9						1.4	317.8			317.8
AGRICULTURAL												
2a. Flour		154.1				1.6			155.7	172.3		328.0
2b. Grains	1,446.3	9.9				143.1		1.7	1,601.0	11.9		1,612.9
2c. Sugar	1,640.3								1,640.3			1,640.3
2d. Fruits						33.9	32.4	29.8	96.1	1.8	2.6	100.5
2e. Coffee		76.3		1.4	1.5	0.3	14.0	113.6	207.1	1.9	0.5	209.5
2f. Other	1,397.0	9.9				4.1	2.6	23.4	1,437.0	2.0		1,439.0
FORESTRY												
2a. Lumber		2.4				3.7		53.4	59.5	0.1		59.6
2b. Extracts	133.0	549.0	63.9		288.4	0.1	533.7	369.9	1,938.0	102.4	263.9	2,304.3
MINERAL												
2a. Metals	368.8					0.8			369.6			369.6
2b. Oil						37.8			37.8	76.7		114.5
TOTAL SEMI-PROCESSED	5,228.4	7,708.1	63.9	1.4	289.9	409.2	1,427.6	1,497.2	16,625.7	372.2	312.8	17,310.7

Table VII-1-2c. *Argentina's Exports to LAFTA Countries, 1960—Manufactured or Processed*

(Thousands of U.S. Dollars)

	Brazil	Chile	Colombia	Ecuador	Mexico	Paraguay	Peru	Uruguay	Total LAFTA	Bolivia	Venezuela	TOTAL
ANIMAL												
3a. Leather	18.5					1.9			20.4	1.8	6.2	28.4
3b. Canned	161.6	25.9		0.6	28.1	0.4	83.6	19.1	319.3	0.6	542.2	862.1
3c. Dairy	288.7	2,273.0		0.8	229.6	358.8	930.7	325.8	4,407.4	560.9	1,962.4	6,930.7
3d. Meal												
3e. Seafood						5.5	0.7		6.2	0.3		6.5
3f. Other	111.0	13.8			0.1	2.0	11.2		138.1			138.1
AGRICULTURAL												
3a. Food	83.5	408.4	3.9		0.1	54.9	4.9	3,192.3	3,748.0	38.3	111.8	3,898.1
3b. Tobacco		1.1					0.5	112.8	114.4			114.4
3c. Beverage	2.2					56.6	0.2		59.0	1.0	0.4	60.4
3d. Oils	210.4	458.0			2.7	167.9	348.2	10.4	1,197.6	181.6	32.8	1,412.0
3e. Textiles	0.1	5.6				28.4		4.8	38.9	73.4	2.1	114.4
3f. Sugar										511.2		511.2
3g. Other		10.4				37.8		8.7	56.9			56.9
FORESTRY												
3a. Wood		1.1				6.4		0.3	7.8	5.7	0.1	13.6
3b. Paper		0.9	0.1			83.8		4.7	89.5	4.2		93.7
MINERAL												
3a. Metals	1,184.7	19.0				97.7		100.4	1,401.8	9.8	1.2	1,412.8
3b. Machinery	110.9	814.0	43.1	4.5	6.5	454.5	81.1	332.1	1,846.7	39.7	104.9	1,991.3
3c. Vehicles		8.2				6.2	0.9	88.1	103.4		0.5	103.9
3d. Cement						63.6		36.7	100.3	4.1		104.4
3e. Chemicals	261.8	48.4	6.4	5.3	72.7	604.1	9.1	252.0	1,259.8	60.6	206.2	1,526.6
3f. Glass		1.2				131.9	0.6	23.4	157.1	0.7	4.3	162.1
MISCELLANEOUS MANUFACTURES	249.3	266.9	10.0	3.3	60.2	586.0	174.3	828.2	2,178.2	227.3	78.7	2,484.2
TOTAL PROCESSED	2,682.7	4,355.9	63.5	14.5	400.0	2,748.4	1,646.0	5,339.9	17,250.8	1,721.2	3,053.8	22,025.8
TOTAL EXPORTS	82,660.7	41,667.8	261.6	57.1	758.2	8,517.8	15,399.9	12,914.1	162,237.2	2,332.9	5,358.0	169,928.1

Table VII-1-3a. *Argentina's Exports to LAFTA Countries, 1961—Raw Materials*

(Thousands of U.S. Dollars)

	Brazil	Chile	Colombia	Ecuador	Mexico	Paraguay	Peru	Uruguay	Total LAFTA	Bolivia	Venezuela	TOTAL
ANIMAL												
1a. Live	113.5	22,297.5	4.9	4.1	64.1	54.9	573.5	257.9	23,306.3	228.1	45.3	23,579.7
1b. Fibers	1,125.7	1,725.9	102.7	26.9		9.6	24.7	14.0	3,094.6	41.3	137.7	3,273.6
1c. Fish												
1d. Other	19.6								19.6			19.6
AGRICULTURAL												
1a. Grains	12,675.0	13.1		0.2		4,454.8	8,709.2	106.2	25,958.5	1,126.0	490.8	27,575.3
1b. Fibers						2.3			2.3		90.8	93.1
1c. Fruits	6,659.3	24.6				301.1	243.1	471.2	7,699.3	101.8	1,382.0	9,183.1
1d. Seeds	2.6	3.5				8.7		62.6	77.4	0.3		77.7
1e. Other												
FORESTRY												
1a. Plants	0.3					0.1		2.9	3.3	0.1		3.4
MINERAL												
1a. Metals	26.6	5-.8							78.4	105.7		184.1
1b. Oil								542.0	542.0			542.0
1c. Stone	6.4								6.4	1.7		8.1
1d. Non-metals	5.7	5.7				29.3			35.0	1.9		36.9
1e. Other	9.4	0.6				197.8		126.2	334.0	0.1		334.1
TOTAL RAW MATERIALS	20,638.4	24,125.7	107.6	31.2	64.1	5,058.6	9,550.5	1,583.0	61,157.1	1,607.0	2,146.6	64,910.7

Source: Secretaría de Estado de Hacienda, Dirección Nacional de Estadística y Censo, *Comercio Exterior, 1961,* Buenos Aires, 1962.

120

Table VII-1-3b. *Argentina's Exports to LAFTA Countries, 1961—Semi-Processed*

(Thousands of U.S. Dollars)

	Brazil	Chile	Colombia	Ecuador	Mexico	Paraguay	Peru	Uruguay	Total LAFTA	Bolivia	Venezuela	TOTAL
ANIMAL												
2a. Hides		28.3				4.0	366.3	0.6	399.2		35.0	434.2
2b. Fat	18.8	4,750.2			49.8	180.4	917.1		5,917.1	1.5	16.0	5,934.6
2c. Meat	140.4	4,023.6			42.5	1.3	1,784.6		5,992.4	1,001.6	7.6	7,001.6
2d. Pelts	0.8	0.6				0.2		0.4	2.0			2.0
2e. Other	2.2							2.0	4.2			4.2
AGRICULTURAL												
2a. Flour						14.7		1.1	15.8	1,789.9		1,805.7
2b. Grains	520.7	46.3				55.9	0.2	8.6	631.7	20.1		651.8
2c. Sugar	1,639.8			0.7		12.2	14.5		1,667.2	7.0		1,674.2
2d. Fruits												
2e. Coffee		18.1		0.6	1.0	1.3	1.3	25.3	47.6	12.2	0.6	60.4
2f. Other	1,331.5	0.1				5.9			1,337.5	8.6		1,346.1
FORESTRY												
2a. Lumber						4.6		92.4	97.0	0.1		97.1
2b. Extracts	148.1	607.4	61.5		376.3		281.5	144.6	1,619.4	100.6	285.7	2,005.7
MINERAL												
2a. Metals	63.8					1.2			65.0			65.0
2b. Oil	3.1	3.4				10.8		230.6	247.9	25.4		273.3
TOTAL SEMI-PROCESSED	3,869.2	9,478.0	61.5	1.3	469.6	292.5	3,365.5	505.6	18,044.0	2,967.0	344.9	21,355.9

Table VII-1-3c. *Argentina's Exports to LAFTA Countries, 1961—Processed or Manufactured*
(Thousands of U.S. Dollars)

	Brazil	Chile	Colombia	Ecuador	Mexico	Paraguay	Peru	Uruguay	Total LAFTA	Bolivia	Venezuela	TOTAL
ANIMAL												
3a. Leather		2,039.1				1.9			2,041.0	5.3	5.8	2,052.1
3b. Canned		1.0	0.7		16.8	1.8	33.0		53.3	42.4	53.9	149.6
3c. Dairy	166.4	250.7		2.3	103.9	385.7	184.8	0.5	1,094.3	190.9	1,643.8	2,929.0
3d. Meal	5.5								5.5			5.5
3e. Seafood						3.7	0.1	0.9	4.7			4.7
3f. Other	27.6	55.4			65.5	0.3	6.8	0.6	156.2	1.1		157.3
AGRICULTURAL												
3a. Food	469.6	2.3	31.5			85.9	4.6	23.2	617.1	63.2	98.7	779.0
3b. Tobacco							0.3	81.3	81.6	0.1		81.7
3c. Beverage	1.1	3.0				387.2			391.3	1.3		392.6
3d. Oils	367.7	97.5	6.0		33.5		581.1	6.5	1,092.3	373.1	59.6	1,525.0
3e. Textiles	20.5	1.1				18.1	1.6	0.1	41.4	5.6		47.0
3f. Sugar		4,733.9				14.5		1,904.5	6,652.9	1,787.5		8,440.4
3g. Other	1.1	9.0	0.6			36.3	8.0	0.7	55.7	24.0		79.7
FORESTRY												
3a. Wood												
3b. Paper	3.3	15.7	2.2	3.5	3.5	198.7	12.8	28.4	268.1	8.7	6.0	282.8
MINERAL												
3a. Metals	600.6	3.8			1.7	371.0	1.0	27.9	1,006.0	97.7	1.0	1,104.7
3b. Machinery	70.4	279.3	38.3	0.7	66.3	192.2	135.3	420.8	1,203.3	21.5	18.9	1,243.7
3c. Vehicles	0.1	34.0				45.0	2.3	52.6	134.0	9.9		143.9
3d. Cement		2.0			7.6	51.5			61.1	45.7		106.8
3e. Chemicals	488.6	111.1	21.6	2.4	75.4	629.9	21.2	401.8	1,752.0	83.8	166.4	2,002.2
3f. Glass												
MISCELLANEOUS MANUFACTURES	131.3	1,785.8	48.6	26.4	234.8	997.5	332.2	754.7	4,311.3	189.1	183.8	4,684.2
TOTAL PROCESSED	2,353.8	9,424.7	149.5	35.3	609.0	3,421.2	1,325.1	3,704.5	21,023.1	2,950.9	2,237.9	26,211.9
TOTAL EXPORTS	26,861.4	43,026.4	318.6	67.8	1,142.7	8,772.3	14,241.1	5,793.1	100,223.4	7,524.9	4,729.4	112,477.7

Table VII-1-4a. *Argentina's Exports to LAFTA Countries, 1962—Raw Materials*

(Thousands of U.S. Dollars)

	Brazil	Chile	Colombia	Ecuador	Mexico	Paraguay	Peru	Uruguay	Total LAFTA	Bolivia	Venezuela	TOTAL
ANIMAL												
1a. live	350.3	19,202.5	1.0	2.0	13.9	697.7	5,756.4	101.9	26,125.7	1,264.3	117.1	27,507.1
1b. Fibers	274.1	1,780.5	1,800.0	60.6	28.0	6.6	5.8		3,955.6	84.9		4,040.5
1c. Fish	1.9					1.6		6.5	10.0			10.0
1d. Other	2.1	1.2		10.3		42.4			56.0	8.6		64.6
AGRICULTURAL												
1a. Grains	42,399.0	14.3				668.8	15,471.0	625.3	59,178.4	1,385.6	1,807.0	62,371.0
1b. Fibers	3.2								3.2	1.2		4.4
1c. Fruits	11,589.4	7.4				392.0	84.0	363.7	12,436.5	110.9	1,148.3	13,695.7
1d. Seeds	5.9	6.6				8.8	0.8	241.6	263.7	0.1	0.1	263.8
1e. Other	81.0					1.2		4.2	86.4	9.1	92.2	187.7
FORESTRY												
1a. Plants	14.9								14.9			14.9
MINERAL												
1a. Metals	279.9	1.2			3.7			6.5	291.3			291.3
1b. Oil						0.9		1,079.3	1,080.2	1,377.1		2,457.3
1c. Stone	88.6	44.1				292.4		188.1	613.2	98.6		711.8
1d. Non-metals		46.2	0.1		16.2	181.9		37.7	282.1	50.7		332.8
1e. Other	3,961.9					6.6			3,968.5	0.4		3,968.9
TOTAL RAW MATERIALS	59,052.2	21,104.0	1,801.1	72.9	61.8	2,300.9	21,318.0	2,654.8	108,365.7	4,391.4	3,164.7	115,921.8

Source: Secretaría de Estado de Hacienda, Dirección Nacional de Estadística y Censo, *Comercio Exterior, 1962*, Buenos Aires, 1963.

123

Table VII-1-4b. *Argentina's Exports to LAFTA Countries, 1962—Semi-Processed*

(Thousands of U.S. Dollars)

	Brazil	Chile	Colombia	Ecuador	Mexico	Paraguay	Peru	Uruguay	Total LAFTA	Bolivia	Venezuela	TOTAL
ANIMAL												
2a. Hides	175.3	1,285.3	2.3			5.2	609.1	38.7	2,116.4	1.7		2,118.1
2b. Fat		2,787.5	208.9			13.1	46.4	0.2	3,056.2	210.4		3,266.6
2c. Meat		3,480.7					2,068.7	238.2	5,787.6	133.7		5,921.4
2d. Pelts	17.6	205.5				0.2	1.1		224.4		0.1	224.4
2e. Other												
AGRICULTURAL												
2a. Flour		16.7				136.8			153.5	1,342.4		1,495.9
2b. Grains	1,888.4		11.8			140.1	135.2		2,175.5	4.8		2,180.3
2c. Sugar	1,673.0	2.1	4.8	0.7		12.9	54.6	4.4	1,752.5	1.9	0.1	1,754.5
2d. Fruits		106.0		0.6	0.2		1.2	43.4	151.4	7.6	1.2	160.2
2e. Coffee												
2f. Other		6.6				7.4		8.4	22.4	10.7		33.1
FORESTRY												
2a. Lumber								41.0	41.0	0.1		41.1
2b. Extracts	157.4	846.0	78.3	1.3	287.5	5.8	464.9	214.1	2,055.3	96.2	299.9	2,451.4
MINERAL												
2a. Metals	368.4					0.9		5.6	374.9			374.9
2b. Oil	1,336.8	6.7				178.7		161.0	1,683.2	0.6		1,683.8
TOTAL SEMI-PROCESSED	5,616.9	8,743.7	306.1	2.6	287.7	501.1	3,381.2	755.0	19,594.3	1,810.1	301.3	21,705.7

Table VII-1-4c. *Argentina's Exports to LAFTA Countries, 1962—Processed or Manufactured*
(Thousands of U.S. Dollars)

	Brazil	Chile	Colombia	Ecuador	Mexico	Paraguay	Peru	Uruguay	Total LAFTA	Bolivia	Venezuela	TOTAL
ANIMAL												
3a. Leather		0.5							0.5			0.5
3b. Canned	173.0	0.3	0.8			0.2	5.3	90.1	269.7	95.9		365.6
3c. Dairy	85.6	772.0			228.7	454.8	520.0		2,061.1	94.2	1,266.8	3,422.1
3d. Meal	9.5								9.5			9.5
3e. Seafood						2.7	0.2	0.9	3.8	8.4		12.2
3f. Other		32.4	0.2		1.9	4.0	20.7		59.2	7.8	24.0	91.0
AGRICULTURAL												
3a. Food	1,084.7	7.7			0.1	111.4	26.0	39.2	1,269.1	10.8	380.4	1,660.3
3b. Tobacco								6.5	6.5			6.5
3c. Beverage	1.0					19.0			20.0	4.4	0.2	24.6
3d. Oils	712.1	43.3	70.3			13.3	0.2	8.1	847.3	388.5		1,235.8
3e. Textiles		2.6				12.1		2.8	17.5	86.6	0.1	104.2
3f. Sugar		13.2						729.3	742.5	203.0		945.5
3g. Other		4.3		0.1		61.7	3.9	5.6	75.6	77.4		153.0
FORESTRY												
3a. Wood	0.2	0.3				1.8	0.1		2.4	3.9		6.3
3b. Paper	1.2	19.5	6.6	0.4	80.7	104.0	56.2	9.7	278.3	2.1	51.0	331.4
MINERAL												
3a. Metals	294.2	48.4				267.9	0.1	211.6	822.2	35.3		857.5
3b. Machinery	646.7	577.6	53.2		2.5	280.4	119.0	1,292.3	2,971.7	39.5	8.6	3,019.8
3c. Vehicles		17.7				61.9	0.7	152.5	232.9	0.6	4.3	237.8
3d. Cement						13.8			13.8	1.6		15.4
3e. Chemicals	622.7	173.9	27.7	10.7	209.6	677.9	19.7	603.2	2,345.4	155.8	41.0	2,542.2
3f. Glass		17.4				2.4	0.1		19.9	0.3		20.2
MISCELLANEOUS MANUFACTURES	153.9	171.9	18.4	6.4	81.4	636.3	180.6	178.4	1,427.3	194.1	312.0	1,933.4
TOTAL PROCESSED	3,784.9	1,903.0	177.2	17.6	604.9	2,725.6	952.8	3,330.2	13,496.2	1,410.2	2,088.4	16,994.8
TOTAL EXPORTS	68,494.0	31,750.7	2,284.4	93.1	954.4	5,527.6	25,652.0	6,740.0	141,456.2	7,611.7	5,554.4	154,622.3

Table VII-1-5a. *Argentina's Exports to LAFTA Countries, 1963—Raw Materials*
(Thousands of U.S. Dollars)

	Brazil	Chile	Colombia	Ecuador	Mexico	Paraguay	Peru	Uruguay	Total LAFTA	Bolivia	Venezuela	TOTAL
ANIMAL												
1a. Live	1,285.9	14,074.2	5,822.3	0.2	38.3	482.6	12,794.3	75.8	34,573.6	960.3	170.5	35,704.4
1b. Fibers	1,785.9	4,680.1		146.1	208.4	3.4	9.3	0.1	6,829.8	237.3		7,067.1
1c. Fish	59.1								62.6			62.6
1d. Other	7.4								7.4			7.4
AGRICULTURAL												
1a. Grains	39,232.8	168.0		72.2		1,999.2	16,774.6	329.7	58,576.5	339.2	660.2	59,575.9
1b. Fibers		101.2							101.2			101.2
1c. Fruits	13,555.7	11.1	0.1		1.2	343.8	105.9	200.0	14,217.8	131.8	1,152.7	15,502.3
1d. Seeds	29.4	2.2		4.9		18.5		453.9	508.9			508.9
1e. Other	41.8				1.3			24.0	67.1		206.2	273.3
FORESTRY												
1a. Plants										2.0		2.0
MINERAL												
1a. Metals	402.2				3.5	0.1		2.1	407.9			407.9
1b. Oil	1,203.2					352.9			1,556.1			1,556.1
1c. Stone	23.2	6.2	16.4		0.3	441.1		409.9	2,436.8	0.2		2,437.0
1d. Non-metals	131.5	97.5			22.8	201.4		103.8	573.4	34.9		608.3
1e. Other	655.3					48.4		13.4	717.1	0.3		717.4
TOTAL RAW MATERIALS	58,413.4	19,140.5	5,838.8	223.4	275.8	3,891.4	29,684.1	1,612.7	119,080.1	1,706.0	2,189.6	122,975.7

<u>Source:</u> Secretaría de Estado de Hacienda, Dirección Nacional de Estadística y Censo, <u>Comercio Exterior</u>, <u>1963</u>, Buenos Aires, 1964.

126

Table VII-1-5b. *Argentina's Exports to LAFTA Countries, 1963—Semi-Processed*
(Thousands of U.S. Dollars)

	Brazil	Chile	Colombia	Ecuador	Mexico	Paraguay	Peru	Uruguay	Total LAFTA	Bolivia	Venezuela	TOTAL
ANIMAL												
2a. Hides	235.6	1,086.8	10.9		1.0	36.0	299.5	88.3	1,758.1			1,758.1
2b. Fat	940.9	2,778.3	1,096.9		11.2	18.0	75.3		4,920.6	84.1		5,004.7
2c. Meat	5.8	6,128.6				3.8	2,813.5	3.0	8,954.7	161.1	1.1	9,116.9
2d. Pelts	15.7	0.6	9.1			7.5		0.7	33.6		0.8	34.4
2e. Other		5.9			2.1	3.9	1.9		13.8		6.2	20.0
AGRICULTURAL												
2a. Flour	1.3	37.0	3.0			128.0			169.3	744.1		913.4
2b. Grains	1,951.2	5.3	1.3			169.2		1.6	2,128.6	34.7		2,163.3
2c. Sugar										0.7		0.7
2d. Fruits	1,545.0		36.1	4.0	35.4	5.8	86.4	1,369.2	3,081.9	4.5		3,086.4
2e. Coffee		696.2		0.3	0.8	0.7	2.5	57.9	758.4	18.6	0.2	777.2
2f. Other	2.9	3.3	0.1			2.4	3.6	3.3	15.6	2.0		17.6
FORESTRY												
2a. Lumber	0.1	23.3				2.0		37.7	63.1	0.3		63.4
2b. Extracts	136.0	556.1	208.6	2.1	245.7	28.5	194.7	183.9	1,555.6	62.1	297.4	1,915.1
MINERAL												
2a. Metals	3,366.1	7.2				82.1	10.4	1,316.8	4,782.6	1.4	404.4	5,188.4
2b. Oil	90.2	23.6				776.9	464.3	1,398.7	2,753.7	9.5		2,763.2
TOTAL SEMI-PROCESSED	8,290.8	11,352.2	1,366.0	6.4	296.2	1,264.8	3,952.1	4,461.1	30,989.6	1,123.1	710.1	32,822.8

127

Table VII-1-5c. *Argentina's Exports to LAFTA Countries, 1963—Processed or Manufactured*

(Thousands of U.S. Dollars)

	Brazil	Chile	Colombia	Ecuador	Mexico	Paraguay	Peru	Uruguay	Total LAFTA	Bolivia	Venezuela	TOTAL
ANIMAL												
3a. Leather						0.6			0.6		1.4	2.0
3b. Canned	216.4	3.3	23.4		4.6	4.0	111.8	16.6	380.1	18.6	1.1	399.8
3c. Dairy	48.4	1,896.4		2.0	341.0	370.4	232.5	276.7	3,167.4	31.7	1,353.7	4,552.8
3d. Meal	8.3								8.3			8.3
3e. Seafood	58.5		0.2			1.6		2.7	63.0	5.7		68.7
3f. Other	28.9	199.8	1.3		70.8	0.4			301.2			301.2
AGRICULTURAL												
3a. Food	2,715.3	3.4	8.8		1.9	136.6	280.5	48.8	3,195.3	66.0	218.6	3,479.9
3b. Tobacco						1.2			1.2			1.2
3c. Beverage	2.3		0.1		0.6	51.3	2.3	114.3	170.9	62.0	0.1	233.0
3d. Oils	1,942.7	44.1	197.0		129.6	11.6	0.4	25.1	2,350.5	137.9	9.4	2,497.8
3e. Textiles	159.4	94.5		0.5	1.0	23.2	2.0	85.8	366.4	420.3	36.6	823.3
3f. Sugar		3,571.9				1,314.4			4,886.3			4,886.3
3g. Other	5.6	4.1				23.9	5.4		39.0	127.1		166.1
FORESTRY												
3a. Wood	41.6	3.9			0.4	15.4	0.1	0.3	61.7	5.2	0.7	67.6
3b. Paper	5.3	203.4	24.4	1.8	253.1	69.7	65.8	151.2	774.7	1.1	67.2	843.0
MINERAL												
3a. Metals	1,824.0	760.8				201.7	14.7	191.9	2,993.1	64.9	2,836.9	5,894.9
3b. Machinery	2,412.4	2,253.4	423.8	16.0	418.4	482.2	567.4	757.4	7,331.0	134.5	196.4	7,661.9
3c. Vehicles	54.8	15.1	4.3	1.5		110.9	38.8	866.5	1,091.9	4.4	32.8	1,129.1
3d. Cement		5.4				9.4			14.8	4.4		19.2
3e. Chemicals	892.3	531.4	71.6	12.5	396.3	782.5	105.8	801.2	3,593.6	235.3	36.4	3,865.3
3f. Glass						8.6			8.6			8.6
MISCELLANEOUS MANUFACTURES	417.3	1,392.3	234.8	54.8	460.6	797.3	470.6	309.0	4,136.7	356.3	500.4	4,993.4
TOTAL PROCESSED	10,833.5	10,983.2	989.7	89.1	2,078.3	4,416.9	1,898.1	3,647.5	34,936.3	1,675.4	5,291.7	41,903.4
TOTAL EXPORTS	77,537.7	41,475.9	8,194.5	318.9	2,650.3	9,573.1	35,534.3	9,721.3	185,006.0	4,504.5	8,191.4	197,701.9

Table VII-2-1a. *Brazil's Exports to LAFTA Countries, 1959—Raw Materials*

(Thousands of U.S. Dollars)

	Argentina	Chile	Colombia	Ecuador	Mexico	Paraguay	Peru	Uruguay	Total LAFTA	Bolivia	Venezuela	TOTAL
ANIMAL												
1a. Live	437.6					11.7		0.4	449.7		13.9	463.6
1b. Fibers												
1c. Fish												
1d. Other												
AGRICULTURAL												
1a. Grains												
1b. Fibers												
1c. Fruits	2.2	4.4					1.2	394.4	397.8			397.8
1d. Seeds	1.6					0.1			6.1		0.8	6.9
1e. Other	3,761.1	1,063.5						5,291.4	10,116.0			10,116.0
FORESTRY												
1a. Plants	0.7								0.7		3.0	3.7
MINERAL												
1a. Metals	213.4							12.8	226.2			226.2
1b. Oil		1.8						602.3	604.1			604.1
1c. Stone	622.8	0.1	7.3		1.7		0.3		632.2		229.2	861.4
1d. Non-metals	83.3	2.1			0.2	0.2			85.8			85.8
1e. Other												
TOTAL RAW MATERIALS	5,122.7	1,071.9	7.3		1.9	12.0	1.5	6,301.3	12,518.6		246.9	12,765.5

Source: Ministerio da Fazenda, Servicio de Estatística Económica e Financiera, Comercio Exterior do Brazil, 1959, Rio de Janeiro, 1960.

129

Table VII-2-1b. *Brazil's Exports to LAFTA Countries, 1959—Semi-Processed*

(Thousands of U.S. Dollars)

	Argentina	Chile	Colombia	Ecuador	Mexico	Paraguay	Peru	Uruguay	Total LAFTA	Bolivia	Venezuela	TOTAL
ANIMAL												
2a. Hides		5.7					22.8	5.7	34.2		0.6	34.8
2b. Fat							0.2		0.2			0.2
2c. Meat												
2d. Pelts												
2e. Other												
AGRICULTURAL												
2a. Flour	28.1	4.2			1.3	1.2		35.8	70.6			70.6
2b. Grains	1.5	25.3				0.3		0.5	25.6		0.7	26.3
2c. Sugar	10.8					0.7			11.5			11.5
2d. Fruits	268.1					1.3			269.4			269.4
2e. Coffee	16,708.7	7,221.7				364.9		10,836.9	35,132.2			35,132.2
2f. Other	54.2					8.7		66.2	129.1			129.1
FORESTRY												
2a. Lumber	19,229.4								19,232.8		0.9	19,233.7
2b. Extracts	22.1					3.4	1.0	2,973.3	2,996.4		339.9	3,336.3
MINERAL												
2a. Metals	59.4								59.4			59.5
2b. Oil										0.1		
TOTAL SEMI-PROCESSED	36,382.3	7,254.9			1.3	380.5	24.0	13,918.4	57,961.4	0.1	342.1	58,303.6

Table VII-2-1c. *Brazil's Exports to LAFTA Countries, 1959—Processed or Manufactured*
(Thousands of U.S. Dollars)

	Argentina	Chile	Colombia	Ecuador	Mexico	Paraguay	Peru	Uruguay	Total LAFTA	Bolivia	Venezuela	TOTAL
ANIMAL												
3a. Leather												
3b. Canned											55.9	55.9
3c. Dairy						0.2			0.2			0.2
3d. Meal												
3e. Seafood												
3f. Other												
AGRICULTURAL												
3a. Food	1.7								1.7			1.7
3b. Tobacco				1.0					1.0			1.0
3c. Beverage	0.6								0.6		2.3	2.9
3d. Oils	21.8	111.4						17.0	150.2		22.9	173.1
3e. Textiles	141.4	290.5	139.9		0.7	139.1		156.5	868.1		108.7	976.8
3f. Sugar												
3g. Other												
FORESTRY												
3a. Wood						1.6			1.6			1.6
3b. Paper	136.4	3.2				1.1	1.3	89.4	231.4	0.1	0.8	232.3
MINERAL												
3a. Metals	60.6	4.9				2.2	3.5	20.8	92.0	0.1		92.1
3b. Machinery	68.9	108.9			9.4	14.0	49.2	8.9	259.3	133.9	4.9	398.1
3c. Vehicles		451.3	10.7	11.0		0.2	2.8	9.0	485.0	23.5	2.2	510.7
3d. Cement						58.4			58.4			58.4
3e. Chemicals	545.3		5.8	6.8	10.5	15.7	4.2	77.4	665.7	1.3	174.4	841.4
3f. Glass						3.1			3.1	0.2		3.3
MISCELLANEOUS MANUFACTURES	360.8	542.2	46.9	12.7	72.3	218.2	109.5	147.7	1,510.3	86.6	241.9	1,838.8
TOTAL PROCESSED	1,337.5	1,512.4	203.3	31.5	92.9	453.8	170.5	526.7	4,328.6	245.7	614.0	5,188.3
TOTAL EXPORTS	42,842.5	9,839.2	210.6	31.5	96.1	846.3	196.0	20,746.4	74,808.6	245.8	1,203.0	76,257.4

Table VII-2-2a. *Brazil's Exports to LAFTA Countries, 1960—Raw Materials*
(Thousands of U.S. Dollars)

	Argentina	Chile	Colombia	Ecuador	Mexico	Paraguay	Peru	Uruguay	Total LAFTA	Bolivia	Venezuela	TOTAL
ANIMAL												
1a. Live	35.1	8.9				2.0			46.0	8.8	0.3	55.1
1b. Fibers												
1c. Fish						1.8		2.3	4.1			4.1
1d. Other						0.7			0.7			0.7
AGRICULTURAL												
1a. Grains										0.2		0.2
1b. Fibers	40.2								40.2	19.2	30.1	89.5
1c. Fruits	92.1							8.0	100.1			100.1
1d. Seeds	3,715.9								3,715.9			3,715.9
1e. Other	5.7							1,204.8	1,210.5			1,210.5
FORESTRY												
1a. Plants	1.4					0.2			1.6		1.2	2.8
MINERAL												
1a. Metals	1,293.0								1,293.0			1,293.0
1b. Oil												
1c. Stone	2.2				0.5		0.2	227.0	229.9	42.5		272.4
1d. Non-metals					108.1	0.2		1.4	109.7			109.7
1e. Other	0.2								0.2			0.2
TOTAL RAW MATERIALS	5,185.8	8.9			108.6	4.9	0.2	1,443.5	6,751.9	70.7	31.6	6,854.2

Source: Ministerio da Fazenda, Servicio de Estatística Económica e Financiera, *Comercio Exterior do Brazil, 1960*, Rio de Janeiro, 1961.

132

Table VII-2-2b. *Brazil's Exports to LAFTA Countries, 1960—Semi-Processed*

(Thousands of U.S. Dollars)

	Argentina	Chile	Colombia	Ecuador	Mexico	Paraguay	Peru	Uruguay	Total LAFTA	Bolivia	Venezuela	TOTAL
ANIMAL												
2a. Hides	0.3						52.5	11.0	63.8	1.2		65.0
2b. Fat												
2c. Meat												
2d. Pelts												
2e. Other										1.0		1.0
AGRICULTURAL												
2a. Flour			7.3		3.9		0.4	93.2	97.5		34.9	132.4
2b. Grains	67.9					2.3			77.5			77.5
2c. Sugar		5,446.5				2.2		1.8	5,450.6	2.0		5,452.6
2d. Fruits				0.4				1.4	1.8			1.8
2e. Coffee	23,123.3	5,335.6				397.1		7,727.0	36,583.0	19.9	1.2	36,604.1
2f. Other	529.7	5.7			0.3	1.0		102.4	639.1	16.5		655.6
FORESTRY												
2a. Lumber	22,192.6						8.9	4,799.1	27,000.6			27,000.6
2b. Extracts	1.6					1.3	83.8		86.7	0.1	629.4	716.2
MINERAL												
2a. Metals	1,554.8								1,554.8			1,554.8
2b. Oil	0.2								0.2			0.2
TOTAL SEMI-PROCESSED	47,470.4	10,787.8	7.3	0.4	4.2	403.9	145.6	12,736.0	71,555.6	40.7	665.5	72,261.8

Table VII-2-2c. *Brazil's Exports to LAFTA Countries, 1960—Processed or Manufactured*
(Thousands of U.S. Dollars)

	Argentina	Chile	Colombia	Ecuador	Mexico	Paraguay	Peru	Uruguay	Total LAFTA	Bolivia	Venezuela	TOTAL
ANIMAL												
3a. Leather	1.1					0.1	4.3		4.4	2.7		7.1
3b. Canned									1.1	0.3		1.4
3c. Dairy						7.0			7.0			7.0
3d. Meal												
3e. Seafood												
3f. Other												
AGRICULTURAL												
3a. Food	125.7				0.1	23.5		1.0	150.2	0.1	4.0	154.3
3b. Tobacco							2.9	1,527.9	1,530.9	174.8		1,705.7
3c. Beverage	5.5							157.0	162.5			162.5
3d. Oils	21.8	86.8			1.4	0.1		40.8	150.9			150.9
3e. Textiles	39.9	12.4	45.9			215.4		122.0	435.6	5.2	44.1	484.9
3f. Sugar												
3g. Other	224.6					9.5			234.1			234.1
FORESTRY												
3a. Wood	181.6	4.2				0.5			186.3	0.2		186.5
3b. Paper	145.1	5.1	0.1			4.1	33.3	154.8	342.5	5.2	5.0	352.7
MINERAL												
3a. Metals	1,155.4					16.0			1,171.4	9.5		1,180.9
3b. Machinery	230.1	21.3	3.0	6.3	0.4	119.3	11.9	160.2	552.5	181.0	11.4	744.9
3c. Vehicles	5.1	209.2	23.4			2.0	3.7	9.4	252.8	31.4	52.8	337.0
3d. Cement	2.5					39.4			41.9			41.9
3e. Chemicals	1,035.2	4.8	37.8	17.4	14.2	11.4	5.1	13.3	1,139.2	15.2	250.8	1,405.2
3f. Glass		3.0				1.4			4.4			4.4
MISCELLANEOUS MANUFACTURES	563.5	422.9	133.8	17.1	59.9	134.4	163.1	217.2	1,711.9	46.9	202.7	1,961.5
TOTAL PROCESSED	3,737.1	769.7	244.0	40.8	76.0	584.1	224.3	2,403.6	8,079.6	472.5	570.8	9,122.9
TOTAL EXPORTS	56,393.3	11,566.4	251.3	41.2	188.8	992.9	370.1	16,583.1	86,387.1	583.9	1,267.9	88,238.9

Table VII-2-3a. *Brazil's Exports to LAFTA Countries, 1961 — Raw Materials*
(Thousands of U.S. Dollars)

	Argen-tina	Chile	Colom-bia	Ecuador	Mexico	Para-guay	Peru	Uruguay	Total LAFTA	Bolivia	Vene-zuela	TOTAL
ANIMAL												
1a. Live	81.5						8.0	3.7	93.3		5.2	98.5
1b. Fibers					0.1				0.1			0.1
1c. Fish	0.1					0.1			0.1		0.1	0.2
1d. Other												
AGRICULTURAL												
1a. Grains												
1b. Fibers	21.7	1,633.1						3,067.4	4,722.2			4,722.2
1c. Fruits	112.4		8.8			0.1	0.1		121.4			121.4
1d. Seeds	2,986.3	70.7				8.8		1,062.8	4,128.6		908.7	5,037.3
1e. Other	645.2	4,387.0		0.2				1,094.9	6,127.3	40.5		6,167.8
FORESTRY												
1a. Plants	8.0								8.0		1.0	9.0
MINERAL												
1a. Metals	682.9								682.9			682.9
1b. Oil												
1c. Stone	128.6	2.9		0.2	6.9	1.3		11.3	151.2		4.2	155.4
1d. Non-metals	165.2								165.2	12.1		177.3
1e. Other	567.3	2.4	19.8		5.1			279.7	874.3			874.3
TOTAL RAW MATERIALS	5,399.2	6,096.1	28.6	0.4	12.1	10.3	8.1	5,519.8	17,074.6	52.6	919.2	18,046.4

Source: Ministerio da Fazenda, Servicio de Estatistica Economica e Financiera, *Comercio Exterior do Brazil, 1961,* Rio de Janeiro, 1962.

135

Table VII-2-3b. *Brazil's Exports to LAFTA Countries, 1961—Semi-Processed*

(Thousands of U.S. Dollars)

	Argentina	Chile	Colombia	Ecuador	Mexico	Paraguay	Peru	Uruguay	Total LAFTA	Bolivia	Venezuela	TOTAL
ANIMAL												
2a. Hides	4.3							0.7	5.2			5.2
2b. Fat		1.3							1.3			1.3
2c. Meat												
2d. Pelts												
2e. Other										0.2		0.2
AGRICULTURAL												
2a. Flour	10.8							16.2	27.0			27.0
2b. Grains	1,084.6	119.6	895.0		1.1	10.6		3.7	2,114.6	13.3		2,127.9
2c. Sugar												
2d. Fruits	149.4				1.1	3.0	0.1		153.6	0.4		154.0
2e. Coffee	22,533.1	1,634.1		0.6		7.9		3,714.7	27,890.4	3.1		27,893.5
2f. Other	50.8	0.3				3.7		16.4	71.2	0.7		71.9
FORESTRY												
2a. Lumber	29,493.7	0.8	22.0			0.9	907.9	3,660.6	33,177.1	0.4		33,177.5
2b. Extracts	29.1								937.9		242.2	1,180.1
MINERAL												
2a. Metals	1,774.3	0.3						16.0	1,790.6			1,790.6
2b. Oil										0.1		0.1
TOTAL SEMI-PROCESSED	55,130.1	1,756.6	917.0	0.6	2.2	26.1	908.0	7,428.3	66,168.9	18.2	242.2	66,429.3

Table VII-2-3c. *Brazil's Exports to LAFTA Countries, 1961—Processed or Manufactured*

(Thousands of U.S. Dollars)

	Argentina	Chile	Colombia	Ecuador	Mexico	Paraguay	Peru	Uruguay	Total LAFTA	Bolivia	Venezuela	TOTAL
ANIMAL												
3a. Leather						3.8	1.0		4.8	1.4		6.2
3b. Canned										0.5		0.5
3c. Dairy										0.2		0.2
3d. Meal	0.1							145.0	145.1			145.1
3e. Seafood												
3f. Other	0.5								0.5			0.5
AGRICULTURAL												
3a. Food	63.6					1.3	5.0	0.5	70.4		2.2	72.6
3b. Tobacco						3.5		1,499.2	1,502.7			1,502.7
3c. Beverage						1.1		92.7	93.8			93.8
3d. Oils	69.4	1.4			3.1			53.3	127.5			127.5
3e. Textiles	76.1	21.8	4.0			97.6	0.3	26.9	226.4	50.7	24.1	301.2
3f. Sugar						0.4			0.4			0.4
3g. Other	20.8					0.5		3.8	25.1			25.1
FORESTRY												
3a. Wood						9.6			9.6	0.1		9.7
3b. Paper	832.7	1.6				5.3	12.2	493.8	1,345.6	3.9	9.0	1,358.5
MINERAL												
3a. Metals	205.8		0.2			28.2			234.2	1.4		235.6
3b. Machinery	339.4	165.7	21.7	8.1	43.5	44.0	26.4	74.2	723.0	22.3	42.2	787.5
3c. Vehicles	3,910.0	2.5	37.4	1.9		38.1	8.1	70.1	4,068.1	5.6	2.9	4,076.6
3d. Cement	3.6	2.5				44.1		1.8	52.0	18.2		70.2
3e. Chemicals	329.0		40.0	13.2	44.6	36.9	3.5	9.5	476.7	13.3	189.3	679.3
3f. Glass	4.8					9.1			13.9		3.8	17.7
MISCELLANEOUS MANUFACTURES	1,049.3	719.4	100.4	50.1	114.7	225.9	266.2	308.7	2,834.7	182.3	196.3	3,213.3
TOTAL PROCESSED	6,905.1	914.9	203.7	73.3	205.9	549.4	322.7	2,779.5	11,954.5	299.9	469.8	12,724.2
TOTAL EXPORTS	67,434.4	8,767.6	1,149.3	74.3	220.2	585.8	1,238.8	15,727.6	95,198.0	370.7	1,631.2	97,199.9

Table VII-2-4a. *Brazil's Exports to LAFTA Countries, 1962—Raw Materials*
(Thousands of U.S. Dollars)

	Argentina	Chile	Colombia	Ecuador	Mexico	Paraguay	Peru	Uruguay	Total LAFTA	Bolivia	Venezuela	TOTAL
ANIMAL												
1a. Live	19.1	3.6			0.1	2.8	20.1	15.8	61.5	2.1	1.5	65.1
1b. Fibers						1.0			1.0			1.0
1c. Fish												
1d. Other						0.2			0.2			0.2
AGRICULTURAL												
1a. Grains						1.0			1.0	0.4		1.4
1b. Fibers	30.2	163.1				1.6		360.5	555.4	37.8	18.8	612.0
1c. Fruits	2,475.1					8.0		1,100.1	3,583.2			3,583.2
1d. Seeds	185.0	51.8			1.9	13.1		23.1	274.9		12.7	287.6
1e. Other						16.7			16.7	0.7		17.4
FORESTRY												
1a. Plants	2.8					0.1		0.8	3.7		3.4	7.1
MINERAL												
1a. Metals	2,160.9							51.6	2,212.5			2,212.5
1b. Oil												
1c. Stone	14.4	1.6			3.0			2.3	21.3	0.2		21.5
1d. Non-metals					3.2				3.2	1.1		4.3
1e. Other												
TOTAL RAW MATERIALS	4,887.5	220.1			8.2	44.5	20.1	1,554.2	6,734.6	42.3	36.4	6,813.3

Source: Ministerio da Fazenda, Servicio de Estatística Económica e Financiera, *Comercio Exterior do Brazil, 1962*, Rio de Janeiro, 1963.

138

Table VII-2-4b. *Brazil's Exports to LAFTA Countries, 1962—Semi-Processed*
(Thousands of U.S. Dollars)

	Argentina	Chile	Colombia	Ecuador	Mexico	Paraguay	Peru	Uruguay	Total LAFTA	Bolivia	Venezuela	TOTAL
ANIMAL												
2a. Hides	0.5					0.1		0.3	0.9	3.3		4.2
2b. Fat										1.1		1.1
2c. Meat												
2d. Pelts												
2e. Other						0.1			0.1			0.1
AGRICULTURAL												
2a. Flour	24.0							62.0	86.0	0.2		86.2
2b. Grains						0.1		614.3	614.4			614.4
2c. Sugar						363.7		2,159.3	2,523.0	24.3		2,547.3
2d. Fruits												
2e. Coffee	19,954.8	7,826.1	2.6	0.9	12.3	3.5	0.2	4,143.2	31,943.6	6.4		31,950.0
2f. Other	161.6					1.6	990.0	39.9	1,193.1	5.4		1,198.5
FORESTRY												
2a. Lumber	16,716.3					18.9	7.8	3,167.1	19,910.1		15.6	19,925.7
2b. Extracts	288.6	1.7				3.3		5.7	299.3		3.7	303.0
MINERAL												
2a. Metals	15.2							5.5	20.7			20.7
2b. Oil						1.4			1.4	1.3		2.7
TOTAL SEMI-PROCESSED	37,161.0	7,827.8	2.6	0.9	12.3	392.7	998.0	10,197.3	56,592.6	42.0	19.3	56,653.9

Table VII-2-4c. *Brazil's Exports to LAFTA Countries, 1962—Processed or Manufactured*
(Thousands of U.S. Dollars)

	Argentina	Chile	Colombia	Ecuador	Mexico	Paraguay	Peru	Uruguay	Total LAFTA	Bolivia	Venezuela	TOTAL
ANIMAL												
3a. Leather						6.5			6.5	0.5		7.0
3b. Canned			39.5			0.1			39.6	8.4	43.4	91.4
3c. Dairy						0.1			0.1			0.1
3d. Meal												
3e. Seafood	0.4					0.1			0.5			0.5
3f. Other			0.2						0.2	3.2		3.4
AGRICULTURAL												
3a. Food	303.4	35.3			6.9	6.6	1.2	2.1	355.5			355.5
3b. Tobacco						1.2		1.4	2.6	41.8		44.4
3c. Beverage						0.2			0.2	6.4		6.6
3d. Oils	24.5	28.0	0.4	7.9	18.1	52.0	0.9	23.6	155.4	0.1		155.5
3e. Textiles	118.9	23.3				352.2		2.3	496.7	71.0	0.7	568.4
3f. Sugar												
3g. Other	32.7	90.9	16.1		19.4	2.7		12.6	174.4	16.2	2.8	193.4
FORESTRY												
3a. Wood	9.9			8.2			16.0	13.0	48.8			48.8
3b. Paper	632.7		21.7		2.6	68.6		19.2	769.0	3.7	21.4	794.1
MINERAL												
3a. Metals	337.9	15.6	0.3			23.5	125.1	46.4	423.7	34.1		457.8
3b. Machinery	323.6	983.1	42.3	0.9		271.5	2.8	271.8	2,069.8	308.6	93.2	2,471.6
3c. Vehicles	3,770.0	2.0	7.8	3.8	51.5	221.8		1,364.2	5,372.4	42.4	45.7	5,460.5
3d. Cement	3.9	3.5				35.8	0.1	0.1	43.3	33.7		77.0
3e. Chemicals	293.9	25.4	19.3	13.2	177.2	74.1	33.5	451.3	1,087.9	42.8	41.5	1,172.2
3f. Glass		10.0				2.1			12.1			12.1
MISCELLANEOUS MANUFACTURES	548.1	85.8	5.7	0.6	8.9	544.2	47.1	64.1	1,304.5	157.5	49.3	1,511.3
TOTAL PROCESSED	6,399.9	1,302.9	153.3	34.6	284.6	1,689.2	226.6	2,272.1	12,363.2	771.0	298.0	13,431.6
TOTAL EXPORTS	48,448.4	9,350.8	155.9	35.5	305.1	2,126.4	1,244.7	14,023.6	75,690.4	855.3	353.7	76,899.4

Table VII-2-5a. Brazil's Exports to LAFTA Countries, 1963—Raw Materials

(Thousands of U.S. Dollars)

	Argentina	Chile	Colombia	Ecuador	Mexico	Paraguay	Peru	Uruguay	Total LAFTA	Bolivia	Venezuela	TOTAL
ANIMAL												
1a. Live	1.8	0.3				4.3		3.5	9.9	77.6	0.9	88.4
1b. Fibers												
1c. Fish	1.8	2.7	51.0		0.2	0.1			55.8		0.1	55.9
1d. Other												
AGRICULTURAL												
1a. Grains	82.6	296.6				1.9		740.1	1,121.2	17.6	0.1	1,138.9
1b. Fibers	31.3					6.1	41.0	13.7	92.1			92.1
1c. Fruits	1.4					0.1		30.0	31.5			31.5
1d. Seeds												
1e. Other	2,326.5	40.2	1.9		53.0	12.3	1.2	960.2	3,395.3		2.9	3,398.2
FORESTRY												
1a. Plants	6.2					1.4			7.6		2.8	10.4
MINERAL												
1a. Metals	3,074.9							33.1	3,108.0			3,108.0
1b. Oil												
1c. Stone	1.0				0.6	2.0		4.6	8.2	0.1		8.3
1d. Non-metals	26.8	0.4			3.2	3.1			33.5			33.5
1e. Other												
TOTAL RAW MATERIALS	5,554.3	340.2	52.9		57.0	31.3	42.2	1,785.2	7,863.1	95.3	6.8	7,965.2

Source: Ministerio da Fazenda, Servicio de Estatística Econômica e Financiera, Comercio Exterior do Brazil, 1963, Rio de Janeiro, 1964.

Table VII-2-5b. *Brazil's Exports to LAFTA Countries, 1963—Semi-Processed*
(Thousands of U.S. Dollars)

	Argentina	Chile	Colombia	Ecuador	Mexico	Paraguay	Peru	Uruguay	Total LAFTA	Bolivia	Venezuela	TOTAL
ANIMAL												
2a. Hides	1.2								1.2			1.2
2b. Fat	0.4					0.1		3.2	3.7			3.7
2c. Meat												
2d. Pelts												
2e. Other						2.8			2.8	3.0		5.8
AGRICULTURAL												
2a. Flour	3.0					1.1		49.9	54.0			54.0
2b. Grains	808.8		80.4		35.0	15.8			940.0	0.1		940.1
2c. Sugar	0.3	1,099.9						114.4	1,214.6			1,214.6
2d. Fruits				0.8		15.2	0.9		16.9	60.0		76.9
2e. Coffee	20,142.4	6,147.7						4,658.0	30,948.1			30,948.1
2f. Other		59.7	0.1						59.8	0.7		60.5
FORESTRY												
2a. Lumber	17,189.5				589.8	4.1	563.1	2,713.7	21,060.2		7.7	21,067.9
2b. Extracts	0.8	7.9						5.2	13.9			13.9
MINERAL												
2a. Metals						1.0			1.0			1.0
2b. Oil		0.4							0.4			0.4
TOTAL SEMI-PROCESSED	38,146.4	7,315.6	80.5	0.8	624.8	40.1	564.0	7,544.4	54,316.6	63.8	7.7	54,388.1

Table VII-2-5c. *Brazil's Exports to LAFTA Countries, 1963—Processed or Manufactured*
(Thousands of U.S. Dollars)

	Argentina	Chile	Colombia	Ecuador	Mexico	Paraguay	Peru	Uruguay	Total LAFTA	Bolivia	Venezuela	TOTAL
ANIMAL												
3a. Leather	3.1	2.4			3.0	2.8	3.0	1.8	2.8	7.2		2.8
3b. Canned						0.2			13.5	0.1	1.5	22.2
3c. Dairy												0.1
3d. Meal												
3e. Seafood												
3f. Other												
AGRICULTURAL												
3a. Food	25.0	15.7			2.2	39.0	4.5	1,376.3	1,462.7	14.4	3.0	1,480.1
3b. Tobacco	7.4					3.7		563.1	574.2			574.2
3c. Beverage			77.4			0.7			0.7	1.2		1.9
3d. Oils	116.3	143.0			50.3	20.8	19.7	93.7	521.2	46.6	20.4	541.6
3e. Textiles	801.1	54.0				309.7	0.9	11.4	1,177.1	1.1	0.6	1,224.3
3f. Sugar	1.9								1.9			3.0
3g. Other												
FORESTRY												
3a. Wood	6.7					12.8	3.6	14.0	37.1	5.3	69.1	111.5
3b. Paper	55.3	0.3			31.8	30.8	20.5	242.0	380.7	2.8	68.7	452.2
MINERAL												
3a. Metals	146.9	10.5	39.5	6.7	34.4	64.1	0.9	18.5	314.8	75.0	729.0	1,118.8
3b. Machinery	207.2	669.6	139.9	1.2	196.0	452.2	49.2	166.7	1,887.5	380.6	27.2	2,295.3
3c. Vehicles	130.1	1.4	43.2		28.5	186.9		864.7	1,256.0	20.8	2,250.0	3,526.8
3d. Cement		1.9			0.3	119.6			121.8	21.3		143.1
3e. Chemicals	763.7	127.2	66.4	1.3	229.0	132.4	36.4	452.7	1,809.1	58.3	57.4	1,924.8
3f. Glass	12.4								12.4			12.4
MISCELLANEOUS MANUFACTURES	228.2	532.9	49.4	16.9	96.3	512.7	297.2	359.9	2,093.5	297.3	153.8	2,544.6
TOTAL PROCESSED	2,505.3	1,558.9	415.8	26.1	671.8	1,888.4	435.9	4,164.8	11,667.0	932.0	3,380.7	15,979.7
TOTAL EXPORTS	46,206.0	9,214.7	549.2	26.9	1,353.6	1,959.8	1,042.1	13,494.4	73,846.7	1,091.1	3,395.2	78,333.0

143

Table VII-3-1a. Chile's Exports to LAFTA Countries, 1959—Raw Materials

(Thousands of U.S. Dollars)

	Argentina	Brazil	Colombia	Ecuador	Mexico	Paraguay	Peru	Uruguay	Total LAFTA	Bolivia	Venezuela	TOTAL
ANIMAL												
1a. live	6.1	0.1	139.1		14.1		47.2		206.6	0.2	186.4	393.2
1b. Fibers												
1c. Fish	0.1								0.1	3.0		3.1
1d. Other			17.5						17.5			17.5
AGRICULTURAL												
1a. Grains		246.2					3.7	524.5	774.4		12.3	786.7
1b. Fibers	111.8								111.8			111.8
1c. Fruits	62.4	457.8	0.7	75.3	115.6		172.3	45.1	929.2	2.9	94.7	1,026.8
1d. Seeds	39.5	203.8	0.5	12.6			87.6	0.1	349.1			349.1
1e. Other							13.8		13.8			13.8
FORESTRY												
1a. Plants												
MINERAL												
1a. Metals	1,099.5	150.7	139.2				143.0		1,532.4		52.4	1,584.8
1b. Oil	4.8								4.8			4.8
1c. Stone							1.6		1.6			1.6
1d. Non-metals	1,995.1	2,422.7	9.1	40.4	301.7	0.2	414.6	35.5	5,219.3	4.9	43.2	5,267.4
1e. Other	266.0								266.0			266.0
TOTAL RAW MATERIALS	3,585.3	3,486.3	306.1	128.3	431.4	0.2	883.8	605.2	9,480.6	11.0	389.0	9,826.6

Source: Dirección de Estadística de Censos, Comercio Exterior, Santiago, 1960.

Table VII-3-1b. *Chile's Exports to LAFTA Countries, 1959—Semi-Processed*
(Thousands of U.S. Dollars)

	Argentina	Brazil	Colombia	Ecuador	Mexico	Paraguay	Peru	Uruguay	Total LAFTA	Bolivia	Venezuela	TOTAL
ANIMAL												
2a. Hides												
2b. Fat												
2c. Meat												
2d. Pelts												
2e. Other												
AGRICULTURAL												
2a. Flour												
2b. Grains		834.0		445.2			488.5		1,767.7	102.4		1,870.1
2c. Sugar												
2d. Fruits		0.1		13.8			161.5		175.4		0.2	175.6
2e. Coffee												
2f. Other	10.1	2.0					8.5		20.6			20.6
FORESTRY												
2a. Lumber	7,512.8	12.4	0.3	1.7	1.0		38.0	0.2	7,566.4		5.8	7,572.2
2b. Extracts												
MINERAL												
2a. Metals	81.7								81.7	2.8		84.5
2b. Oil	409.5								409.5			409.5
TOTAL SEMI-PROCESSED	8,014.1	848.5	0.3	460.7	1.0		696.5	0.2	10,021.3	105.2	6.0	10,132.5

145

Table VII-3-1c. Chile's Exports to LAFTA Countries, 1959—Processed or Manufactured

(Thousands of U.S. Dollars)

	Argentina	Brazil	Colombia	Ecuador	Mexico	Paraguay	Peru	Uruguay	Total LAFTA	Bolivia	Venezuela	TOTAL
ANIMAL												
3a. Leather												
3b. Canned												
3c. Dairy								0.3	0.3	22.6		22.9
3d. Meat			7.0		87.6				94.6	0.1	125.3	220.0
3e. Seafood	0.2	0.5		1.9			2.8		5.4	4.6	0.2	10.2
3f. Other		20.0							20.0		1.2	21.2
AGRICULTURAL												
3a. Food		0.4		9.0	23.2		313.9		346.5			346.5
3b. Tobacco												
3c. Beverage	33.5	57.0	1.6	14.3	1.5	2.0	31.6	4.8	146.3	0.7	23.3	170.3
3d. Oils							0.4		0.4			0.4
3e. Textiles	325.4		1.2				9.4		336.0	6.3		342.3
3f. Sugar												
3g. Other												
FORESTRY												
3a. Wood	2.8	7.6	1.8	2.5			2.2	0.6	17.5	0.1	0.5	18.1
3b. Paper	1,622.5	1,586.5	51.3	246.1	719.1		253.0	290.3	4,768.8	142.7	124.4	5,035.9
MINERAL												
3a. Metals	9,590.6	2,128.9	89.4	102.4			608.3	300.2	12,819.8	4.8	143.4	12,968.0
3b. Machinery	8.0		383.3	3.1	0.1		2.9	11.0	408.4	4.6	48.0	461.0
3c. Vehicles	77.2	19.4		5.2			4.8	1.0	107.6	0.8		108.4
3d. Cement	0.6						0.6		1.2			1.2
3e. Chemicals	542.6		2.8	8.1		0.7	40.6	1.3	596.1	1,386.4		1,982.5
3f. Glass												
MISCELLANEOUS MANUFACTURES	137.5	22.6	13.2	11.7	25.4	0.8	95.4	9.7	316.3	12.3	31.0	359.6
TOTAL PROCESSED	12,340.9	3,842.9	551.6	404.3	856.9	3.5	1,365.9	619.2	19,985.2	1,586.0	497.3	22,068.5
TOTAL EXPORTS	23,940.3	8,177.7	858.0	993.3	1,289.3	3.7	2,946.2	1,224.6	39,433.1	1,702.2	892.3	42,027.6

Table VII-3-2a. *Chile's Exports to LAFTA Countries, 1960—Raw Materials*

(Thousands of U.S. Dollars)

	Argentina	Brazil	Colombia	Ecuador	Mexico	Paraguay	Peru	Uruguay	Total LAFTA	Bolivia	Venezuela	TOTAL
ANIMAL												
1a. Live	3.5		1.7	130.6	13.0		47.1		195.9	0.6	7.2	203.7
1b. Fibers			140.1						140.1			140.1
1c. Fish	16.7								16.7	3.1		19.8
1d. Other												
AGRICULTURAL												
1a. Grains												
1b. Fibers												
1c. Fruits	478.4	207.8	0.7	122.0		49.0	412.2	12.8	1,282.9	9.4	114.4	1,406.7
1d. Seeds	4.4								4.4			4.4
1e. Other							0.2	1.4	1.6			1.6
FORESTRY												
1a. Plants												
MINERAL												
1a. Metals	1,630.0	71.0	259.0				153.7		2,113.7		45.5	2,159.2
1b. Oil												
1c. Stone												
1d. Non-metals	445.3	1,564.4	10.5	56.5	327.5		547.7	30.2	2,982.1	7.1	16.1	3,005.3
1e. Other												
TOTAL RAW MATERIALS	2,578.3	1,843.2	412.0	309.1	340.5	49.0	1,160.9	44.4	6,737.4	20.2	183.2	6,940.8

Source: Dirección de Estadística de Censos, *Comercio Exterior*, Santiago, 1961.

147

Table VII-3-2b. *Chile's Exports to LAFTA Countries, 1960—Semi-Processed*
(Thousands of U.S. Dollars)

	Argentina	Brazil	Colombia	Ecuador	Mexico	Paraguay	Peru	Uruguay	Total LAFTA	Bolivia	Venezuela	TOTAL
ANIMAL												
2a. Hides												
2b. Fat		17.2							17.2			17.2
2c. Meat										1.0		1.0
2d. Pelts		144.0							144.0			144.0
2e. Other											3.2	3.2
AGRICULTURAL												
2a. Flour							247.4		247.6			247.6
2b. Grains		475.5					235.3		710.8	51.0		761.8
2c. Sugar												
2d. Fruits												
2e. Coffee		6.7							6.7			6.7
2f. Other	14.0	399.0					0.8		413.8			413.8
FORESTRY												
2a. Lumber	1,314.3	3.6	0.1	0.6	0.3		58.1		1,378.6			1,378.6
2b. Extracts		5.0					13.4	2.2	19.0			19.0
MINERAL												
2a. Metals	10,115.7		164.4	11.3			329.0	192.4	10,812.8		233.7	11,046.5
2b. Oil	68.0								68.0			68.0
TOTAL SEMI-PROCESSED	11,512.0	1,051.0	164.5	12.1	0.3		884.0	194.6	13,818.5	52.0	236.9	14,107.4

148

Table VII-3-2c. *Chile's Exports to LAFTA Countries, 1960—Processed or Manufactured*

(Thousands of U.S. Dollars)

	Argentina	Brazil	Colombia	Ecuador	Mexico	Paraguay	Peru	Uruguay	Total LAFTA	Bolivia	Venezuela	TOTAL
ANIMAL												
3a. Leather												
3b. Canned												
3c. Dairy							0.9		0.9			0.9
3d. Meal	0.1				6.8				6.9	0.2		7.1
3e. Seafood				0.1			13.0		13.1			13.1
3f. Other												
AGRICULTURAL												
3a. Food				8.0			537.9		545.9	0.3		546.2
3b. Tobacco												
3c. Beverage	4.4	0.7	1.1	9.6	6.0	1.2	43.8	3.5	70.3	0.6	23.7	94.6
3d. Oils												
3e. Textiles	99.2	0.1					0.8		100.1	0.1		100.2
3f. Sugar												
3g. Other							0.2	9.2	9.4			9.4
FORESTRY												
3a. Wood	1.5						16.9		18.4			18.4
3b. Paper	736.8	1,446.2	119.6	251.4			367.8	646.5	3,568.3	223.9	159.8	3,952.0
MINERAL												
3a. Metals	323.2	605.6	184.8	47.8			198.3	68.0	1,427.7	1.2	224.8	1,653.7
3b. Machinery	17.2	1.0	104.4	31.4	0.4		9.3	71.0	234.7	0.1	1.0	235.8
3c. Vehicles	18.7						0.4		19.1	8.0		27.1
3d. Cement	0.9						18.9		19.7			19.7
3e. Chemicals	1,467.3	22.1	4.3	14.9		0.4	8.8	5.1	1,522.9	1,445.7	0.2	2,968.8
3f. Glass				1.8					1.8		0.9	2.7
MISCELLANEOUS MANUFACTURES	1,109.0	848.9	8.0	17.5	15.6	0.7	94.8	22.8	2,117.3	18.6	32.8	2,168.7
TOTAL PROCESSED	3,778.3	2,924.6	422.2	382.5	28.8	2.3	1,311.8	826.1	9,676.5	1,698.7	443.2	11,818.4
TOTAL EXPORTS	17,868.6	5,818.8	998.7	703.7	369.6	51.3	3,356.7	1,065.1	30,232.5	1,770.9	863.3	32,866.7

Table VII-3-3a. *Chile's Exports to LAFTA Countries, 1961—Raw Materials*
(Thousands of U.S. Dollars)

	Argentina	Brazil	Colombia	Ecuador	Mexico	Paraguay	Peru	Uruguay	Total LAFTA	Bolivia	Venezuela	TOTAL
ANIMAL												
1a. Live	17.9	89.9	0.2	18.3		0.1	57.0		183.4	0.4	1.0	184.8
1b. Fibers	33.1		52.3				5.8	12.6	103.8			103.8
1c. Fish												
1d. Other												
AGRICULTURAL												
1a. Grains												
1b. Fibers	12.3	24.4		62.8			448.1		547.6		108.2	655.8
1c. Fruits	864.7	7.3	0.2	2.0			65.7		939.9			939.9
1d. Seeds												
1e. Other												
FORESTRY												
1a. Plants	6.1			1.0					7.1		0.2	7.3
MINERAL												
1a. Metals	1,899.6	763.0			14.6		80.8		2,778.0		74.4	2,852.4
1b. Oil												
1c. Stone												
1d. Non-metals	770.3	2,365.0	35.8	27.0	267.2		286.2	16.8	3,768.3	33.6	32.8	3,834.7
1e. Other												
TOTAL RAW MATERIALS	3,604.0	3,269.6	88.5	111.1	281.8	0.1	943.6	29.4	8,328.1	34.0	216.6	8,578.7

Source: Cámara de Comercio de Santiago, *Comercio Exterior de Chile*, 1962.

Table VII-3-3b. *Chile's Exports to LAFTA Countries, 1961—Semi-Processed*

(Thousands of U.S. Dollars)

	Argentina	Brazil	Colombia	Ecuador	Mexico	Paraguay	Peru	Uruguay	Total LAFTA	Bolivia	Venezuela	TOTAL
ANIMAL												
2a. Hides												
2b. Fat												
2c. Meat							1.5		1.5	2.1		3.6
2d. Pelts	16.9								16.9	4.2		21.1
2e. Other												
AGRICULTURAL												
2a. Flour										6.5		6.5
2b. Grains	1.7	73.6							75.3	76.6		151.9
2c. Sugar										3.2		3.2
2d. Fruits	8.5						187.0		195.5			195.5
2e. Coffee	1.4			3.9					5.3			5.3
2f. Other											395.7	395.7
FORESTRY												
2a. Lumber	2,449.2	1.4					65.1	10.3	2,527.0			2,527.0
2b. Extracts	7.7	4.3		0.4	1.0		15.8	2.7	30.9	40.4	5.6	76.9
MINERAL												
2a. Metals	583.5	33.5	30.5				56.2	10.1	713.8			713.8
2b. Oil	70.0			13.0					83.0	8.2		91.2
TOTAL SEMI-PROCESSED	3,138.9	112.8	30.5	17.3	1.0		325.6	23.1	3,649.2	141.2	401.3	4,191.7

Table VII-3-3c. *Chile's Exports to LAFTA Countries, 1961—Processed or Manufactured*

(Thousands of U.S. Dollars)

	Argentina	Brazil	Colombia	Ecuador	Mexico	Paraguay	Peru	Uruguay	Total LAFTA	Bolivia	Venezuela	TOTAL
ANIMAL												
3a. Leather												
3b. Canned		13.8							13.8			13.8
3c. Dairy												
3d. Meal												
3e. Seafood												
3f. Other												
AGRICULTURAL												
3a. Food	105.3	162.8		3.2			647.5	17.5	936.3	11.7	76.2	1,024.2
3b. Tobacco							0.7		0.7			0.7
3c. Beverage	18.2	0.6	3.9	10.5	0.9	0.9	57.1	1.8	93.9	0.5	0.1	94.5
3d. Oils				28.9					28.9			28.9
3e. Textiles	67.0		52.3				5.8	12.5	137.6			137.6
3f. Sugar												
3g. Other												
FORESTRY												
3a. Wood												
3b. Paper	1,548.5	1,378.2	5.1	189.0			472.4	757.9	4,351.1	0.3	121.0	4,472.4
MINERAL												
3a. Metals	9,472.7	88.6	65.8	55.3			58.3	471.9	10,212.6		1.0	10,213.6
3b. Machinery	10.0			14.8			18.0	0.8	43.6			43.6
3c. Vehicles	26.6	9.8		3.0				3.0	42.4	16.9		59.3
3d. Cement	18.8						6.3		25.1			25.1
3e. Chemicals	3,215.4	997.3	2.0			1.9	60.3	10.0	4,286.9	1,536.9		5,823.8
3f. Glass				2.4					2.4	0.1		2.5
MISCELLANEOUS MANUFACTURES	1,960.5	248.8	24.9	43.5	2.2	22.2	246.2	106.5	2,654.8	175.6	235.1	3,065.5
TOTAL PROCESSED	16,443.0	2,899.9	154.0	350.6	3.1	25.0	1,572.6	1,381.9	22,830.1	1,742.0	433.4	25,005.5
TOTAL EXPORTS	23,185.9	6,282.3	273.0	479.0	285.9	25.1	2,841.8	1,434.4	34,807.4	1,917.2	1,051.3	37,775.9

152

Table VII-3-4a. *Chile's Exports to LAFTA Countries, 1962—Raw Materials*
(Thousands of U.S. Dollars)

	Argentina	Brazil	Colombia	Ecuador	Mexico	Paraguay	Peru	Uruguay	Total LAFTA	Bolivia	Venezuela	TOTAL
ANIMAL												
1a. Live	13.5	2.9		3.0	21.3		57.5		98.2		34.6	132.8
1b. Fibers					0.1				0.1			0.1
1c. Fish												
1d. Other	11.0								11.0	0.3		11.3
AGRICULTURAL												
1a. Grains		282.0		0.2			39.1		321.3	197.7		519.0
1b. Fibers	7.7							3.0	10.7			10.7
1c. Fruits	693.4	158.4		108.8			624.2	53.3	1,638.1		66.9	1,708.0
1d. Seeds	507.0	443.2		4.5			46.9	3.5	1,005.1	3.0		1,005.1
1e. Other	19.5	38.5		2.2			15.5		75.7		0.2	75.9
FORESTRY												
1a. Plants												
MINERAL												
1a. Metals	1,955.4	60.3							2,015.7			2,015.7
1b. Oil												
1c. Stone	9.8								9.8	27.3		37.1
1d. Non-metals	388.0	1,552.5	20.8	34.2	348.5		402.4	16.6	2,763.0	4.9	5.7	2,773.6
1e. Other												
TOTAL RAW MATERIALS	3,605.3	2,537.8	20.8	152.9	369.9		1,185.6	76.4	7,948.7	233.2	107.4	8,289.3

Source: Dirección de Estadística de Censos, Comercio Exterior, Santiago, 1963.

153

Table VII-3-4b. *Chile's Exports to LAFTA Countries, 1962—Semi-Processed*

(Thousands of U.S. Dollars)

	Argentina	Brazil	Colombia	Ecuador	Mexico	Paraguay	Peru	Uruguay	Total LAFTA	Bolivia	Venezuela	TOTAL
ANIMAL												
2a. Hides		55.5							55.5			55.5
2b. Fat												
2c. Meat							24.3		24.3	0.5		24.8
2d. Pelts												
2e. Other												
AGRICULTURAL												
2a. Flour	0.1								0.1			0.1
2b. Grains		305.5							305.5	13.7		319.2
2c. Sugar												
2d. Fruits		1.9		1.7			86.1		89.7			89.7
2e. Coffee												
2f. Other												
FORESTRY												
2a. Lumber	2,071.4	3.9			2.3		50.5	8.8	2,141.9			2,141.9
2b. Extracts												
MINERAL												
2a. Metals	2,614.9	14,049.6	20.1				3.1		16,687.7	19.9		16,707.6
2b. Oil	100.9		4.0					3.0	107.9	5.8		113.7
TOTAL SEMI-PROCESSED	4,787.3	14,421.4	24.1	1.7	2.3		164.0	11.8	19,412.6	39.9		19,452.5

Table VII-3-4c. *Chile's Exports to LAFTA Countries, 1962—Processed or Manufactured*
(Thousands of U.S. Dollars)

	Argentina	Brazil	Colombia	Ecuador	Mexico	Paraguay	Peru	Uruguay	Total LAFTA	Bolivia	Venezuela	TOTAL
ANIMAL												
3a. Leather		21.6							21.6			21.6
3b. Canned	0.4								0.4			0.4
3c. Dairy												
3d. Meal											653.7	653.7
3e. Seafood	2.4	1.0					2.7	2.3	8.4		0.1	8.5
3f. Other												
AGRICULTURAL												
3a. Food		7.3	0.1	2.1			608.3	1.0	618.8	2.5	0.1	621.4
3b. Tobacco												
3c. Beverage	4.1	9.5	22.3	7.9	5.6	2.3	45.8	2.0	99.5	1.6	6.8	107.9
3d. Oils												
3e. Textiles	0.9	77.0				2.8	0.6	6.1	87.4	12.4	2.4	102.2
3f. Sugar												
3g. Other										0.6		0.6
FORESTRY												
3a. Wood	0.5			6.1			2.2		8.8			8.8
3b. Paper	1,048.9	603.7	22.9	227.9	295.4	3.0	608.5	351.2	3,161.5	174.9	162.2	3,498.6
MINERAL												
3a. Metals	1,853.0	15.6	43.3	34.0		18.3	186.5	523.3	2,674.0	8.0	216.4	2,898.4
3b. Machinery	16.2	2.7	24.8	2.1	2.4		40.9		89.1	23.2		112.3
3c. Vehicles	945.5	13.4					77.0		1,035.9	1.9		1,037.8
3d. Cement							2.8		2.8			2.8
3e. Chemicals	2,498.0	766.8	92.0	2.9		1.4	140.0	68.1	3,569.2	1,211.5		4,780.7
3f. Glass				0.1					0.1			0.1
MISCELLANEOUS MANUFACTURES	94.6	35.3	412.4	15.8	8.1	2.2	51.6	19.8	639.8	13.3	218.9	872.0
TOTAL PROCESSED	6,464.5	1,553.9	617.8	298.9	311.5	30.0	1,766.9	973.8	12,017.3	1,449.9	1,260.6	14,727.8
TOTAL EXPORTS	14,857.1	18,513.1	662.7	453.5	683.7	30.0	3,116.5	1,062.0	39,378.6	1,723.0	1,368.0	42,469.6

Table VII-3-5a. *Chile's Exports to LAFTA Countries, 1963—Raw Materials*
(Thousands of U.S. Dollars)

	Argentina	Brazil	Colombia	Ecuador	Mexico	Paraguay	Peru	Uruguay	Total LAFTA	Bolivia	Venezuela	TOTAL
ANIMAL												
1a. Live	10.2	19.3					1.1		31.1	0.3		31.4
1b. Fibers	4.7	0.7		0.8	26.0		20.6		52.8		60.0	112.8
1c. Fish	4.5						0.5		5.0			5.0
1d. Other												
AGRICULTURAL												
1a. Grains		93.7	111.9	6.0			47.2		258.8			258.8
1b. Fibers	21.0	144.3				2.7		5.0	173.0			173.0
1c. Fruits	499.5	298.6	2.6	115.6		7.1	593.8	1.6	1,518.8	4.4	78.6	1,601.8
1d. Seeds	331.6	301.6	2.2	0.1			10.8	184.3	830.6			830.6
1e. Other												
FORESTRY												
1a. Plants												
MINERAL												
1a. Metals	1,824.5	4.4						2.3	1,831.2			1,831.2
1b. Oil												
1c. Stone												
1d. Non-metals	390.4	1,737.4	89.6	41.7	377.9		295.8	24.1	2,956.9	31.0		2,987.9
1e. Other												
TOTAL RAW MATERIALS	3,086.4	2,600.5	206.3	164.2	403.9	9.8	969.8	217.3	7,658.2	35.7	138.6	7,832.5

Source: Cámara de Comercio de Santiago de Chile, *Comercio Exterior de Chile, 1963*, Santiago, April, 1964.

156

Table VII-3-5b. *Chile's Exports to LAFTA Countries, 1963—Semi-Processed*

(Thousands of U.S. Dollars)

	Argentina	Brazil	Colombia	Ecuador	Mexico	Paraguay	Peru	Uruguay	Total LAFTA	Bolivia	Venezuela	TOTAL
ANIMAL												
2a. Hides												
2b. Fat												
2c. Meat							19.7		19.7			19.7
2d. Pelts		19.5							19.5			19.5
2e. Other												
AGRICULTURAL												
2a. Flour												
2b. Grains		331.6	1.8				38.4		371.8	62.6		434.4
2c. Sugar												
2d. Fruits												
2e. Coffee	20.8	7.6	0.6		10.4		50.2		89.6			89.6
2f. Other							4.2		4.2			4.2
FORESTRY												
2a. Lumber	1,230.2						106.3	17.2	1,353.7	0.8		1,354.5
2b. Extracts												
MINERAL												
2a. Metals	4,440.9	20,242.7	25.5				2.9	141.5	24,853.5	9.3		24,862.8
2b. Oil	86.0								86.0	0.3		86.3
TOTAL SEMI-PROCESSED	5,777.9	20,601.4	27.9		10.4		221.7	158.7	26,798.0	73.0		26,871.0

157

Table VII-3-5c. Chile's Exports to LAFTA Countries, 1963—Processed or Manufactured

(Thousands of U.S. Dollars)

	Argentina	Brazil	Colombia	Ecuador	Mexico	Paraguay	Peru	Uruguay	Total LAFTA	Bolivia	Venezuela	TOTAL
ANIMAL												
3a. Leather	1.5								1.5			1.5
3b. Canned		8.0							8.0			8.0
3c. Dairy												
3d. Meal		5.1					0.5		5.6		1,097.0	1,102.6
3e. Seafood	0.7	5.1							5.8			5.8
3f. Other												
AGRICULTURAL												
3a. Food	25.6	1.1		4.4			550.5		581.6			581.6
3b. Tobacco					12.6		57.9		70.5			70.5
3c. Beverage	4.2	111.8	37.5	12.6		2.1		2.4	170.6		7.7	178.3
3d. Oils												
3e. Textiles								16.6	16.6			16.6
3f. Sugar												
3g. Other	11.5	10.8	1.2	0.6	0.3		0.5	5.8	30.7		0.7	31.4
FORESTRY												
3a. Wood							7.0		7.0			7.0
3b. Paper							25.2		25.2			25.2
MINERAL												
3a. Metals	2,795.9	1,678.2	236.1	91.8	0.1	5.2	852.3	471.8	6,131.4	33.8	74.6	6,239.8
3b. Machinery	3.7	1.1	22.0		2.8		76.2		105.8	0.4		106.2
3c. Vehicles	211.7	4.4	2.2	2.8			10.9		232.0	2.4		234.4
3d. Cement												
3e. Chemicals	650.1	561.6	8.3	5.6		2.1	38.2	12.2	1,278.1	96.4		1,374.5
3f. Glass												
MISCELLANEOUS MANUFACTURES	1,897.7	1,366.3	329.8	457.6	725.7	8.5	893.6	496.7	6,175.9	244.6	45.6	6,466.1
TOTAL PROCESSED	5,602.6	3,753.5	637.1	575.4	741.5	17.9	2,512.8	1,005.5	14,846.3	377.6	1,225.6	16,449.5
TOTAL EXPORTS	14,466.9	26,955.4	871.3	739.6	1,155.8	27.7	3,704.3	1,381.5	49,302.5	486.3	1,364.2	51,153.0

Table VII-4-1a. *Colombia's Exports to LAFTA Countries, 1959—Raw Materials*
(Thousands of U.S. Dollars)

	Argen-tina	Brazil	Chile	Ecuador	Mexico	Para-guay	Peru	Uruguay	Total LAFTA	Bolivia	Vene-zuela	TOTAL
ANIMAL												
1a. Live					1.1				1.1		48.3	49.4
1b. Fibers										0.4		0.4
1c. Fish												
1d. Other												
AGRICULTURAL												
1a. Grains											0.5	0.5
1b. Fibers					0.2				0.2		9.3	9.5
1c. Fruits											37.6	37.6
1d. Seeds											0.6	0.6
1e. Other											49.7	49.7
FORESTRY												
1a. Plants												
MINERAL												
1a. Metals											4.2	4.2
1b. Oil												
1c. Stone											2.9	2.9
1d. Non-metals												
1e. Other								0.1	0.1			0.1
TOTAL RAW MATERIALS					1.3			0.1	1.4	0.4	153.1	154.9

Source: Departamento Administrativo Nacional de Estadística, *Anuario de Comercio Exterior, 1959,* Colombia, 1960.

Table VII-4-1b. *Colombia's Exports to LAFTA Countries, 1959—Semi-Processed*

(Thousands of U.S. Dollars)

	Argentina	Brazil	Chile	Ecuador	Mexico	Paraguay	Peru	Uruguay	Total LAFTA	Bolivia	Venezuela	TOTAL
ANIMAL												
2a. Hides												
2b. Fat												
2c. Meat												
2d. Pelts												
2e. Other												
AGRICULTURAL												
2a. Flour				2.4					2.4			2.4
2b. Grains											0.6	0.6
2c. Sugar												
2d. Fruits												
2e. Coffee	55.6		137.1				0.1	14.0	206.7			206.7
2f. Other											2.6	2.6
FORESTRY												
2a. Lumber					12.4				12.4		42.2	54.6
2b. Extracts											15.4	15.4
MINERAL												
2a. Metals												
2b. Oil			707.3				1,316.4		2,023.7	0.9		2,024.6
TOTAL SEMI-PROCESSED	55.6		844.4	2.4	12.4		1,316.5	14.0	2,245.2	0.9	60.8	2,306.9

160

Table VII-4-1c. *Colombia's Exports to LAFTA Countries, 1959–Processed or Manufactured*
(Thousands of U.S. Dollars)

	Argentina	Brazil	Chile	Ecuador	Mexico	Paraguay	Peru	Uruguay	Total LAFTA	Bolivia	Venezuela	TOTAL
ANIMAL												
3a. Leather												
3b. Canned				0.3	1.6				1.9		5.2	7.1
3c. Dairy												
3d. Meal												
3e. Seafood												
3f. Other					2.2				2.2		24.7	26.8
AGRICULTURAL												
3a. Food				0.1					0.1			0.1
3b. Tobacco					1.6				1.6		0.6	2.2
3c. Beverage											0.1	0.1
3d. Oils											2.0	2.0
3e. Textiles				2.2			9.9		12.1		14.2	26.3
3f. Sugar												
3g. Other			1.4	3.2					4.6		4.3	8.9
FORESTRY												
3a. Wood											59.7	59.7
3b. Paper				6.3			3.8		10.1		9.3	19.4
MINERAL												
3a. Metals										1.0	163.1	164.0
3b. Machinery			0.9	178.2	8.5		32.4		220.0	2.0	570.1	792.1
3c. Vehicles			1.7				5.4		7.1	0.2	31.1	38.5
3d. Cement				0.4					0.4		19.5	19.9
3e. Chemicals	3.8	31.9		136.9	7.7		10.5		190.8		22.8	213.8
3f. Glass										0.1	5.4	5.4
MISCELLANEOUS MANUFACTURES		0.3	13.3	3.9	0.5		64.7	1.8	84.5	0.2	392.8	477.4
TOTAL PROCESSED	3.8	32.2	17.3	331.5	22.1		126.7	1.8	535.4	3.5	1,324.9	1,863.7
TOTAL EXPORTS	59.4	32.2	861.7	334.0	35.8		1,443.3	15.9	2,782.0	4.8	1,538.8	4,325.5

Table VII-4-2a. *Colombia's Exports to LAFTA Countries, 1960—Raw Materials*
(Thousands of U.S. Dollars)

	Argentina	Brazil	Chile	Ecuador	Mexico	Paraguay	Peru	Uruguay	Total LAFTA	Bolivia	Venezuela	TOTAL
ANIMAL												
1a. Live				0.5	1.0				1.5		61.8	63.3
1b. Fibers												
1c. Fish												
1d. Other												
AGRICULTURAL												
1a. Grains											1.1	1.1
1b. Fibers												
1c. Fruits											4.5	4.5
1d. Seeds											3.2	3.2
1e. Other												
FORESTRY												
1a. Plants												
MINERAL												
1a. Metals												
1b. Oil											0.7	0.7
1c. Stone												
1d. Non-metals				0.2					0.2		4.2	4.4
1e. Other												
TOTAL RAW MATERIALS				0.7	1.0				1.7		75.5	77.2

Source: Departamento Administrativo Nacional de Estadística, *Anuario de Comercio Exterior, 1960*, Colombia, 1961.

Table VII-4-2b. *Colombia's Exports to LAFTA Countries, 1960—Semi-Processed*
(Thousands of U.S. Dollars)

	Argentina	Brazil	Chile	Ecuador	Mexico	Paraguay	Peru	Uruguay	Total LAFTA	Bolivia	Venezuela	TOTAL
ANIMAL												
2a. Hides	0.1								0.1		4.4	4.5
2b. Fat												
2c. Meat												
2d. Pelts												
2e. Other												
AGRICULTURAL												
2a. Flour												
2b. Grains												
2c. Sugar												
2d. Fruits												
2e. Coffee	102.8		528.5									
2f. Other									631.3			631.3
FORESTRY												
2a. Lumber												
2b. Extracts					39.1		3.7		42.8		11.8	54.6
MINERAL												
2a. Metals												
2b. Oil			206.5				3,142.1		3,348.6			3,348.6
TOTAL SEMI-PROCESSED	102.9		735.0		39.1		3,145.8		4,022.8		16.2	4,039.0

Table VII-4-2c. *Colombia's Exports to LAFTA Countries, 1960—Processed or Manufactured*

(Thousands of U.S. Dollars)

	Argen-tina	Brazil	Chile	Ecuador	Mexico	Para-guay	Peru	Uruguay	Total LAFTA	Bolivia	Vene-zuela	TOTAL
ANIMAL												
3a. Leather												
3b. Canned												
3c. Dairy												
3d. Meal												
3e. Seafood												
3f. Other												
AGRICULTURAL												
3a. Food												
3b. Tobacco								13.5	13.5			13.5
3c. Beverage				1.0					1.0		1.1	2.1
3d. Oils												
3e. Textiles												
3f. Sugar												
3g. Other											4.2	4.2
FORESTRY												
3a. Wood											19.6	19.6
3b. Paper			0.7	0.2			4.8		5.7		9.4	15.1
MINERAL												
3a. Metals	17.2	0.2	196.0	66.5	11.5		34.2		325.6	2.0	770.0	1,097.6
3b. Machinery			14.4	4.4	5.4				24.2	0.2	0.5	24.9
3c. Vehicles											9.2	9.2
3d. Cement												
3e. Chemicals	20.4	46.6		236.0	2.7		15.1		320.8	0.2	112.0	433.0
3f. Glass				2.4					2.4		2.7	5.1
MISCELLANEOUS MANUFACTURES	0.2	1.1	9.8	57.0	8.6		27.7		104.4		321.3	425.7
TOTAL PROCESSED	37.8	47.9	220.9	367.5	28.2		81.8	13.5	796.7	2.4	1,250.0	2,050.0
TOTAL EXPORTS	140.7	47.9	955.9	368.2	68.3		3,227.6	13.5	4,822.1	2.4	1,341.7	6,166.2

Table VII-4-3a. *Colombia's Exports to LAFTA Countries, 1961—Raw Materials*

(Thousands of U.S. Dollars)

	Argentina	Brazil	Chile	Ecuador	Mexico	Paraguay	Peru	Uruguay	Total LAFTA	Bolivia	Venezuela	TOTAL
ANIMAL												
1a. Live												
1b. Fibers												
1c. Fish												
1d. Other				0.5			0.1		0.6		40.3	40.9
AGRICULTURAL												
1a. Grains												
1b. Fibers				697.7					697.7		36.3	734.0
1c. Fruits		0.5					0.1		0.6		62.7	63.3
1d. Seeds							0.5		0.5		0.2	0.7
1e. Other			231.7						231.7		62.7	294.4
FORESTRY												
1a. Plants												
MINERAL												
1a. Metals										1.0		1.0
1b. Oil												
1c. Stone								3.9	3.9			3.9
1d. Non-metals											0.7	0.7
1e. Other												
TOTAL RAW MATERIALS		0.5	231.7	698.2			0.7	3.9	935.0	1.0	202.9	1,138.9

Source: Departamento Administrativo Nacional de Estadística, *Anuario de Comercio Exterior, 1961*, Colombia, 1962.

Table VII-4-3b. *Colombia's Exports to LAFTA Countries, 1961—Semi-Processed*
(Thousands of U.S. Dollars)

	Argentina	Brazil	Chile	Ecuador	Mexico	Paraguay	Peru	Uruguay	Total LAFTA	Bolivia	Venezuela	TOTAL
ANIMAL												
2a. Hides												
2b. Fat												
2c. Meat											6.0	6.0
2d. Pelts												
2e. Other												
AGRICULTURAL												
2a. Flour												
2b. Grains											1.4	1.4
2c. Sugar												
2d. Fruits												
2e. Coffee	150.6		29.5	0.3	93.2		0.1	6.4	280.1			280.1
2f. Other												
FORESTRY												
2a. Lumber					60.7				60.7		1.4	62.1
2b. Extracts											0.1	0.1
MINERAL												
2a. Metals												
2b. Oil				15.3			3,140.5		3,155.8			3,155.8
TOTAL SEMI-PROCESSED	150.6		29.5	15.6	153.9		3,140.6	6.4	3,496.6		8.9	3,505.5

Table VII-4-3c. *Colombia's Exports to LAFTA Countries, 1961–Processed or Manufactured*
(Thousands of U.S. Dollars)

	Argentina	Brazil	Chile	Ecuador	Mexico	Paraguay	Peru	Uruguay	Total LAFTA	Bolivia	Venezuela	TOTAL
ANIMAL												
3a. Leather							0.2		0.2		10.6	10.8
3b. Canned												
3c. Dairy												
3d. Meal												
3e. Seafood												
3f. Other											0.1	0.1
AGRICULTURAL												
3a. Food												
3b. Tobacco				0.9			3.1	58.6	62.6		144.2	206.8
3c. Beverage							0.3		0.3		2.9	3.2
3d. Oils				1.0					1.0			1.0
3e. Textiles				112.5			37.8		150.3		5.0	155.3
3f. Sugar												
3g. Other							0.6		0.6			0.6
FORESTRY												
3a. Wood							99.7		99.7		10.7	110.4
3b. Paper	5.1		5.7	5.9	10.1		11.0	1.7	39.5	4.4	13.1	57.0
MINERAL												
3a. Metals				0.3			2.8		3.1			3.1
3b. Machinery	15.9			32.7			306.7		355.3	7.0	609.3	971.6
3c. Vehicles			12.2	0.8			220.8		233.8			233.8
3d. Cement			14.1				0.3		14.4		6.3	20.7
3e. Chemicals	3.3	212.5		283.8	38.1		32.1		569.8		73.7	643.5
3f. Glass				4.0			1.7		5.7		0.6	6.3
MISCELLANEOUS MANUFACTURES	24.3	2.7	32.0	61.4	14.2		48.5	0.1	126.9	0.7	210.0	337.6
TOTAL PROCESSED	174.9	215.2	293.2	503.3	62.4		765.6	60.4	1,663.2	12.1	1,086.3	2,761.6
TOTAL EXPORTS	174.9	215.7	293.2	1,217.3	216.3		3,906.9	70.7	6,095.0	13.1	1,298.1	7,406.2

Table VII-4-4a. *Colombia's Exports to LAFTA Countries, 1962—Raw Materials*
(Thousands of U.S. Dollars)

	Argentina	Brazil	Chile	Ecuador	Mexico	Paraguay	Peru	Uruguay	Total LAFTA	Bolivia	Venezuela	TOTAL
ANIMAL												
1a. Live				0.1			0.4		0.5		22.7	23.2
1b. Fibers												
1c. Fish												
1d. Other												
AGRICULTURAL												
1a. Grains			72.8	362.6					435.4		0.1	435.4
1b. Fibers	65.6								65.6		0.7	66.3
1c. Fruits				1.4					1.4		4.7	6.1
1d. Seeds												
1e. Other											64.3	64.3
FORESTRY												
1a. Plants												
MINERAL												
1a. Metals												
1b. Oil												
1c. Stone											3.9	3.9
?d. Non-metals											2.8	2.8
1e. Other												
TOTAL RAW MATERIALS	65.6		72.8	364.1			0.4		502.9		99.2	602.0

Source: Departamento Administrativo Nacional de Estadística, *Anuario de Comercio Exterior, 1962*, Colombia, 1963.

168

Table VII-4-4b. *Colombia's Exports to LAFTA Countries, 1962—Semi-Processed*
(Thousands of U.S. Dollars)

	Argentina	Brazil	Chile	Ecuador	Mexico	Paraguay	Peru	Uruguay	Total LAFTA	Bolivia	Venezuela	TOTAL
ANIMAL												
2a. Hides											2.0	2.0
2b. Fat												
2c. Meat												
2d. Pelts												
2e. Other												
AGRICULTURAL												
2a. Flour												
2b. Grains												
2c. Sugar			652.4						652.4		0.4	652.8
2d. Fruits												
2e. Coffee	554.9		235.7				10.1		800.7	6.6		807.3
2f. Other				3.4					3.4		4.6	8.0
FORESTRY												
2a. Lumber					52.3				52.3		0.8	53.1
2b. Extracts							0.3		0.3		0.1	0.4
MINERAL												
2a. Metals												
2b. Oil			176.2				3,149.3		3,325.5		0.1	3,325.6
TOTAL SEMI-PROCESSED	554.9		1,064.3	3.4	52.3		3,159.7		4,834.6	6.6	8.0	4,849.2

169

Table VII-4-4c. *Colombia's Exports to LAFTA Countries, 1962—Processed or Manufactured*

(Thousands of U.S. Dollars)

	Argentina	Brazil	Chile	Ecuador	Mexico	Paraguay	Peru	Uruguay	Total LAFTA	Bolivia	Venezuela	TOTAL
ANIMAL												
3a. Leather												
3b. Canned												
3c. Dairy				0.3					0.3			0.3
3d. Meal												
3e. Seafood												
3f. Other												
AGRICULTURAL												
3a. Food	3.4								3.4			3.4
3b. Tobacco								34.3	34.3			34.3
3c. Beverage											0.7	0.7
3d. Oils											0.5	0.5
3e. Textiles				445.8			261.9	50.2	757.9		101.1	859.0
3f. Sugar				1.5					1.5			1.5
3g. Other				0.2			0.3		0.5		1.0	1.5
FORESTRY												
3a. Wood			0.6	6.0		10.2	6.4	47.4	70.6		6.2	76.7
3b. Paper										0.1	6.0	6.2
MINERAL												
3a. Metals	0.2			1.5			4.6		6.8	5.6	0.5	12.9
3b. Machinery		1.3		38.1			155.9		196.0		490.3	686.3
3c. Vehicles				29.9	0.4	0.1	0.3		30.2		0.1	30.3
3d. Cement							22.2		22.2		9.9	32.1
3e. Chemicals		3.6	24.2	510.0	15.5		28.5		581.8		64.3	646.1
3f. Glass				23.8					23.8			23.8
MISCELLANEOUS MANUFACTURES	10.9	10.0	36.8	129.9	34.3	3.6	38.2	7.2	270.9	16.3	248.8	536.0
TOTAL PROCESSED	14.5	14.9	61.6	1,187.0	50.2	13.9	518.3	139.8	2,000.2	22.0	929.4	2,951.6
TOTAL EXPORTS	635.0	14.9	1,198.7	1,554.5	102.5	13.9	3,678.4	139.8	7,337.7	28.6	1,036.6	8,402.9

Table VII-4-5a. *Colombia's Exports to LAFTA Countries, 1963—Raw Materials*
(Thousands of U.S. Dollars)

	Argentina	Brazil	Chile	Ecuador	Mexico	Paraguay	Peru	Uruguay	Total LAFTA	Bolivia	Venezuela	TOTAL
ANIMAL												
1a. Live				1.0	19.8				20.8		24.9	45.7
1b. Fibers							1.6		1.6		0.4	2.0
1c. Fish												
1d. Other												
AGRICULTURAL												
1a. Grains												
1b. Fibers												
1c. Fruits			97.2	933.7					1,030.9			1,030.9
1d. Seeds	54.4								54.4			54.4
1e. Other											61.2	61.2
FORESTRY												
1a. Plants												
MINERAL												
1a. Metals	231.5								231.5			231.5
1b. Oil												
1c. Stone					0.1				0.1		0.6	0.7
1d. Non-metals											7.5	7.5
1e. Other												
TOTAL RAW MATERIALS	285.9		97.2	934.7	19.9		1.6		1,339.3		94.6	1,433.9

Source: Departamento Administrativo Nacional de Estadística, <u>Anuario de Comercio Exterior</u>, <u>1963</u>, Colombia, 1964.

Table VII-4-5b. *Colombia's Exports to LAFTA Countries, 1963—Semi-Processed*
(Thousands of U.S. Dollars)

	Argentina	Brazil	Chile	Ecuador	Mexico	Paraguay	Peru	Uruguay	Total LAFTA	Bolivia	Venezuela	TOTAL
ANIMAL												
2a. Hides											3.8	3.8
2b. Fat												
2c. Meat												
2d. Pelts												
2e. Other												
AGRICULTURAL												
2a. Flour												
2b. Grains												
2c. Sugar												
2d. Fruits												
2e. Coffee	218.5		139.3						358.2	0.1		358.3
2f. Other							0.2	0.2				
FORESTRY												
2a. Lumber					39.3				39.3		0.9	40.2
2b. Extracts							0.3		0.3			0.3
MINERAL												
2a. Metals				1.7					30.9			30.9
2b. Oil		29.2		50.6			1,000.7		1,051.3			1,051.3
TOTAL SEMI-PROCESSED	218.5	29.2	139.3	52.3	39.3		1,001.2	0.2	1,480.0	0.1	4.7	1,484.8

Table VII-4-5c. *Colombia's Exports to LAFTA Countries, 1963—Processed or Manufactured*
(Thousands of U.S. Dollars)

	Argentina	Brazil	Chile	Ecuador	Mexico	Paraguay	Peru	Uruguay	Total LAFTA	Bolivia	Venezuela	TOTAL
ANIMAL												
3a. Leather												
3b. Canned												
3c. Dairy												
3d. Meal												
3e. Seafood												
3f. Other												
AGRICULTURAL												
3a. Food	2.1			0.6					2.7			2.7
3b. Tobacco								64.3	64.3			64.3
3c. Beverage												
3d. Oils												
3e. Textiles				735.5			460.5	188.8	1,384.8		8.7	1,393.5
3f. Sugar											6.2	6.2
3g. Other	0.9								0.9			0.9
FORESTRY												
3a. Wood							2.5		2.5		3.0	5.5
3b. Paper				17.3	2.1	32.2	88.1	14.2	153.9		26.8	180.7
MINERAL												
3a. Metals				3.2			0.5		3.7		1.5	5.2
3b. Machinery		46.7	5.2	118.4	2.3		133.4	8.5	314.5		532.5	847.0
3c. Vehicles				75.5			31.2		106.7		1.6	108.3
3d. Cement				0.6			1.6		2.2		5.0	7.2
3e. Chemicals		55.8	14.2	486.3	29.1		64.3		649.7	1.6	16.0	667.3
3f. Glass				88.1					88.1			88.1
MISCELLANEOUS MANUFACTURES	34.3	0.6	12.4	167.2	127.0	6.3	37.1	11.2	396.1	11.8	216.4	624.3
TOTAL PROCESSED	37.3	103.1	31.8	1,692.7	160.5	38.5	819.2	287.0	3,170.1	13.4	817.7	4,001.2
TOTAL EXPORTS	541.7	132.3	268.3	2,679.7	219.7	38.5	1,822.0	287.2	5,989.4	13.5	917.0	6,919.2

Table VII-5-1a. *Ecuador's Exports to LAFTA Countries, 1959—Raw Materials*
(Thousands of U.S. Dollars)

	Argentina	Brazil	Chile	Colombia	Mexico	Paraguay	Peru	Uruguay	Total LAFTA	Bolivia	Venezuela	TOTAL
ANIMAL												
1a. Live												
1b. Fibers												
1c. Fish				5.5			0.3		5.8			5.8
1d. Other												
AGRICULTURAL												
1a. Grains											1,391.1	1,391.1
1b. Fibers			1,956.1				129.3		2,085.4		6.5	2,091.9
1c. Fruits												
1d. Seeds												
1e. Other							41.4		41.4			41.4
FORESTRY												
1a. Plants												
MINERAL												
1a. Metals												
1b. Oil												
1c. Stone												
1d. Non-metals												
1e. Other												
TOTAL RAW MATERIALS			1,956.1	5.5			171.0		2,132.6		1,397.6	3,530.2

Source: Banco Central de Ecuador, <u>Comercio Exterior Ecuatoriano</u>, October, November, and December, 1959.

Table VII-5-1b. *Ecuador's Exports to LAFTA Countries, 1959—Semi-Processed*
(Thousands of U.S. Dollars)

	Argentina	Brazil	Chile	Colombia	Mexico	Paraguay	Peru	Uruguay	Total LAFTA	Bolivia	Venezuela	TOTAL
ANIMAL												
2a. Hides												
2b. Fat												
2c. Meat												
2d. Pelts												
2e. Other												
AGRICULTURAL												
2a. Flour												
2b. Grains			10.7	0.8					11.5		376.9	388.4
2c. Sugar												
2d. Fruits												
2e. Coffee	45.6		72.5	4,436.1				10.6	4,564.8			4,564.8
2f. Other												
FORESTRY												
2a. Lumber												
2b. Extracts			12.1				0.4		12.5			12.5
MINERALS												
2a. Metals												
2b. Oil												
TOTAL SEMI-PROCESSED	45.6		95.3	4,436.9			0.4	10.6	4,588.8		376.9	4,965.7

Table VII-5-1c. *Ecuador's Exports to LAFTA Countries, 1959—Processed or Manufactured*
(Thousands of U.S. Dollars)

	Argentina	Brazil	Chile	Colombia	Mexico	Paraguay	Peru	Uruguay	Total LAFTA	Bolivia	Venezuela	TOTAL
ANIMAL												
3a. Leather												
3b. Canned												
3c. Dairy												
3d. Meal												
3e. SeaFood												
3f. Other												
AGRICULTURAL												
3a. Food												
3b. Tobacco												
3c. Beverage												
3d. Oils												
3e. Textiles												
3f. Sugar												
3g. Other												
FORESTRY												
3a. Wood												
3b. Paper			6.5				6.4		12.9			12.9
MINERAL												
3a. Metals												
3b. Machinery												
3c. Vehicles												
3d. Cement												
3e. Chemicals				819.2					819.2	15.5	11.5	846.2
3f. Glass												
MISCELLANEOUS MANUFACTURES	0.2		4.5	0.6	1.5	7.1	6.0	2.0	21.9	4.0	45.5	71.4
TOTAL PROCESSED	0.2		11.0	819.8	1.5	7.1	12.4	2.0	854.0	19.5	57.0	930.5
TOTAL EXPORTS	45.8		2,062.4	5,262.2	1.5	7.1	183.8	12.6	7,575.4	19.5	1,831.5	9,426.4

Table VII-5-2a. *Ecuador's Exports to LAFTA Countries, 1960—Raw Materials*

(Thousands of U.S. Dollars)

	Argentina	Brazil	Chile	Colombia	Mexico	Paraguay	Peru	Uruguay	Total LAFTA	Bolivia	Venezuela	TOTAL
ANIMAL												
1a. Live							41.8		41.8			41.8
1b. Fibers												
1c. Fish				3.0					3.0			3.0
1d. Other												
AGRICULTURAL												
1a. Grains											2,798.2	2,798.2
1b. Fibers											1.0	1.0
1c. Fruits	1.1		2,082.3				126.1		2,209.5		3.4	2,212.9
1d. Seeds			12.6						12.6			12.6
1e. Other							38.9		38.9			38.9
FORESTRY												
1a. Plants												
MINERAL												
1a. Metals												
1b. Oil												
1c. Stone												
1d. Non-metals												
1e. Other												
TOTAL RAW MATERIALS	1.1		2,094.9	3.0			206.8		2,305.8		2,802.6	5,108.4

Source: Banco Central de Ecuador, <u>Comercio Exterior Ecuatoriano</u>, October, November, and December, 1960.

Table VII-5-2b. *Ecuador's Exports to LAFTA Countries, 1960—Semi-Processed*
(Thousands of U.S. Dollars)

	Argentina	Brazil	Chile	Colombia	Mexico	Paraguay	Peru	Uruguay	Total LAFTA	Bolivia	Venezuela	TOTAL
ANIMAL												
2a. Hides												
2b. Fat												
2c. Meat												
2d. Pelts												
2e. Other												
AGRICULTURAL												
2a. Flour												
2b. Grains			1.4						1.4			1.4
2c. Sugar												
2d. Fruits												
2e. Coffee	16.2		66.2					5.6				
2f. Other				1,502.7					1,590.7	20.7		1,611.4
FORESTRY												
2a. Lumber	2.2		2.6									
2b. Extracts							2.9		7.7			7.7
MINERAL												
2a. Metals												
2b. Oil				0.6					0.6			0.6
TOTAL SEMI-PROCESSED	18.4		70.2	1,503.3			2.9	5.6	1,600.4	20.7		1,621.1

Table VII-5-2c. *Ecuador's Exports to LAFTA Countries, 1960—Processed or Manufactured*
(Thousands of U.S. Dollars)

	Argentina	Brazil	Chile	Colombia	Mexico	Paraguay	Peru	Uruguay	Total LAFTA	Bolivia	Venezuela	TOTAL
ANIMAL												
3a. Leather												
3b. Canned												
3c. Dairy												
3d. Meal												
3e. Seafood							5.4		5.4			5.4
3f. Other												
AGRICULTURAL												
3a. Food												
3b. Tobacco												
3c. Beverage												
3d. Oils												
3e. Textiles												
3f. Sugar										10.0		10.0
3g. Other												
FORESTRY												
3a. Wood												
3b. Paper		0.4							0.4			0.4
MINERAL												
3a. Metals												
3b. Machinery												
3c. Vehicles												
3d. Cement												
3e. Chemicals							0.2		0.2			0.2
3f. Glass	0.2	0.5	6.1	952.2					952.9	16.0	14.4	983.3
MISCELLANEOUS MANUFACTURES	7.6	0.7		213.9	133.9	8.2	20.7	0.8	391.9	7.0	40.0	438.9
TOTAL PROCESSED	7.8	1.6	6.1	1,166.1	133.9	8.2	26.3	0.8	1,350.8	33.0	54.4	1,438.2
TOTAL EXPORTS	27.3	1.6	2,171.2	2,672.4	133.9	8.2	236.0	6.4	5,257.0	53.7	2,857.0	8,167.7

Table VII-5-3a. *Ecuador's Exports to LAFTA Countries, 1961—Raw Materials*
(Thousands of U.S. Dollars)

	Argen-tina	Brazil	Chile	Colom-bia	Mexico	Para-guay	Peru	Uruguay	Total LAFTA	Bolivia	Vene-zuela	TOTAL
ANIMAL												
1a. Live							18.9		18.9			18.9
1b. Fibers												
1c. Fish				14.0					14.0			14.0
1d. Other												
AGRICULTURAL												
1a. Grains												
1b. Fibers												
1c. Fruits		0.6	2,531.0				320.8		2,852.4			2,852.4
1d. Seeds												
1e. Other							22.6		22.6			22.6
FORESTRY												
1a. Plants												
MINERAL												
1a. Metals												
1b. Oil												
1c. Stone												
1d. Non-metals												
1e. Other												
TOTAL RAW MATERIALS		0.6	2,531.0	14.0			362.3		2,907.9			2,907.9

Source: Banco Central de Ecuador, *Comercio Exterior Ecuatoriano*, October, November, and December, 1961.

Table VII-5-3b. *Ecuador's Exports to LAFTA Countries, 1961—Semi-Processed*
(Thousands of U.S. Dollars)

	Argentina	Brazil	Chile	Colombia	Mexico	Paraguay	Peru	Uruguay	Total LAFTA	Bolivia	Venezuela	TOTAL
ANIMAL												
2a. Hides												
2b. Fat												
2c. Meat												
2d. Pelts												
2e. Other												
AGRICULTURAL												
2a. Flour												
2b. Grains				1,341.0					1,341.0		587.0	1,928.0
2c. Sugar												
2d. Fruits												
2e. Coffee	32.8	19.2	103.0	1,793.8			14.5		1,963.3		29.8	1,993.1
2f. Other												
FORESTRY												
2a. Lumber	5.6		5.3				5.0		15.9			15.9
2b. Extracts			34.6						34.6			34.6
MINERAL												
2a. Metals												
2b. Oil												
TOTAL SEMI-PROCESSED	38.4	19.2	142.9	3,134.8			19.5		3,354.8		616.8	3,971.6

181

Table VII-5-3c. *Ecuador's Exports to LAFTA Countries, 1961—Processed or Manufactured*
(Thousands of U.S. Dollars)

	Argentina	Brazil	Chile	Colombia	Mexico	Paraguay	Peru	Uruguay	Total LAFTA	Bolivia	Venezuela	TOTAL
ANIMAL												
3a. Leather												
3b. Canned												
3c. Dairy												
3d. Meal												
3e. Seafood												
3f. Other												
AGRICULTURAL												
3a. Food												
3b. Tobacco												
3c. Beverage												
3d. Oils												
3e. Textiles												
3f. Sugar												
3g. Other												
FORESTRY												
3a. Wood												
3b. Paper												
MINERAL												
3a. Metals												
3b. Machinery												
3c. Vehicles												
3d. Cement												
3e. Chemicals	1.6	0.4		1,014.6					1,016.6	21.3		1,037.9
3f. Glass												
MISCELLANEOUS MANUFACTURES	21.2		8.9	23.0	25.6	8.1	17.7	7.5	112.0	14.6	29.8	156.4
TOTAL PROCESSED	22.8	0.4	8.9	1,037.6	25.6	8.1	17.7	7.5	1,128.6	35.9	29.8	1,194.3
TOTAL EXPORTS	61.2	20.2	2,682.8	4,186.4	25.6	8.1	399.5	7.5	7,391.3	35.9	646.6	8,073.8

Table VII-5-4a. *Ecuador's Exports to LAFTA Countries, 1962—Raw Materials*
(Thousands of U.S. Dollars)

	Argentina	Brazil	Chile	Colombia	Mexico	Paraguay	Peru	Uruguay	Total LAFTA	Bolivia	Venezuela	TOTAL
ANIMAL												
1a. Live												
1b. Fibers												
1c. Fish											8.1	8.1
1d. Other												
AGRICULTURAL												
1a. Grains												
1b. Fibers												
1c. Fruits			2,237.5				434.7		2,672.2			2,672.2
1d. Seeds			5.7				2.7		8.4			8.4
1e. Other												
FORESTRY												
1a. Plants												
MINERAL												
1a. Metals												
1b. Oil	163.1								163.1			163.1
1c. Stone												
1d. Non-metals												
1e. Other												
TOTAL RAW MATERIALS	163.1		2,243.2				437.4		2,843.7		8.1	2,851.8

Source: Ministerio de Finanzas, Dirección de Financiamiento y Asesoría Fiscal, *Anuario de Comercio Exterior, 1962,* Quito, 1963.

Table VII-5-4b. *Ecuador's Exports to LAFTA Countries, 1962—Semi-Processed*
(Thousands of U.S. Dollars)

	Argentina	Brazil	Chile	Colombia	Mexico	Paraguay	Peru	Uruguay	Total LAFTA	Bolivia	Venezuela	TOTAL
ANIMAL												
2a. Hides												
2b. Fat												
2c. Meat												
2d. Pelts												
2e. Other												
AGRICULTURAL												
2a. Flour												
2b. Grains												
2c. Sugar												
2d. Fruits												
2e. Coffee	30.3		15.2	2,229.0			17.9		2,292.4			2,292.4
2f. Other												
FORESTRY												
2a. Lumber	2.0		1.8				1.1		4.9			4.9
2b. Extracts							70.6		70.6			70.6
MINERAL												
2a. Metals												
2b. Oil							0.1		0.1			0.1
TOTAL SEMI-PROCESSED	32.3		17.0	2,229.0			89.7		2,368.0			2,368.0

184

Table VII-5-4c. *Ecuador's Exports to LAFTA Countries, 1962—Processed or Manufactured*
(Thousands of U.S. Dollars)

	Argentina	Brazil	Chile	Colombia	Mexico	Paraguay	Peru	Uruguay	Total LAFTA	Bolivia	Venezuela	TOTAL
ANIMAL												
3a. Leather												
3b. Canned												
3c. Dairy												
3d. Meal							0.2		0.2			0.2
3e. Seafood							0.8		0.8	0.1		0.9
3f. Other												
AGRICULTURAL												
3a. Food							0.1		0.1			0.1
3b. Tobacco												
3c. Beverage												
3d. Oils												
3e. Textiles												
3f. Sugar												
3g. Other												
FORESTRY												
3a. Wood			0.6				0.4		1.0		2.9	3.9
3b. Paper							5.0		5.0			5.0
MINERAL												
3a. Metals												
3b. Machinery			0.2						0.4			0.4
3c. Vehicles					0.5				0.5			0.5
3d. Cement												
3e. Chemicals												
3f. Glass	1.8	2.5		877.9			0.8		883.0	20.2	11.9	915.1
MISCELLANEOUS MANUFACTURES	1.0					0.9		2.2	6.2	4.3	13.0	23.5
TOTAL PROCESSED	2.8	2.5	2.9	878.1	0.5	0.9	7.3	2.2	897.2	24.6	27.8	949.6
TOTAL EXPORTS	198.2	2.5	2,263.1	3,107.1	0.5	0.9	534.4	2.2	6,108.9	24.6	35.9	6,169.4

Table VII-5-5a. *Ecuador's Exports to LAFTA Countries, 1963—Raw Materials*
(Thousands of U.S. Dollars)

	Argentina	Brazil	Chile	Colombia	Mexico	Paraguay	Peru	Uruguay	Total LAFTA	Bolivia	Venezuela	TOTAL
ANIMAL												
1a. Live				0.6			116.5		117.1		6.9	124.0
1b. Fibers												
1c. Fish							2.0		2.0	0.1		2.1
1d. Other												
AGRICULTURAL												
1a. Grains							624.5		624.5			624.5
1b. Fibers	10.0		1,730.5				483.8		2,224.3			2,224.3
1c. Fruits			42.2				1.1		43.3			43.3
1d. Seeds												
1e. Other	19.5	3.1		6.7			30.5		59.8		5.3	65.1
FORESTRY												
1a. Plants												
MINERAL												
1a. Metals	172.1								172.1			172.1
1b. Oil												
1c. Stone												
1d. Non-metals												
1e. Other												
TOTAL RAW MATERIALS	201.6	3.1	1,772.7	7.3			1,258.4		3,243.1	0.1	12.2	3,255.4

Source: Ministerio de Finanzas, Dirección de Financiamiento y Asesoría Fiscal, *Anuario de Comercio Exterior, 1963*, Quito, 1964.

186

Table VII-5-5b. *Ecuador's Exports to LAFTA Countries, 1963—Semi-Processed*

(Thousands of U.S. Dollars)

	Argentina	Brazil	Chile	Colombia	Mexico	Paraguay	Peru	Uruguay	Total LAFTA	Bolivia	Venezuela	TOTAL
ANIMAL												
2a. Hides												
2b. Fat												
2c. Meat												
2d. Pelts												
2e. Other												
AGRICULTURAL												
2a. Flour							0.2		0.2			0.2
2b. Grains												
2c. Sugar												
2d. Fruits							1.4		1.4			1.4
2e. Coffee	61.6	0.1	201.6	3,364.9			16.2	25.1	3,669.5			3,669.5
2f. Other			45.4						45.4			45.4
FORESTRY												
2a. Lumber												
2b. Extracts	3.0	1.9					3.8		8.7		0.1	8.8
MINERAL												
2a. Metals												
2b. Oil												
TOTAL SEMI-PROCESSED	64.6	2.0	247.0	3,364.9			21.6	25.1	3,725.2		0.1	3,725.3

187

Table VII-5-5c. *Ecuador's Exports to LAFTA Countries, 1963—Processed or Manufactured*
(Thousands of U.S. Dollars)

	Argentina	Brazil	Chile	Colombia	Mexico	Paraguay	Peru	Uruguay	Total LAFTA	Bolivia	Venezuela	TOTAL
ANIMAL												
3a. Leather												
3b. Canned												
3c. Dairy							0.4		0.4			0.4
3d. Meal												
3e. Seafood												
3f. Other												
AGRICULTURAL												
3a. Food												
3b. Tobacco												
3c. Beverage			8.0						8.0			8.0
3d. Oils												
3e. Textiles												
3f. Sugar												
3g. Other												
FORESTRY												
3a. Wood												
3b. Paper							77.9		77.9			77.9
MINERAL												
3a. Metals							10.3		10.3			10.3
3b. Machinery				0.1					0.1			0.1
3c. Vehicles							1.5		1.5			1.5
3d. Cement												
3e. Chemicals		8.4	49.7	869.7					927.7	18.7	8.2	954.7
3f. Glass												
MISCELLANEOUS MANUFACTURES	3.8		9.3	0.4	6.9	0.7		2.8	23.9	8.1	16.8	48.8
TOTAL PROCESSED	3.8	8.4	67.0	870.2	6.9	0.7	90.1	2.8	1,049.9	26.8	25.0	1,101.7
TOTAL EXPORTS	270.0	13.5	2,086.7	4,242.4	6.9	0.7	1,370.1	27.9	8,018.2	26.9	37.3	8,082.4

Table VII-6-1a. Mexico's Exports to LAFTA Countries, 1959—Raw Materials

(Thousands of U.S. Dollars)

	Argentina	Brazil	Chile	Colombia	Ecuador	Paraguay	Peru	Uruguay	Total LAFTA	Bolivia	Venezuela	TOTAL
ANIMAL												
1a. Live												
1b. Fibers												
1c. Fish												
1d. Other												
AGRICULTURAL												
1a. Grains											480.0	480.0
1b. Fibers	12.7	39.2	265.7	41.3			22.9	1.7	383.5		1.2	384.7
1c. Fruits											71.0	71.0
1d. Seeds												
1e. Other			566.2						566.2		15.8	582.0
FORESTRY												
1a. Plants		0.1							0.1		0.4	0.5
MINERAL												
1a. Metals	7.5	171.3	362.9	412.6				39.0	993.3		140.7	1,134.0
1b. Oil												
1c. Stone	137.0			0.7			39.1		176.8		87.2	264.0
1d. Non-metals				6.2	1.3		3.4		10.9		220.2	231.1
1e. Other												
TOTAL RAW MATERIALS	157.2	210.6	1,194.8	460.8	1.3		65.4	40.7	2,130.8		1,016.5	3,147.3

Source: Secretaría de Industria y Comercio, Dirección General de Estadística, *Anuario Estadístico del Comercio Exterior de los Estados Unidos Mexicanos, 1959*, México, D.F., 1960.

Table VII-6-1b. *Mexico's Exports to LAFTA Countries, 1959—Semi-Processed*
(Thousands of U.S. Dollars)

	Argen-tina	Brazil	Chile	Colom-bia	Ecuador	Para-guay	Peru	Uruguay	Total LAFTA	Bolivia	Vene-zuela	TOTAL
ANIMAL												
2a. Hides											52.6	52.6
2b. Fat												
2c. Meat												
2d. Pelts												
2e. Other												
AGRICULTURAL												
2a. Flour												
2b. Grains												
2c. Sugar												
2d. Fruits												
2e. Coffee												
2f. Other												
FORESTRY												
2a. Lumber												
2b. Extracts	25.1	32.5	73.2	48.9			7.4		187.1		3.2	190.3
MINERAL												
2a. Metals												
2b. Oil							3.8		3.8			3.8
TOTAL SEMI-PROCESSED	25.1	32.5	73.2	48.9			11.2		190.9		55.8	246.7

Table VII-6-1c. *Mexico's Exports to LAFTA Countries, 1959—Processed or Manufactured*
(Thousands of U.S. Dollars)

	Argentina	Brazil	Chile	Colombia	Ecuador	Paraguay	Peru	Uruguay	Total LAFTA	Bolivia	Venezuela	TOTAL
ANIMAL												
3a. Leather	0.1						0.6		0.8	0.2	12.4	13.4
3b. Canned								0.1	0.2		1.5	1.7
3c. Dairy												
3d. Meal												
3e. Seafood				0.2							0.3	0.3
3f. Other												
AGRICULTURAL												
3a. Food	0.6		0.1	0.1	2.1		0.2	0.1	3.2		7.0	10.2
3b. Tobacco		0.1					0.1		0.1			0.1
3c. Beverage	0.1		0.1				0.4	0.1	0.7		0.5	1.2
3d. Oils		0.1										
3e. Textiles	2.2		1.4	7.9	11.7	8.0	49.5		80.9	7.4	60.5	148.8
3f. Sugar											0.4	0.4
3g. Other											8.1	8.1
FORESTRY												
3a. Wood	0.2			0.2			0.2		0.4		17.8	18.2
3b. Paper			7.2	2.4	1.1		20.9		31.9	0.4	149.0	181.3
MINERAL												
3a. Metals	124.8			236.7	21.5		2.7		385.7		113.9	499.6
3b. Machinery	8.3	1.7	1.9	76.6	3.5		81.8		174.2		597.7	771.9
3c. Vehicles	31.3		7.6	51.5	55.6		22.0	0.4	168.0		152.8	320.8
3d. Cement											1.9	1.9
3e. Chemicals	24.0	24.0	9.9	60.1	90.8	65.0	236.8		510.6	10.7	848.5	1,369.8
3f. Glass											0.1	0.1
MISCELLANEOUS MANUFACTURES	102.3	52.0	155.1	358.6	179.9	0.4	354.4	52.4	1,255.1	11.1	1,604.3	2,870.5
TOTAL PROCESSED	293.9	77.9	183.3	794.3	366.2	73.4	769.6	53.2	2,611.8	29.8	3,576.7	6,218.3
TOTAL EXPORTS	476.2	321.0	1,451.3	1,304.0	367.5	73.4	846.2	93.9	4,933.5	29.8	4,649.0	9,612.3

Table VII-6-2a. *Mexico's Exports to LAFTA Countries, 1960—Raw Materials*
(Thousands of U.S. Dollars)

	Argentina	Brazil	Chile	Colombia	Ecuador	Paraguay	Peru	Uruguay	Total LAFTA	Bolivia	Venezuela	TOTAL
ANIMAL												
1a. Live												
1b. Fibers												
1c. Fish												
1d. Other												
AGRICULTURAL												
1a. Grains	22.9	12.1	26.5				35.6		98.1			98.1
1b. Fibers			89.6						89.6			89.6
1c. Fruits				0.7							0.4	0.4
1d. Seeds												
1e. Other												
FORESTRY												
1a. Plants			6.7		3.7				10.4			10.4
MINERAL												
1a. Metals		436.4	431.6	221.6	0.8			1.9	1,092.3		120.4	1,212.7
1b. Oil	0.2								0.2			0.2
1c. Stone		89.9		2.5			18.2		110.6			110.6
1d. Non-metals				2.6		9.6	8.0		20.2		190.6	210.8
1e. Other	0.2								0.2			0.2
TOTAL RAW MATERIALS	23.3	538.7	554.4	227.4	4.5	9.6	61.8	1.9	1,421.6		311.4	1,733.0

Source: Secretaría de Industria y Comercio, Dirección General de Estadística, *Anuario Estadístico del Comercio Exterior de los Estados Unidos Mexicanos, 1960*, México, D.F., 1961.

Table VII-6-2b. *Mexico's Exports to LAFTA Countries, 1960—Semi-Processed*
(Thousands of U.S. Dollars)

	Argentina	Brazil	Chile	Colombia	Ecuador	Paraguay	Peru	Uruguay	Total LAFTA	Bolivia	Venezuela	TOTAL
ANIMAL												
2a. Hides											91.5	91.5
2b. Fat												
2c. Meat												
2d. Pelts												
2e. Other											1.8	1.8
AGRICULTURAL												
2a. Flour							0.2		0.2			0.2
2b. Grains												
2c. Sugar			0.1									
2d. Fruits				0.3					0.4			0.4
2e. Coffee				30.5					30.5			30.5
2f. Other												
FORESTRY												
2a. Lumber												
2b. Extracts	260.2	457.2	183.1	34.1			7.3	31.7	973.6		1.0	974.6
MINERAL												
2a. Metals												
2b. Oil	0.7	2.5	0.6	3.2			33.0	3.0	43.0			43.0
TOTAL SEMI-PROCESSED	260.9	459.7	183.8	68.1			40.5	34.7	1,047.7		94.3	1,142.0

Table VII-6c. *Mexico's Exports to LAFTA Countries, 1960—Processed or Manufactured*
(Thousands of U.S. Dollars)

	Argentina	Brazil	Chile	Colombia	Ecuador	Paraguay	Peru	Uruguay	Total LAFTA	Bolivia	Venezuela	TOTAL
ANIMAL												
3a. Leather	0.1			0.2					0.3		12.7	13.0
3b. Canned							0.1		0.1		0.9	1.0
3c. Dairy												
3d. Meal												
3e. Seafood												
3f. Other								0.1	0.1			0.1
AGRICULTURAL												
3a. Food	0.4		0.2	4.0	2.2		1.3		8.1		3.8	11.9
3b. Tobacco	0.1		0.2					0.1	0.4		0.3	0.7
3c. Beverage						0.6			0.6			0.6
3d. Oils												
3e. Textiles	5.0	0.3	5.0	6.9	12.2	3.8	32.8	0.2	66.2	17.4	66.6	150.2
3f. Sugar			70.4						70.4			70.4
3g. Other			0.1				4.3		4.4		0.4	4.8
FORESTRY												
3a. Wood				0.1	4.0		27.6		31.7	0.1	6.8	38.5
3b. Paper	6.4	0.7	5.6	2.2	0.7		3.6	0.1	19.3		71.8	91.2
MINERAL												
3a. Metals		55.7		254.4	16.9				327.0		0.8	327.8
3b. Machinery	37.2	4.7	7.6	114.8	39.8	1.4	76.1	9.6	291.2		288.4	579.6
3c. Vehicles	14.4		16.9	2.3	63.0		4.4	32.5	133.5	212.2	50.8	396.5
3d. Cement					87.5				87.5			87.5
3e. Chemicals			4.6	130.4	32.2	10.1	215.7		393.0		652.1	1,045.1
3f. Glass					0.1				0.1			0.1
MISCELLANEOUS MANUFACTURES	283.4	153.8	488.6	429.0	170.7	1.0	232.8	58.1	1,817.4	19.0	1,308.1	3,144.5
TOTAL PROCESSED	347.0	215.2	599.2	944.3	429.3	16.9	594.4	105.0	3,251.3	248.7	2,463.5	5,963.5
TOTAL EXPORTS	631.2	1,213.6	1,337.4	1,239.8	433.8	26.5	696.7	141.6	5,720.6	248.7	2,869.2	8,838.5

Table VII-6-3a. *Mexico's Exports to LAFTA Countries, 1961 — Raw Materials*
(Thousands of U.S. Dollars)

	Argentina	Brazil	Chile	Colombia	Ecuador	Paraguay	Peru	Uruguay	Total LAFTA	Bolivia	Venezuela	TOTAL
ANIMAL												
1a. Live	0.3	11.2			4.4				15.9		6.2	22.1
1b. Fibers												
1c. Fish												
1d. Other												
AGRICULTURAL												
1a. Grains	17.5	1.8	0.6				0.5		20.4		192.0	212.4
1b. Fibers	0.1								0.1			0.1
1c. Fruits			2.5	114.2					116.7			116.7
1d. Seeds	7.5								7.5			7.5
1e. Other												
FORESTRY												
1a. Plants												
MINERAL												
1a. Metals		36.1					4.2		40.3			40.3
1b. Oil												
1c. Stone				1.0					1.0			1.0
1d. Non-metals		54.5		5.8	0.5		1.2		62.0		191.4	253.4
1e. Other												
TOTAL RAW MATERIALS	25.4	103.6	3.1	122.1	4.9		5.9		265.0		389.6	654.6

Source: Secretaría de Industria y Comercio, Dirección General de Estadística, Anuario Estadístico del Comercio Exterior de los Estados Unidos Mexicanos, 1961, México, D.F., 1962.

195

Table VII-6-3b. *Mexico's Exports to LAFTA Countries, 1961—Semi-Processed*

(Thousands of U.S. Dollars)

	Argentina	Brazil	Chile	Colombia	Ecuador	Paraguay	Peru	Uruguay	Total LAFTA	Bolivia	Venezuela	TOTAL
ANIMAL												
2a. Hides											47.4	47.4
2b. Fat						4.9			4.9		1.2	6.1
2c. Meat												
2d. Pelts												
2e. Other				4.9					4.9			4.9
AGRICULTURAL												
2a. Flour												
2b. Grains												
2c. Sugar												
2d. Fruits												
2e. Coffee												
2f. Other												
FORESTRY												
2a. Lumber							1.5		1.5			1.5
2b. Extracts	396.4	537.4	339.3	62.6			7.7	91.9	1,435.3		3.1	1,438.4
MINERAL												
2a. Metals		781.4	459.3	280.0				4.0	1,524.7		254.7	1,779.4
2b. Oil					2.1				2.1	1.8		3.9
TOTAL SEMI-PROCESSED	396.4	1,318.8	798.6	347.5	2.1	4.9	9.2	95.9	2,973.4	1.8	306.4	3,281.6

Table VII-6-3c. *Mexico's Exports to LAFTA Countries, 1961—Processed or Manufactured*

(Thousands of U.S. Dollars)

	Argentina	Brazil	Chile	Colombia	Ecuador	Paraguay	Peru	Uruguay	Total LAFTA	Bolivia	Venezuela	TOTAL
ANIMAL												
3a. Leather												
3b. Canned											0.8	0.8
3c. Dairy												
3d. Meal												
3e. Seafood												
3f. Other						7.3			7.3			7.3
AGRICULTURAL												
3a. Food	5.2						4.0		14.9	0.1	3.9	18.9
3b. Tobacco								12.7	12.7			12.7
3c. Beverage												
3d. Oils				0.1					0.1		0.1	0.2
3e. Textiles	21.0		31.9	0.2	20.3	17.4	141.3	1.9	245.3	20.0	7.2	272.5
3f. Sugar												
3g. Other			5.0		0.1				5.1			5.1
FORESTRY												
3a. Wood	0.5			0.2			0.1		0.8	0.2	4.1	5.1
3b. Paper	3.0	1.2	5.6	7.6	4.3	0.1	9.8		31.6		30.5	62.1
MINERAL												
3a. Metals	105.6	342.2	0.5	310.7	19.9	0.4	23.2		696.9	0.2	43.0	740.1
3b. Machinery	18.1	10.1	50.4	67.7	24.1	1.6	217.7	10.3	487.5		522.5	1,010.0
3c. Vehicles		0.8	46.8	1.4	90.4		0.5		158.0	3.6	54.8	216.4
3d. Cement							0.2		0.2		0.9	1.1
3e. Chemicals	31.2		4.0	135.7	112.1		34.1	4.1	321.2		535.6	856.8
3f. Glass	0.1			0.4	2.1		3.2		5.8		1.6	7.4
MISCELLANEOUS MANUFACTURES	527.3	17.6	544.0	616.1	323.1	1.1	385.6	88.4	2,503.2	20.2	1,153.1	3,676.5
TOTAL PROCESSED	712.0	383.2	688.4	1,144.0	597.1	27.9	819.7	118.3	4,490.6	44.3	2,358.1	6,893.0
TOTAL EXPORTS	1,133.8	1,805.6	1,490.1	1,613.6	604.1	32.8	834.8	214.2	7,729.0	46.1	3,054.1	10,829.2

Table VII-6-4a. *Mexico's Exports to LAFTA Countries, 1962—Raw Materials*
(Thousands of U.S. Dollars)

	Argentina	Brazil	Chile	Colombia	Ecuador	Paraguay	Peru	Uruguay	Total LAFTA	Bolivia	Venezuela	TOTAL
ANIMAL												
1a. Live	0.1			2.9	3.4		0.1		6.5		5.1	11.6
1b. Fibers												
1c. Fish	0.3								0.3			0.3
1d. Other												
AGRICULTURAL												
1a. Grains		104.7		10.5					115.2		162.5	277.7
1b. Fibers	6.1	16.6	161.0	7.2			83.8	144.8	419.5			419.5
1c. Fruits						0.3			0.3		3.0	3.3
1d. Seeds		49.6			4.1		0.2		53.9		277.2	331.1
1e. Other		188.9							188.9		1.4	190.3
FORESTRY												
1a. Plants				0.1					0.1			0.1
MINERAL												
1a. Metals	42.0		395.8	142.8					580.6		20.4	601.0
1b. Oil												
1c. Stone				3.8			1.1		4.9		0.5	5.4
1d. Non-metals		261.3		19.8				1.2	282.3			282.3
1e. Other												
TOTAL RAW MATERIALS	48.5	621.1	556.8	187.1	7.5	0.3	85.2	146.0	1,652.5		470.1	2,122.6

Source: Secretaría de Industria y Comercio, Dirección General de Estadística, Anuario Estadístico del Comercio Exterior de los Estados Unidos Mexicanos, 1962, México, D.F., 1963.

Table VII-6-4b. *Mexico's Exports to LAFTA Countries, 1962—Semi-Processed*
(Thousands of U.S. Dollars)

	Argentina	Brazil	Chile	Colombia	Ecuador	Paraguay	Peru	Uruguay	Total LAFTA	Bolivia	Venezuela	TOTAL
ANIMAL												
2a. Hides	0.2								0.2			0.2
2b. Fat												
2c. Meat												
2d. Pelts												
2e. Other												
AGRICULTURAL												
2a. Flour												
2b. Grains												
2c. Sugar												
2d. Fruits		163.2							163.2			163.2
2e. Coffee	21.9		15.7						37.6			37.6
2f. Other	1.9	6.5		8.3			1.1		17.8		0.1	17.9
FORESTRY												
2a. Lumber												
2b. Extracts	370.2	1,202.9	143.9	185.9			31.6	38.4	1,972.9		74.8	2,047.7
MINERAL												
2a. Metals		1,610.2	17.3	93.7				40.5	1,761.7		908.2	2,669.9
2b. Oil			14.2				9.7		23.9			23.9
TOTAL SEMI-PROCESSED	394.2	2,982.8	191.1	287.9			42.4	78.9	3,977.3		983.1	4,960.4

199

Table VII-6-4c. Mexico's Exports to LAFTA Countries, 1962—Processed or Manufactured
(Thousands of U.S. Dollars)

	Argentina	Brazil	Chile	Colombia	Ecuador	Paraguay	Peru	Uruguay	Total LAFTA	Bolivia	Venezuela	TOTAL
ANIMAL												
3a. Leather											2.1	2.1
3b. Canned			0.2				0.1		0.3		0.5	0.8
3c. Dairy												
3d. Meal												
3e. Seafood							7.8		7.8			7.8
3f. Other												
AGRICULTURAL												
3a. Food	7.7	0.1	0.6				1.7		10.1		2.8	12.9
3b. Tobacco			0.5				0.1	16.8	17.4			17.4
3c. Beverage	0.1		6.5	0.2	0.1		2.1		9.0		0.2	9.2
3d. Oils												
3e. Textiles				53.8	99.6	5.3	7.6		167.0	18.0	13.9	198.9
3f. Sugar												
3g. Other			0.7	15.4	2.0				17.4		0.7	18.1
FORESTRY												
3a. Wood	0.2		0.3	6.8	8.9		0.1		0.6		4.5	5.1
3b. Paper	18.9	0.2	4.6			0.1	394.2	0.1	433.8	0.2	36.2	470.2
MINERAL												
3a. Metals	291.6	3,339.9	58.7	293.5	96.9		541.3	136.4	4,758.3		254.7	5,013.0
3b. Machinery	808.2	160.8	38.0	314.7	20.1		253.2	62.4	1,657.4	2.6	910.8	2,570.8
3c. Vehicles	91.5	0.1	21.4	9.1	98.1			3.1	223.3		117.7	341.0
3d. Cement											6.7	6.7
3e. Chemicals	15.4	298.6	902.1	165.5	63.2		206.9	6.9	1,658.8	15.0	561.0	2,234.8
3f. Glass	0.3	2.7	18.7	38.4			3.3		63.4		30.2	93.6
MISCELLANEOUS MANUFACTURES	570.0	51.2	545.6	548.7	253.1	9.5	108.9	69.5	2,156.5	30.2	994.9	3,398.1
TOTAL PROCESSED	1,803.9	3,853.8	1,597.9	1,446.1	642.0	14.9	1,527.3	295.2	11,181.1	66.0	2,936.9	14,184.0
TOTAL EXPORTS	2,246.6	7,457.7	2,345.8	1,921.1	649.5	15.2	1,654.9	520.1	16,810.9	66.0	4,390.1	21,267.0

Table VII-6-5a. *Mexico's Exports to LAFTA Countries, 1963—Raw Materials*
(Thousands of U.S. Dollars)

	Argentina	Brazil	Chile	Colombia	Ecuador	Paraguay	Peru	Uruguay	Total LAFTA	Bolivia	Venezuela	TOTAL
ANIMAL												
1a. Live				2.5	8.4		1.0		11.9		19.9	31.8
1b. Fibers												
1c. Fish	0.1								0.1			0.1
1d. Other												
AGRICULTURAL												
1a. Grains				171.0					171.0			171.0
1b. Fibers	31.0	0.2	700.0	1.9	17.6		38.1	49.4	838.2			838.2
1c. Fruits	117.0	151.2		59.6			0.1	42.4	370.3	1.6	1.5	373.4
1d. Seeds	49.5		17.7	9.6	10.7				87.5		942.3	1,029.8
1e. Other												
FORESTRY												
1a. Plants												
MINERAL												
1a. Metals	10.9	3,377.8		7.3			0.3		3,396.3		9.9	3,406.2
1b. Oil												
1c. Stone				1.8			0.5		2.3		0.2	2.5
1d. Non-metals		359.9	728.6	79.2				6.6	1,174.3		255.0	1,429.3
1e. Other												
TOTAL RAW MATERIALS	208.5	3,889.1	1,446.3	332.9	36.7		40.0	98.4	6,051.9	1.6	1,228.8	7,282.3

Source: Secretaría de Industria y Comercio, Dirección General de Estadística, *Anuario Estadístico del Comercio Exterior de los Estados Unidos Mexicanos, 1963,* México, D.F., 1964.

Table VII-6-5b. *Mexico's Exports to LAFTA Countries, 1963 – Semi-Processed*
(Thousands of U.S. Dollars)

	Argentina	Brazil	Chile	Colombia	Ecuador	Paraguay	Peru	Uruguay	Total LAFTA	Bolivia	Venezuela	TOTAL
ANIMAL												
2a. Hides												
2b. Fat												
2c. Meat												
2d. Pelts												
2e. Other											6.3	6.3
AGRICULTURAL												
2a. Flour												
2b. Grains												
2c. Sugar												
2d. Fruits	1.1								1.1			1.1
2e. Coffee	21.0		62.0						83.0			83.0
2f. Other	2.5	94.2	3.4	17.7			13.8		131.6		12.6	144.2
FORESTRY												
2a. Lumber												
2b. Extracts	606.1	899.9	93.3	242.2			24.5	41.2	1,907.2		90.4	1,997.6
MINERAL												
2a. Metals		1,051.3	496.0	575.8	0.7			10.9	2,134.7		80.8	2,215.5
2b. Oil	0.1	440.3		12.6			2.9		455.9		248.9	704.8
TOTAL SEMI-PROCESSED	630.8	2,485.7	654.7	848.3	0.7		41.2	52.1	4,713.5		439.0	5,152.5

Table VII-6-5c. Mexico's Exports to LAFTA Countries, 1963—Processed or Manufactured

(Thousands of U.S. Dollars)

	Argentina	Brazil	Chile	Colombia	Ecuador	Paraguay	Peru	Uruguay	Total LAFTA	Bolivia	Venezuela	TOTAL
ANIMAL												
3a. Leather	0.2						0.1		0.3		0.6	0.9
3b. Canned												
3c. Dairy												
3d. Meal												
3e. Seafood	1.2					0.3	9.3		10.8			10.8
3f. Other												
AGRICULTURAL												
3a. Food	50.8	1.0	108.6		0.1		2.5		163.0		1.0	164.0
3b. Tobacco	0.2	36.0						18.1	18.1			18.1
3c. Beverage			10.2				2.1	0.2	48.7		0.3	49.0
3d. Oils			0.4				3.8		4.2			4.2
3e. Textiles	11.5	7.3	1.9	0.4	221.2	4.8	27.0	0.3	274.4	17.0	51.1	342.5
3f. Sugar												
3g. Other												
FORESTRY												
3a. Wood												
3b. Paper	9.5	1.5	6.8	46.4	8.6	0.6	30.6	1.2	105.2	1.8	80.0	187.0
MINERAL												
3a. Metals	2.8	758.7		445.6	103.2		794.0	63.6	2,167.9	3.6	111.2	2,282.7
3b. Machinery	59.5	685.9	95.3	309.7	21.0		158.1	0.8	1,328.3	1.3	683.5	2,013.1
3c. Vehicles	116.5		1.4	164.0	113.5		208.8	3.2	607.4	6.7	101.8	715.9
3d. Cement												
3e. Chemicals	140.0	809.8	1,680.5	720.4	96.5		195.0	18.7	3,660.9	31.2	367.7	4,059.8
3f. Glass	0.2	0.2			2.6		2.1		5.1		3.5	8.6
MISCELLANEOUS MANUFACTURES	1,231.9	1,469.0	991.1	1,293.3	318.8	44.9	1,468.4	236.3	7,053.7	144.4	2,685.3	9,883.4
TOTAL PROCESSED	1,622.3	3,769.4	2,896.2	2,979.8	885.5	50.6	2,901.8	342.4	15,448.0	206.0	4,086.0	19,740.0
TOTAL EXPORTS	2,461.6	10,144.2	4,997.2	4,161.0	922.9	50.6	2,983.0	492.9	26,213.4	207.6	5,753.8	32,174.8

Table VII-7-1a. *Paraguay's Exports to LAFTA Countries, 1959—Raw Materials*

(Thousands of U.S. Dollars)

	Argen- tina	Brazil	Chile	Colom- bia	Ecuador	Mexico	Peru	Uruguay	Total LAFTA	Bolivia	Vene- zuela	TOTAL
ANIMAL												
1a. Live	0.7								0.7			0.7
1b. Fibers												
1c. Fish												
1d. Other												
AGRICULTURAL												
1a. Grains	115.2								115.2			115.2
1b. Fibers		3.1						49.9	53.0			53.0
1c. Fruits	219.0							7.1	226.1			226.1
1d. Seeds	4.2							0.1	4.3			4.3
1e. Other	1.2	1.1						2.3	4.6	5.2		9.8
FORESTRY												
1a. Plants												
MINERAL												
1a. Metals												
1b. Oil												
1c. Stone												
1d. Non-metals												
1e. Other												
TOTAL RAW MATERIALS	340.3	4.2						59.4	403.9	5.2		409.1

Source: Banco Central del Paraguay, Departamento de Estudios Económicos, *Boletín Estadístico Mensual*, No. 67, Asunción, December, 1963.

Table VII-7-1b. *Paraguay's Exports to LAFTA Countries, 1959—Semi-Processed*
(Thousands of U.S. Dollars)

	Argentina	Brazil	Chile	Colombia	Ecuador	Mexico	Peru	Uruguay	Total LAFTA	Bolivia	Venezuela	TOTAL
ANIMAL												
2a. Hides	14.9							35.6	50.5			50.5
2b. Fat												
2c. Meat												
2d. Pelts	8.7								8.7			8.7
2e. Other												
AGRICULTURAL												
2a. Flour												
2b. Grains												
2c. Sugar	6.1		170.1					115.5	291.7	310.2		601.9
2d. Fruits												
2e. Coffee	1,756.0							5.3	1,761.3			1,761.3
2f. Other												
FORESTRY												
2a. Lumber	3,705.6	21.7						329.9	4,057.2			4,057.2
2b. Extracts								76.0	76.0			76.0
MINERAL												
2a. Metals												
2b. Oil												
TOTAL SEMI-PROCESSED	5,491.3	21.7	170.1					562.3	6,245.4	310.2		6,555.6

Table VII-7-1c. *Paraguay's Exports to LAFTA Countries, 1959—Processed or Manufactured*
(Thousands of U.S. Dollars)

	Argen-tina	Brazil	Chile	Colom-bia	Ecuador	Mexico	Peru	Uruguay	Total	Bolivia	Vene-zuela	TOTAL
ANIMAL												
3a. Leather	0.6							2.2	2.8	17.7		20.5
3b. Canned												
3c. Dairy												
3d. Meal												
3e. Seafood												
3f. Other												
AGRICULTURAL												
3a. Food	14.4	1.0							15.4			15.4
3b. Tobacco	0.5							50.9	51.4			51.4
3c. Beverage												
3d. Oils	592.7	6.5						180.8	780.0			780.0
3e. Textiles												
3f. Sugar												
3g. Other												
FORESTRY												
3a. Wood												
3b. Paper												
MINERAL												
3a. Metals												
3b. Machinery												
3c. Vehicles												
3d. Cement												
3e. Chemicals												
3f. Glass												
MISCELLANEOUS MANUFACTURES												
TOTAL PROCESSED	608.2	7.5						233.9	849.6	17.7		867.3
TOTAL EXPORTS	6,439.8	33.4	170.1					855.6	7,498.9	333.1		7,832.0

Table VII-7-2a. *Paraguay's Exports to LAFTA Countries, 1960—Raw Materials*
(Thousands of U.S. Dollars)

	Argentina	Brazil	Chile	Colombia	Ecuador	Mexico	Peru	Uruguay	Total LAFTA	Bolivia	Venezuela	TOTAL
ANIMAL												
1a. Live	1.0	37.0							38.0			38.0
1b. Fibers												
1c. Fish												
1d. Other												
AGRICULTURAL												
1a. Grains	35.5								35.5			35.5
1b. Fibers	7.1							3.6	10.7			10.7
1c. Fruits	287.5							5.5	293.0			293.0
1d. Seeds	0.6								0.6			0.6
1e. Other	3.0								3.0			3.0
FORESTRY												
1a. Plants												
MINERAL												
1a. Metals												
1b. Oil												
1c. Stone												
1d. Non-metals												
1e. Other												
TOTAL RAW MATERIALS	334.7	37.0						9.1	380.8			380.8

Source: Banco Central del Paraguay, Departamento de Estudios Económicos, *Boletín Estadístico Mensual*, No. 67, Asunción, December, 1963.

207

Table VII-7-2b. *Paraguay's Exports to LAFTA Countries, 1960—Semi-Processed*

(Thousands of U.S. Dollars)

	Argentina	Brazil	Chile	Colombia	Ecuador	Mexico	Peru	Uruguay	Total LAFTA	Bolivia	Venezuela	TOTAL
ANIMAL												
2a. Hides	6.0								6.0			6.0
2b. Fat	12.8								12.8			12.8
2c. Meat												
2d. Pelts	19.3								19.3			19.3
2e. Other												
AGRICULTURAL												
2a. Flour												
2b. Grains	4.5								4.5			4.5
2c. Sugar	1.5								1.5	64.7		66.2
2d. Fruits												
2e. Coffee	2,699.4							17.2	2,716.6			2,716.6
2f. Other												
FORESTRY												
2a. Lumber	4,142.8	21.0						847.4	5,011.2			5,011.2
2b. Extracts								9.0	9.0			9.0
MINERAL												
2a. Metals												
2b. Oil												
TOTAL SEMI-PROCESSED	6,886.3	21.0						873.6	7,780.9	64.7		7,845.6

208

Table VII-7-2c. *Paraguay's Exports to LAFTA Countries, 1960—Processed or Manufactured*
(Thousands of U.S. Dollars)

	Argentina	Brazil	Chile	Colombia	Ecuador	Mexico	Peru	Uruguay	Total LAFTA	Bolivia	Venezuela	TOTAL
ANIMAL												
3a. Leather	0.5	0.5							1.0			1.0
3b. Canned												
3c. Dairy												
3d. Meal												
3e. Seafood												
3f. Other												
AGRICULTURAL												
3a. Food	1.4	0.5							1.9			1.9
3b. Tobacco	78.1							113.0	191.1			191.1
3c. Beverage												
3d. Oils	323.9	21.4					0.8	170.5	516.6			516.6
3e. Textiles												
3f. Sugar												
3g. Other												
FORESTRY												
3a. Wood												
3b. Paper												
MINERAL												
3a. Metals												
3b. Machinery												
3c. Vehicles												
3d. Cement												
3e. Chemicals	26.4								26.4			26.4
3f. Glass												
MISCELLANEOUS MANUFACTURES												
TOTAL PROCESSED	430.3	22.4					0.8	283.5	737.0			737.0
TOTAL EXPORTS	7,651.3	80.4					0.8	1,166.2	8,898.7	64.7		8,963.4

Table VII-7-3a. *Paraguay's Exports to LAFTA Countries, 1961—Raw Materials*
(Thousands of U.S. Dollars)

	Argentina	Brazil	Chile	Colombia	Ecuador	Mexico	Peru	Uruguay	Total LAFTA	Bolivia	Venezuela	TOTAL
ANIMAL												
1a. Live												
1b. Fibers												
1c. Fish												
1d. Other												
AGRICULTURAL												
1a. Grains	8.8								8.8			8.8
1b. Fibers	15.4							85.3	100.7			100.7
1c. Fruits	350.5							6.0	356.5			356.5
1d. Seeds	0.2								0.2			0.2
1e. Other	51.4	4.3						2.0	57.7			57.7
FORESTRY												
1a. Plants												
MINERAL												
1a. Metals												
1b. Oil												
1c. Stone												
1d. Non-metals												
1e. Other												
TOTAL RAW MATERIALS	426.3	4.3						93.3	523.9			523.9

Source: Banco Central del Paraguay, Departamento de Estudios Económicos, Boletín Estadístico Mensual, No. 67, Asunción, December, 1963.

Table VII-7-3b. *Paraguay's Exports to LAFTA Countries, 1961—Semi-Processed*
(Thousands of U.S. Dollars)

	Argentina	Brazil	Chile	Colombia	Ecuador	Mexico	Peru	Uruguay	Total LAFTA	Bolivia	Venezuela	TOTAL
ANIMAL												
2a. Hides	1.1							4.0	5.1			5.1
2b. Fat	17.8							1.2	19.0			19.0
2c. Meat												
2d. Pelts	26.6								26.6			26.6
2e. Other	3.5								3.5			3.5
AGRICULTURAL												
2a. Flour												
2b. Grains												
2c. Sugar										21.8		21.8
2d. Fruits												
2e. Coffee	1,796.1							74.1	1,870.2			1,870.2
2f. Other												
FORESTRY												
2a. Lumber												
2b. Extracts	5,875.0	33.2						551.3	6,459.5			6,459.5
MINERAL												
2a. Metals												
2b. Oil												
TOTAL SEMI-PROCESSED	7,720.1	33.2						630.6	8,383.9	21.8		8,405.7

Table VII-7-3c. *Paraguay's Exports to LAFTA Countries, 1961 —Processed or Manufactured*

(Thousands of U.S. Dollars)

	Argentina	Brazil	Chile	Colombia	Ecuador	Mexico	Peru	Uruguay	Total LAFTA	Bolivia	Venezuela	TOTAL
ANIMAL												
3a. Leather												
3b. Canned												
3c. Dairy												
3d. Meal												
3e. Seafood												
3f. Other												
AGRICULTURAL												
3a. Food												
3b. Tobacco								357.0	357.0			357.0
3c. Beverage	525.3	30.2						17.3	574.8			574.8
3d. Oils							2.0					
3e. Textiles												
3f. Sugar												
3g. Other												
FORESTRY												
3a. Wood												
3b. Paper												
MINERAL												
3a. Metals												
3b. Machinery												
3c. Vehicles												
3d. Cement	48.2								48.2			48.2
3e. Chemicals												
3f. Glass												
MISCELLANEOUS MANUFACTURES												
TOTAL PROCESSED	573.5	30.2						374.3	980.0			980.0
TOTAL EXPORTS	8,719.9	67.7					2.0	1,098.2	9,887.8	21.8		9,909.6

Table VII-7-4a. *Paraguay's Exports to LAFTA Countries, 1962—Raw Materials*

(Thousands of U.S. Dollars)

	Argentina	Brazil	Chile	Colombia	Ecuador	Mexico	Peru	Uruguay	Total LAFTA	Bolivia	Venezuela	TOTAL
ANIMAL												
1a. Live		2.0							2.0			2.0
1b. Fibers												
1c. Fish												
1d. Other												
AGRICULTURAL												
1a. Grains								263.1	263.1			263.1
1b. Fibers												
1c. Fruits	418.4		1.8					6.0	426.2			426.2
1d. Seeds	6.0								6.0			6.0
1e. Other	20.3	5.0							25.3			25.3
FORESTRY												
1a. Plants												
MINERAL												
1a. Metals												
1b. Oil												
1c. Stone	1.6								1.6			1.6
1d. Non-metals												
1e. Other												
TOTAL RAW MATERIALS	446.3	7.0	1.8					269.1	724.2			724.2

Source: Banco Central del Paraguay, Departamento de Estudios Económicos, <u>Boletín Estadístico Mensual</u>,
No. 67, Asunción, December, 1963.

Table VII-7-4b. *Paraguay's Exports to LAFTA Countries, 1962—Semi-Processed*
(Thousands of U.S. Dollars)

	Argentina	Brazil	Chile	Colombia	Ecuador	Mexico	Peru	Uruguay	Total LAFTA	Bolivia	Venezuela	TOTAL
ANIMAL												
2a. Hides	2.8	1.0						9.7	41.3			41.3
2b. Fat												
2c. Meat	24.2	0.8							25.6			25.6
2d. Pelts	27.8		0.6						27.8			27.8
2e. Other												
AGRICULTURAL												
2a. Flour												
2b. Grains								4.0	4.0			4.0
2c. Sugar												
2d. Fruits												
2e. Coffee	2,240.0							189.7	2,429.7			2,429.7
2f. Other	21.3	2.0							23.3			23.3
FORESTRY												
2a. Lumber	6,160.4	40.0						417.0	6,617.4			6,617.4
2b. Extracts	30.6								30.6			30.6
MINERAL												
2a. Metals												
2b. Oil												
TOTAL SEMI-PROCESSED	8,507.1	43.8	0.6					620.4	9,171.9			9,171.9

Table VII-7-4c. Paraguay's Exports to LAFTA Countries, 1962—Processed or Manufactured

(Thousands of U.S. Dollars)

	Argentina	Brazil	Chile	Colombia	Ecuador	Mexico	Peru	Uruguay	Total LAFTA	Bolivia	Venezuela	TOTAL
ANIMAL												
3a. Leather												
3b. Canned												
3c. Dairy												
3d. Meal												
3e. Seafood												
3f. Other												
AGRICULTURAL												
3a. Food	8.6							61.9	70.5			70.5
3b. Tobacco												
3c. Beverage	608.5	57.2	19.5			0.7		191.5	877.4			877.4
3d. Oils												
3e. Textiles												
3f. Sugar	17.6								17.6			17.6
3g. Other	2.3							3.6	5.9			5.9
FORESTRY												
3a. Wood												
3b. Paper												
MINERAL												
3a. Metals												
3b. Machinery												
3c. Vehicles												
3d. Cement	19.5								19.5			19.5
3e. Chemicals												
3f. Glass												
MISCELLANEOUS MANUFACTURES								0.2	0.2	3.3		3.5
TOTAL PROCESSED	656.5	57.2	19.5			0.7		257.2	991.9	3.3		994.4
TOTAL EXPORTS	9,609.9	108.0	21.9			0.7		1,146.7	10,887.2	3.3		10,890.5

Table VII-7-5a. *Paraguay's Exports to LAFTA Countries, 1963—Raw Materials*
(Thousands of U.S. Dollars)

	Argentina	Brazil	Chile	Colombia	Ecuador	Mexico	Peru	Uruguay	Total LAFTA	Bolivia	Venezuela	TOTAL
ANIMAL												
1a. Live												
1b. Fibers												
1c. Fish												
1d. Other												
AGRICULTURAL												
1a. Grains												
1b. Fibers	561.0							414.0	975.0			975.0
1c. Fruits	313.0								313.0			313.0
1d. Seeds	8.0								8.0			8.0
1e. Other	1.0								1.0			1.0
FORESTRY												
1a. Plants												
MINERAL												
1a. Metals												
1b. Oil												
1c. Stone												
1d. Non-metals												
1e. Other												
TOTAL RAW MATERIALS	883.0							414.0	1,297.0			1,297.0

Source: Banco Central del Paraguay, Departamento de Estudios Económicos, *Boletín Estadístico Mensual*, No. 77, Asunción, October, 1964.

Table VII-7-5b. *Paraguay's Exports to LAFTA Countries, 1963—Semi-Processed*
(Thousands of U.S. Dollars)

	Argen-tina	Brazil	Chile	Colom-bia	Ecuador	Mexico	Peru	Uruguay	Total LAFTA	Bolivia	Vene-zuela	TOTAL
ANIMAL												
2a. Hides	65.0	1.0							66.0			66.0
2b. Fat												
2c. Meat	45.0	42.0	2.0						89.0			89.0
2d. Pelts	25.0								25.0			25.0
2e. Other	3.0								3.0			3.0
AGRICULTURAL												
2a. Flour												
2b. Grains												
2c. Sugar	14.0		1.0						15.0			15.0
2d. Fruits												
2e. Coffee												
2f. Other	2,281.0							279.0	2,560.0			2,560.0
FORESTRY												
2a. Lumber	4,274.0	40.0						557.0	4,871.0			4,871.0
2b. Extracts								6.0	6.0			6.0
MINERAL												
2a. Metals												
2b. Oil												
TOTAL SEMI-PROCESSED	6,707.0	83.0	3.0					842.0	7,635.0			7,635.0

Table VII-7-5c. *Paraguay's Exports to LAFTA Countries, 1963—Processed or Manufactured*
(Thousands of U.S. Dollars)

	Argentina	Brazil	Chile	Colombia	Ecuador	Mexico	Peru	Uruguay	Total LAFTA	Bolivia	Venezuela	TOTAL
ANIMAL												
3a. Leather												
3b. Canned												
3c. Dairy												
3d. Meal												
3e. Seafood												
3f. Other												
AGRICULTURAL												
3a. Food			24.0						24.0			24.0
3b. Tobacco	8.0							115.0	123.0			123.0
3c. Beverage		310.0							310.0			310.0
3d. Oils	770.0		138.0			8.0		104.0	1,020.0			1,020.0
3e. Textiles												
3f. Sugar												
3g. Other												
FORESTRY												
3a. Wood												
3b. Paper												
MINERAL												
3a. Metals												
3b. Machinery												
3c. Vehicles												
3d. Cement	2.0								2.0			2.0
3e. Chemicals												
3f. Glass												
MISCELLANEOUS MANUFACTURES	225.0	3.0						18.0	246.0			246.0
TOTAL PROCESSED	1,005.0	313.0	162.0			8.0		237.0	1,725.0			1,725.0
TOTAL EXPORTS	8,595.0	396.0	165.0			8.0		1,493.0	10,657.0			10,657.0

Table VII-8-1a. *Peru's Exports to LAFTA Countries, 1959—Raw Materials*
(Thousands of U.S. Dollars)

	Argentina	Brazil	Chile	Colombia	Ecuador	Mexico	Paraguay	Uruguay	Total LAFTA	Bolivia	Venezuela	TOTAL
ANIMAL												
1a. Live	2.4			0.1	21.8	2.2			26.5		2.2	28.7
1b. Fibers										8.5		8.5
1c. Fish												
1d. Other				4.8		0.9			5.7	70.5	0.9	77.1
AGRICULTURAL												
1a. Grains	5,070.8		10,911.4	909.7	117.4			595.6	17,604.9			17,604.9
1b. Fibers		6.2	127.5		12.8	0.2			146.7	2.4		149.1
1c. Fruits	0.2		24.4			2.6			27.2	0.1	0.9	28.2
1d. Seeds					0.1				0.1	4.3		4.4
1e. Other												
FORESTRY												
1a. Plants	1.8								1.8			1.8
MINERAL												
1a. Metals	991.3		26.3		13.3				1,030.9		36.6	1,067.5
1b. Oil	2,104.9	1,331.5							3,436.4			3,436.4
1c. Stone	648.9		10.5						659.4		1.8	661.2
1d. Non-metals					2.4				2.4			2.4
1e. Other			30.1		32.7				62.8			62.8
TOTAL RAW MATERIALS	8,820.3	1,337.7	11,130.2	914.6	200.5	5.9		595.6	23,004.8	85.8	42.4	23,133.0

Source: Ministerio de Hacienda y Comercio Superintendencia General de Aduanas, *Estadística del Comercio Exterior, 1959*, Lima, 1960.

219

Table VII-8-1b. *Peru's Exports to LAFTA Countries, 1959—Semi-Processed*
(Thousands of U.S. Dollars)

	Argentina	Brazil	Chile	Colombia	Ecuador	Mexico	Paraguay	Uruguay	Total LAFTA	Bolivia	Venezuela	TOTAL
ANIMAL												
2a. Hides												
2b. Fat												
2c. Meat												
2d. Pelts												
2e. Other											135.3	135.3
AGRICULTURAL												
2a. Flour												
2b. Grains												
2c. Sugar			11,087.1						11,087.1	277.8		11,364.9
2d. Fruits												
2e. Coffee												
2f. Other			0.4		0.4				0.8	8.2		9.0
FORESTRY												
2a. Lumber	0.7		0.4		0.1				0.5		2.0	2.5
2b. Extracts					0.4				1.1			1.1
MINERAL												
2a. Metals	58.1	18.6	427.6	20.9	17.7				720.9			720.9
2b. Oil		11.8	7,615.9	11.4	890.3			178.0	8,529.4	0.8	1.8	8,532.0
TOTAL SEMI-PROCESSED	58.8	30.4	19,131.4	32.3	908.9			178.0	20,339.8	286.8	139.1	20,765.7

220

Table VII-8-1c. *Peru's Exports to LAFTA Countries, 1959—Processed or Manufactured*
(Thousands of U.S. Dollars)

	Argentina	Brazil	Chile	Colombia	Ecuador	Mexico	Paraguay	Uruguay	Total LAFTA	Bolivia	Venezuela	TOTAL
ANIMAL												
3a. Leather												
3b. Canned												
3c. Dairy				2.6					2.6	9.2		11.8
3d. Meal												
3e. Seafood				0.3	9.5				9.8	69.7	30.0	109.5
3f. Other	13.2								13.2			13.2
AGRICULTURAL												
3a. Food			0.6		0.6				1.2	0.3		1.5
3b. Tobacco												
3c. Beverage			137.9		3.5				141.4	0.1	0.4	141.9
3d. Oils										0.1		0.1
3e. Textiles			0.5		40.6				41.1	25.7		66.8
3f. Sugar	3.2		376.6						379.8	2,609.1		2,988.9
3g. Other												
FORESTRY												
3a. Wood					0.3				0.3	0.1	2.0	2.4
3b. Paper	0.2		0.1	117.8	17.6	0.1		0.1	135.9	29.2	76.4	241.5
MINERAL												
3a. Metals					0.1				0.1	0.1		0.2
3b. Machinery					0.4				0.4	0.5		0.9
3c. Vehicles			31.5						31.5			31.5
3d. Cement			16.1		0.5				16.6	2.4		19.0
3e. Chemicals	41.1		4.8	59.4	92.3	589.2			786.8	69.8	48.2	904.8
3f. Glass												
MISCELLANEOUS MANUFACTURES	35.6	5.1	28.0	85.4	1,467.1	5.3	5.4	2.3	1,634.2	77.2	209.8	1,921.2
TOTAL PROCESSED	93.3	5.1	596.1	265.5	1,632.5	594.6	5.4	2.4	3,194.9	2,893.5	366.8	6,455.2
TOTAL EXPORTS	8,972.4	1,373.2	30,857.7	1,212.4	2,741.9	600.5	5.4	776.0	46,539.5	3,266.1	548.3	50,353.9

Table VII-8-2a. *Peru's Exports to LAFTA Countries, 1960—Raw Materials*
(Thousands of U.S. Dollars)

	Argentina	Brazil	Chile	Colombia	Ecuador	Mexico	Paraguay	Uruguay	Total LAFTA	Bolivia	Venezuela	TOTAL
ANIMAL												
1a. Live	0.9			0.1	10.7	2.2			14.3	2.0	1.9	18.2
1b. Fibers												
1c. Fish												
1d. Other			21.0	6.9		1.5			29.4	116.8		146.2
AGRICULTURAL												
1a. Grains	4,931.9		4,322.5	454.7	378.6			261.0	10,348.7			10,348.7
1b. Fibers	0.2		148.4		21.4	28.2			198.2	0.5		198.7
1c. Fruits		0.4	13.0		6.8	1.4			21.6	1.1		22.7
1d. Seeds												
1e. Other	3.2		0.2		0.8				4.2	1.3	4.1	9.6
FORESTRY												
1a. Plants												
MINERAL												
1a. Metals	708.5		10.8		14.8				734.1	7.3		741.4
1b. Oil	1,744.6	1,528.6	43.0						3,316.2			3,316.2
1c. Stone			0.4						0.4			0.4
1d. Non-metals			0.2		8.3				8.5			8.5
1e. Other			33.6		4.0				37.6			37.6
TOTAL RAW MATERIALS	7,389.3	1,529.0	4,593.5	461.7	445.4	33.3		261.0	14,713.2	129.0	6.0	14,848.2

Source: Ministerio de Hacienda y Comercio Superintendencia General de Aduanas, *Estadística del Comercio Exterior, 1960,* Lima, 1961.

222

Table VII-8-2b. *Peru's Exports to LAFTA Countries, 1960—Semi-Processed*
(Thousands of U.S. Dollars)

	Argentina	Brazil	Chile	Colombia	Ecuador	Mexico	Paraguay	Uruguay	Total LAFTA	Bolivia	Venezuela	TOTAL
ANIMAL												
2a. Hides											61.4	61.4
2b. Fat												
2c. Meat												
2d. Pelts												
2e. Other										0.2		0.2
AGRICULTURAL												
2a. Flour					30.6				30.6	66.4		97.0
2b. Grains			4,700.1		0.4				4,700.5	1,614.0		6,314.5
2c. Sugar										0.6		0.6
2d. Fruits												
2e. Coffee	23.0		1.8						24.8	1.6		26.4
2f. Other			1.9		17.9				19.8	6.9		26.7
FORESTRY												
2a. Lumber												
2b. Extracts	0.4				0.3				0.7			0.7
MINERAL												
2a. Metals		142.6	289.4	24.4	33.7			398.7	888.8			888.8
2b. Oil	3.0	267.5	6,536.0	21.4	596.2				7,424.1	548.2		7,972.3
TOTAL SEMI-PROCESSED	26.4	410.1	11,529.2	45.8	679.1			398.7	13,089.3	2,237.9	61.4	15,388.6

Table VII-8-2c. *Peru's Exports to LAFTA Countries, 1960—Processed or Manufactured*
(Thousands of U.S. Dollars)

	Argentina	Brazil	Chile	Colombia	Ecuador	Mexico	Paraguay	Uruguay	Total LAFTA	Bolivia	Venezuela	TOTAL
ANIMAL												
3a. Leather					0.4				0.4			0.4
3b. Canned					1.9				1.9			1.9
3c. Dairy		151.1		69.3		788.9			1,009.3	3.9	324.7	1,337.9
3d. Meal				0.5	25.8				26.3	98.6	28.7	153.6
3e. Seafood											12.8	12.8
3f. Other												
AGRICULTURAL												
3a. Food										1.1	1.5	2.6
3b. Tobacco			158.0		6.8			0.1	164.9	8.8		173.7
3c. Beverage												
3d. Oils					0.1				0.1	2.2		2.3
3e. Textiles			2.7		106.0				108.7	53.2		161.9
3f. Sugar			18.7				1.4		20.1	2.6		22.7
3g. Other			0.1		6.4				6.5	1.4		7.9
FORESTRY												
3a. Wood	0.2		0.5		0.1				0.6		0.6	1.2
3b. Paper			0.6	0.1	26.4	0.1			27.4	19.6	0.4	47.4
MINERAL												
3a. Metals		17.9	0.4						18.3	0.2		18.5
3b. Machinery					0.3				0.3	0.2		0.5
3c. Vehicles			50.8						50.8			50.8
3d. Cement			9.3		8.9				18.2	21.1		39.3
3e. Chemicals	58.9		20.7	2.1	87.6				169.2	56.8	0.3	226.3
3f. Glass										0.1		0.1
MISCELLANEOUS MANUFACTURES	1,900.0	14.8	86.7	32.5	1,558.0	3.4	4.4	13.3	3,613.1	206.0	81.7	3,900.8
TOTAL PROCESSED	1,959.0	183.8	348.5	104.5	1,828.7	792.4	5.8	13.4	5,236.3	475.8	450.7	6,163.0
TOTAL EXPORTS	9,374.7	2,122.9	16,471.2	612.0	2,953.2	825.7	5.8	673.1	33,038.8	2,842.7	518.1	36,399.6

Table VII-8-3a. *Peru's Exports to LAFTA Countries, 1961—Raw Materials*

(Thousands of U.S. Dollars)

	Argentina	Brazil	Chile	Colombia	Ecuador	Mexico	Paraguay	Uruguay	Total LAFTA	Bolivia	Venezuela	TOTAL
ANIMAL												
1a. Live	15.7		3.2		7.5	0.1			26.5	3.4	2.4	32.3
1b. Fibers												
1c. Fish												
1d. Other			23.9	7.1				1.4	40.8	88.2		129.0
AGRICULTURAL												
1a. Grains			0.3						0.3			0.3
1b. Fibers	4,465.2		10,227.9	524.2	261.7			1,249.8	16,728.8		212.3	16,941.1
1c. Fruits	0.1		161.8		17.2				179.1	0.6		179.7
1d. Seeds	0.3		2.6		3.2				6.1	11.2		17.3
1e. Other	7.1	81.7	0.2		16.6				105.6	2.1	0.2	107.9
FORESTRY												
1a. Plants												
MINERAL												
1a. Metals	826.2								826.2			826.2
1b. Oil	1,448.2	1,170.3	152.2						2,770.7			2,770.7
1c. Stone			28.9		3.6				32.5			32.5
1d. Non-metals			0.8		9.5				10.3			10.3
1e. Other			26.6						26.6			26.6
TOTAL RAW MATERIALS	6,762.8	1,252.0	10,628.4	531.3	319.3	8.5		1,251.2	20,753.5	105.5	214.9	21,073.9

Source: Ministerio de Hacienda y Comercio Superintendencia General de Aduanas, *Estadística del Comercio Exterior,* 1961, Lima, 1962.

Table VII-8-3b. *Peru's Exports to LAFTA Countries, 1961—Semi-Processed*
(Thousands of U.S. Dollars)

	Argentina	Brazil	Chile	Colombia	Ecuador	Mexico	Paraguay	Uruguay	Total LAFTA	Bolivia	Venezuela	TOTAL
ANIMAL												
2a. Hides				9.2					9.2		72.0	81.2
2b. Fat			103.8		1.1				104.9			104.9
2c. Meat												
2d. Pelts												
2e. Other												
AGRICULTURAL												
2a. Flour					54.6				54.6	24.9		79.5
2b. Grains										167.8		167.8
2c. Sugar												
2d. Fruits												
2e. Coffee	76.7		1.5					65.0	143.2	0.1		143.3
2f. Other			1.5		49.1				50.6	43.5		94.1
FORESTRY												
2a. Lumber			5.8						5.8	0.4		6.2
2b. Extracts					0.4				0.4			0.4
MINERAL												
2a. Metals	175.3	2,300.8	214.6	195.4	25.3			99.0	3,010.4			3,010.4
2b. Oil	29.8	41.9	2,751.4		13.0				2,836.1	154.3		2,990.4
TOTAL SEMI-PROCESSED	281.9	2,342.7	3,078.7	204.6	143.6			164.0	6,215.5	391.1	72.0	6,678.6

Table VII-8-3c. *Peru's Exports to LAFTA Countries, 1961—Processed or Manufactured*
(Thousands of U.S. Dollars)

	Argentina	Brazil	Chile	Colombia	Ecuador	Mexico	Paraguay	Uruguay	Total LAFTA	Bolivia	Venezuela	TOTAL
ANIMAL												
3a. Leather			0.5						0.5			0.5
3b. Canned												
3c. Dairy					0.1				0.1			0.1
3d. Meal		295.1		52.9		901.4			1,249.4	0.6	433.8	1,683.8
3e. Seafood	4.1		3.5		18.2				25.8	146.5	42.2	214.5
3f. Other										19.4	11.8	31.2
AGRICULTURAL												
3a. Food										0.1	2.4	2.5
3b. Tobacco										0.6		0.6
3c. Beverage			185.4		5.1				190.5	14.8		205.3
3d. Oils										18.8		18.8
3e. Textiles			41.8		65.8		0.1		107.7	79.7	0.1	187.5
3f. Sugar			19.4						19.4	4.7		24.1
3g. Other			0.6		13.9				14.5			14.5
FORESTRY												
3a. Wood			0.8		0.2				1.0	0.1	0.1	1.2
3b. Paper	22.4		3.6	1.1	7.3	1.3			35.7	25.0		60.8
MINERAL												
3a. Metals				136.9	0.2				137.1	0.2	0.1	137.3
3b. Machinery					0.7				0.7	2.8		3.5
3c. Vehicles												
3d. Cement	1.6		36.1						37.7	34.5		72.2
3e. Chemicals	73.6		238.1	2.5	87.2				401.4	53.6		455.0
3f. Glass												
MISCELLANEOUS MANUFACTURES	1,116.4	10.4	134.8	24.1	1,029.7	5.5	16.9	11.2	2,349.0	384.5	45.1	2,778.6
TOTAL PROCESSED	1,218.1	305.5	664.6	217.5	1,228.4	908.2	17.0	11.2	4,570.5	785.9	535.6	5,892.0
TOTAL EXPORTS	8,262.8	3,900.2	14,371.7	953.4	1,691.3	916.7	17.0	1,426.4	31,539.5	1,282.5	822.5	33,614.5

Table VII-8-4a. *Peru's Exports to LAFTA Countries, 1962–Raw Materials*

(Thousands of U.S. Dollars)

	Argentina	Brazil	Chile	Colombia	Ecuador	Mexico	Paraguay	Uruguay	Total LAFTA	Bolivia	Venezuela	TOTAL
ANIMAL												
1a. Live	15.2	0.1	4.3	5.2	2.4	0.1		1.8	29.1	39.0	0.8	68.9
1b. Fibers	11.9	4.1	38.0			4.5			58.5	173.4		231.9
1c. Fish												
1d. Other												
AGRICULTURAL												
1a. Grains	4,171.2	10.2	18,466.1	458.9	246.4	0.8		1,105.8	24,459.4	15.9	894.2	25,369.5
1b. Fibers			490.4		21.0			0.1	511.5	0.7		512.2
1c. Fruits	3.0	29.6			4.8				37.4			37.4
1d. Seeds												
1e. Other	2.0		0.6		1.3				3.9	31.2	1.9	37.0
FORESTRY												
1a. Plants												
MINERAL												
1a. Metals	2,140.2								2,140.2			2,140.2
1b. Oil	638.1	1,670.7	98.5						2,407.3			2,407.3
1c. Stone			14.8		26.1				40.9	11.3		52.2
1d. Non-metals												
1e. Other		43.0	1.5		5.7				50.2			50.2
TOTAL RAW MATERIALS	6,981.6	1,757.7	19,114.2	464.1	307.7	5.4		1,107.7	29,738.4	271.5	896.9	30,906.8

Source: Ministerio de Hacienda y Comercio Superintendencia General de Aduanas, *Estadística del Comercio Exterior, 1962,* Lima, 1963.

Table VII-8-4b. *Peru's Exports to LAFTA Countries, 1962—Semi-Processed*
(Thousands of U.S. Dollars)

	Argen-tina	Brazil	Chile	Colom-bia	Ecuador	Mexico	Para-guay	Uruguay	Total LAFTA	Bolivia	Vene-zuela	TOTAL
ANIMAL												
2a. Hides												
2b. Fat											57.2	57.2
2c. Meat										0.1		0.1
2d. Pelts										0.2		0.2
2e. Other												
AGRICULTURAL												
2a. Flour		0.1			64.4				64.5	204.1		268.6
2b. Grains												
2c. Sugar										83.9		83.9
2d. Fruits												
2e. Coffee			74.0					7.8	81.8		2.1	83.9
2f. Other		0.2	2.1		49.6				51.9	52.5		104.4
FORESTRY												
2a. Lumber			4.2						4.2			4.2
2b. Extracts			0.4	0.2					0.6			0.6
MINERAL												
2a. Metals	530.9	8,222.2	562.6		55.4			92.4	9,463.5			9,463.5
2b. Oil			2,608.0		18.9				2,626.9	3.0		2,629.9
TOTAL SEMI-PROCESSED	530.9	8,222.5	3,251.3	0.2	188.3			100.2	12,293.4	343.8	59.3	12,696.5

Table VII-8-4c. *Peru's Exports to LAFTA Countries, 1962–Processed or Manufactured*
(Thousands of U.S. Dollars)

	Argentina	Brazil	Chile	Colombia	Ecuador	Mexico	Paraguay	Uruguay	Total LAFTA	Bolivia	Venezuela	TOTAL
ANIMAL												
3a. Leather			2.0						2.0			2.0
3b. Canned			29.2		0.1				29.3	46.0		75.3
3c. Dairy	14.3	71.7	9.5	258.0		1,802.0			2,155.5	6.3	675.3	2,837.1
3d. Meal	1.7		11.2	12.5	42.9				68.3	132.1	45.2	245.6
3e. Seafood				254.3	0.1				254.4		7.6	262.0
3f. Other												
AGRICULTURAL												
3a. Food							0.4		0.4			0.4
3b. Tobacco		0.2	7.2		15.0				22.4	41.6	0.1	64.1
3c. Beverage					2.8				2.8	23.3		26.1
3d. Oils			6.0		19.4				25.4	59.5		84.9
3e. Textiles			0.2		0.5		1.1		1.8	14.1		15.9
3f. Sugar												
3g. Other	71.3	161.8	21.5		16.0				270.6	0.1		270.7
FORESTRY												
3a. Wood	0.3		29.7		0.2	0.2			30.4	1.0	0.1	31.5
3b. Paper	0.7		1.2	0.4	0.9	0.2			3.5	28.2	0.1	31.8
MINERAL												
3a. Metals	349.6	1,002.6	17.8		1.0				1,371.0	0.6		1,371.6
3b. Machinery					1.1				1.1	10.8		11.9
3c. Vehicles			364.6						364.6			364.6
3d. Cement			24.6		5.6				30.2	39.0		69.2
3e. Chemicals	58.1	29.6	470.2	5.1	57.3	0.8		260.6	881.7	83.6		965.3
3f. Glass												
MISCELLANEOUS MANUFACTURES	360.4	10.4	157.5	9.9	736.7	7.1	6.6	5.5	1,294.1	370.3	39.5	1,703.9
TOTAL PROCESSED	856.4	1,276.5	1,152.4	540.2	899.6	1,810.3	8.1	266.2	6,809.5	856.5	767.9	8,433.9
TOTAL EXPORTS	8,368.9	11,256.5	23,517.9	1,004.5	1,395.6	1,815.7	8.1	1,474.1	48,841.3	1,471.8	1,724.1	52,037.2

230

Table VII-8-5a. *Peru's Exports to LAFTA Countries, 1963—Raw Materials*

(Thousands of U.S. Dollars)

	Argentina	Brazil	Chile	Colombia	Ecuador	Mexico	Paraguay	Uruguay	Total LAFTA	Bolivia	Venezuela	TOTAL
ANIMAL												
1a. Live	11.6	0.1	9.7	0.4	15.6	0.3			37.7	40.6	1.9	80.2
1b. Fibers	6.5	3.2	59.1	4.5		1.5			74.8	170.3	2,378.8	2,623.9
1c. Fish												
1d. Other												
AGRICULTURAL												
1a. Grains	3,611.2		11,888.5	532.8	518.4			1,184.0	17,734.9			17,734.9
1b. Fibers			272.2		65.5				337.7	0.8		338.5
1c. Fruits	3.3		42.1		4.4				49.8	3.4		53.2
1d. Seeds										0.6		0.6
1e. Other												
FORESTRY												
1a. Plants	0.9								0.9			0.9
MINERAL												
1a. Metals	813.7	12.2	1.0	27.9					854.8			854.8
1b. Oil	1,648.0	1,586.8							3,234.8			3,234.8
1c. Stone			0.3		11.0				11.3	0.2		11.5
1d. Non-metals												
1e. Other												
TOTAL RAW MATERIALS	6,095.2	1,602.3	12,272.9	565.6	614.9	1.8		1,184.0	22,336.7	215.9	2,380.7	24,933.3

Source: Ministerio de Hacienda y Comercio Superintendencia General de Aduanas, *Estadística del Comercio Exterior, 1963,* Lima, 1964.

Table VII-8-5b. *Peru's Exports to LAFTA Countries, 1963—Semi-Processed*
(Thousands of U.S. Dollars)

	Argentina	Brazil	Chile	Colombia	Ecuador	Mexico	Paraguay	Uruguay	Total LAFTA	Bolivia	Venezuela	TOTAL
ANIMAL												
2a. Hides												
2b. Fat			0.6						0.6			0.6
2c. Meat	27.7								27.7	0.3		28.0
2d. Pelts			1.3						1.3			1.3
2e. Other												
AGRICULTURAL												
2a. Flour					74.1				74.1			74.1
2b. Grains					0.7				0.7			0.7
2c. Sugar			8,545.1					980.7	9,525.8			9,525.8
2d. Fruits												
2e. Coffee	8.3		62.0			25.4			95.7		6.4	102.1
2f. Other	30.5		0.6		15.7		0.1		46.9	28.2		75.1
FORESTRY												
2a. Lumber												
2b. Extracts				0.4				0.3	0.7			0.7
MINERAL												
2a. Metals	25.0	7,611.4	517.6	8.1				239.1	8,401.2	0.2		8,401.4
2b. Oil	17.6	50.6	1,813.2		5.9				1,887.3	1.0		1,888.3
TOTAL SEMI-PROCESSED	109.1	7,662.0	10,940.4	8.5	96.4	25.4	0.1	1,220.1	20,062.0	29.7	6.4	20,098.1

Table VII-8-5c. *Peru's Exports to LAFTA Countries, 1963—Processed or Manufactured*
(Thousands of U.S. Dollars)

	Argentina	Brazil	Chile	Colombia	Ecuador	Mexico	Paraguay	Uruguay	Total LAFTA	Bolivia	Venezuela	TOTAL
ANIMAL												
3a. Leather												
3b. Canned												
3c. Dairy			8.6		0.3				8.9	31.2		40.1
3d. Meat		191.2		259.5		2,323.5			2,774.2	40.3	626.5	3,441.0
3e. Seafood		6.5	3.6		22.6	40.0		61.6	134.3	79.0		213.3
3f. Other				822.2	11.2				833.4			833.4
AGRICULTURAL												
3a. Food					16.3				16.3	0.4		16.7
3b. Tobacco											1.1	1.1
3c. Beverage					19.0				19.0	6.4		25.4
3d. Oils			97.3						97.3	2.9		100.2
3e. Textiles	34.0	62.5	77.8	27.6	6.0	23.3			231.2	16.4		247.6
3f. Sugar										327.6		327.6
3g. Other					0.5				0.5	0.9		1.4
FORESTRY												
3a. Wood	0.1		0.5	0.1	30.9				31.6		0.1	31.7
3b. Paper	0.1		0.1	0.1	0.6	0.3		0.1	1.3	23.9	0.1	25.3
MINERAL												
3a. Metals	13.9	387.9	0.8		1.2				403.8	2.7		406.5
3b. Machinery			295.9		1.0				296.9	2.6	9.2	308.7
3c. Vehicles			564.5						564.5	3.5		568.0
3d. Cement			9.0		3.9				12.9	46.3		59.2
3e. Chemicals	91.0	113.1	211.7	44.8	75.0				535.6	41.6		577.2
3f. Glass												
MISCELLANEOUS MANUFACTURES	19.4	11.7	181.6	22.9	542.9	53.9	6.4	5.8	844.6	637.1	44.4	1,526.1
TOTAL PROCESSED	158.5	772.9	1,451.4	1,177.2	731.4	2,441.0	6.4	67.5	6,806.3	1,262.8	681.4	8,750.5
TOTAL EXPORTS	6,362.8	10,037.2	24,664.7	1,751.3	1,442.7	2,468.2	6.5	2,471.6	49,205.0	1,508.4	3,068.5	53,781.9

Table VII-9-1a. *Uruguay's Exports to LAFTA Countries, 1959—Raw Materials*
(Thousands of U.S. Dollars)

	Argentina	Brazil	Chile	Colombia	Ecuador	Mexico	Paraguay	Peru	Total LAFTA	Bolivia	Venezuela	TOTAL
ANIMAL												
1a. Live	41.8	293.8					2.6		338.2		10.2	348.4
1b. Fibers				237.5	100.3		9.5		347.3	64.5	8.6	420.4
1c. Fish												
1d. Other												
AGRICULTURAL												
1a. Grains		1,072.0					29.6	546.0	1,647.6		26.1	1,673.7
1b. Fibers												
1c. Fruits							1.5					
1d. Seeds		4.8							6.3			6.3
1e. Other		3.0							3.0			3.0
FORESTRY												
1a. Plants												
MINERAL												
1a. Metals												
1b. Oil												
1c. Stone	17.3								17.3			17.3
1d. Non-metals												
1e. Other												
TOTAL RAW MATERIALS	59.1	1,373.6		237.5	100.3		43.2	546.0	2,359.7	64.5	44.9	2,469.1

Source: Banco Comercial, *Información Económica del Uruguay*, June, 1960.

234

Table VII-9-1b. *Uruguay's Exports to LAFTA Countries, 1959—Semi-Processed*
(Thousands of U.S. Dollars)

	Argentina	Brazil	Chile	Colombia	Ecuador	Mexico	Paraguay	Peru	Total LAFTA	Bolivia	Venezuela	TOTAL
ANIMAL												
2a. Hides	15.2								15.2		156.2	171.4
2b. Fat												
2c. Meat												
2d. Pelts												
2e. Other												
AGRICULTURAL												
2a. Flour												
2b. Grains												
2c. Sugar												
2d. Fruits												
2e. Coffee												
2f. Other												
FORESTRY												
2a. Lumber												
2b. Extracts												
MINERAL												
2a. Metals												
2b. Oil												
TOTAL SEMI-PROCESSED	15.2								15.2		156.2	171.4

Table VII-9-1c. *Uruguay's Exports to LAFTA Countries, 1959—Processed or Manufactured*
(Thousands of U.S. Dollars)

	Argentina	Brazil	Chile	Colombia	Ecuador	Mexico	Paraguay	Peru	Total LAFTA	Bolivia	Venezuela	TOTAL
ANIMAL												
3a. Leather												
3b. Canned												
3c. Dairy												
3d. Meal												
3e. Seafood												
3f. Other												
AGRICULTURAL												
3a. Food							0.7		0.7			0.7
3b. Tobacco						19.3			19.3		4.0	23.3
3c. Beverage												
3d. Oils							2.4		2.4			2.4
3e. Textiles												
3f. Sugar							0.6		0.6			0.6
3g. Other												
FORESTRY												
3a. Wood	0.1								0.3			0.3
3b. Paper						0.2						
MINERAL												
3a. Metals	33.5								33.5			33.5
3b. Machinery			0.1						0.1			0.1
3c. Vehicles												
3d. Cement												
3e. Chemicals								1.0	1.0			1.0
3f. Glass		4.0					21.7		25.7			25.7
MISCELLANEOUS MANUFACTURES	249.6		0.1	0.1		0.2	9.6	0.4	260.0		0.2	260.2
TOTAL PROCESSED	283.2	4.0	0.2	0.1		19.7	35.0	1.4	343.6		4.2	347.8
TOTAL EXPORTS	357.5	1,377.6	0.2	237.6	100.3	19.7	78.2	547.4	2,718.5	64.5	205.3	2,988.3

Table VII-9-2a. *Uruguay's Exports to LAFTA Countries, 1960—Raw Materials*

(Thousands of U.S. Dollars)

	Argentina	Brazil	Chile	Colombia	Ecuador	Mexico	Paraguay	Peru	Total LAFTA	Bolivia	Venezuela	TOTAL
ANIMAL												
1a. Live	146.8	287.2	1.2				32.5	47.1	514.8		11.8	526.6
1b. Fibers			249.1	136.8	122.5		13.2		521.6	180.3	3.7	705.6
1c. Fish												
1d. Other												
AGRICULTURAL												
1a. Grains	0.4						0.5		0.9			0.9
1b. Fibers												
1c. Fruits												
1d. Seeds		10.0							10.0		1.2	11.2
1e. Other												
FORESTRY												
1a. Plants												
MINERAL												
1a. Metals												
1b. Oil												
1c. Stone												
1d. Non-metals	148.7								148.7			148.7
1e. Other												
TOTAL RAW MATERIALS	295.9	297.2	250.3	136.8	122.5		46.2	47.1	1,196.0	180.3	16.7	1,393.0

Source: Banco Comercial, *Información Económica del Uruguay*, April, 1961.

Table VII-9-2b. *Uruguay's Exports to LAFTA Countries, 1960—Semi-Processed*

(Thousands of U.S. Dollars)

	Argen-tina	Brazil	Chile	Colom-bia	Ecuador	Mexico	Para-guay	Peru	Total LAFTA	Bolivia	Vene-zuela	TOTAL
ANIMAL												
2a. Hides								3.7	3.7			3.7
2b. Fat												
2c. Meat												
2d. Pelts												
2e. Other												
AGRICULTURAL												
2a. Flour												
2b. Grains												
2c. Sugar												
2d. Fruits												
2e. Coffee												
2f. Other												
FORESTRY												
2a. Lumber	6.4								6.4			6.4
2b. Extracts												
MINERAL												
2a. Metals												
2b. Oil												
TOTAL SEMI-PROCESSED	6.4							3.7	10.1			10.1

Table VII-9-2c. *Uruguay's Exports to LAFTA Countries, 1960—Processed or Manufactured*
(Thousands of U.S. Dollars)

	Argentina	Brazil	Chile	Colombia	Ecuador	Mexico	Paraguay	Peru	Total LAFTA	Bolivia	Venezuela	TOTAL
ANIMAL												
3a. Leather			0.2						0.2		10.7	10.9
3b. Canned		0.1						25.3	25.4		1.1	26.5
3c. Dairy												
3d. Meal												
3e. Seafood												
3f. Other												
AGRICULTURAL												
3a. Food							2.7		2.7			2.7
3b. Tobacco												
3c. Beverage												
3d. Oils												
3e. Textiles					3.7		5.8		9.5			9.5
3f. Sugar												
3g. Other							0.9		0.9			0.9
FORESTRY												
3a. Wood												
3b. Paper	152.4								152.4			152.4
MINERAL												
3a. Metals	53.1								53.1			53.1
3b. Machinery	9.1	0.1				2.6			11.8			11.8
3c. Vehicles												
3d. Cement	0.7						9.7		10.4			10.4
3e. Chemicals							1.1	0.1	1.2			1.2
3f. Glass		10.0					25.5		35.5			35.5
MISCELLANEOUS MANUFACTURES	1,851.0		5.5	0.3		7.5	46.8	9.3	1,920.4	0.7		1,921.1
TOTAL PROCESSED	2,066.3	10.2	5.7	0.3	3.7	10.1	92.5	34.7	2,223.5	0.7	11.8	2,236.0
TOTAL EXPORTS	2,368.6	307.4	256.0	137.1	126.2	10.1	138.7	85.5	3,429.6	181.0	28.5	3,639.1

Table VII-9-3a. *Uruguay's Exports to LAFTA Countries, 1961—Raw Materials*
(Thousands of U.S. Dollars)

	Argentina	Brazil	Chile	Colombia	Ecuador	Mexico	Paraguay	Peru	Total LAFTA	Bolivia	Venezuela	TOTAL
ANIMAL												
1a. Live	114.5	507.2					34.6	14.5	670.8		12.3	683.1
1b. Fibers			727.1	537.5	145.6	19.5	76.5	111.7	1,617.9	191.0	0.4	1,809.3
1c. Fish	42.2								42.2			42.2
1d. Other												
AGRICULTURAL												
1a. Grains	0.4	1,275.7	26.0						1,302.1			1,302.1
1b. Fibers												
1c. Fruits	1.5								1.5			1.5
1d. Seeds												
1e. Other												
FORESTRY												
1a. Plants												
MINERAL												
1a. Metals												
1b. Oil												
1c. Stone	324.7								324.7			324.7
1d. Non-metals												
1e. Other												
TOTAL RAW MATERIALS	483.3	1,782.9	753.1	537.5	145.6	19.5	111.1	126.2	3,959.2	191.0	12.7	4,162.9

<u>Source:</u> Banco Comercial, <u>Información Económica del Uruguay</u>, August, 1962.

240

Table VII-9-3b. *Uruguay's Exports to LAFTA Countries, 1961—Semi-Processed*
(Thousands of U.S. Dollars)

	Argentina	Brazil	Chile	Colombia	Ecuador	Mexico	Paraguay	Peru	Total LAFTA	Bolivia	Venezuela	TOTAL
ANIMAL												
2a. Hides							0.1		0.1	0.3	10.6	11.0
2b. Fat												
2c. Meat		2.0						7.1	9.1			9.1
2d. Pelts												
2e. Other												
AGRICULTURAL												
2a. Flour												
2b. Grains												
2c. Sugar												
2d. Fruits												
2e. Coffee												
2f. Other												
FORESTRY												
2a. Lumber												
2b. Extracts												
MINERAL												
2a. Metals												
2b. Oil	32.1								32.1			32.1
TOTAL SEMI-PROCESSED	32.1	2.0					0.1	7.1	41.3	0.3	10.6	52.2

Table VII-9-3c. *Uruguay's Exports to LAFTA Countries, 1961—Processed or Manufactured*
(Thousands of U.S. Dollars)

	Argentina	Brazil	Chile	Colombia	Ecuador	Mexico	Paraguay	Peru	Total LAFTA	Bolivia	Venezuela	TOTAL
ANIMAL												
3a. Leather												
3b. Canned												
3c. Dairy												
3d. Meal												
3e. Seafood												
3f. Other												
AGRICULTURAL												
3a. Food							3.2		3.2			3.2
3b. Tobacco							113.0		113.0			113.0
3c. Beverage												
3d. Oils												
3e. Textiles												
3f. Sugar												
3g. Other												
FORESTRY												
3a. Wood												
3b. Paper	492.2	18.9							511.1			511.1
MINERAL												
3a. Metals							3.7		3.7			3.7
3b. Machinery	13.7	1.1	9.8			1.3	65.8	1.1	92.8			92.8
3c. Vehicles												
3d. Cement	87.7						53.7		141.4			141.4
3e. Chemicals	8.7		2.5				0.9		12.1			12.1
3f. Glass		36.9					50.5		87.4			87.4
MISCELLANEOUS MANUFACTURES	712.0		8.0	0.2	0.2	12.5	117.6	10.5	861.0	1.1		862.1
TOTAL PROCESSED	1,314.3	56.9	20.3	0.2	0.2	13.8	408.4	11.6	1,825.7	1.1		1,826.8
TOTAL EXPORTS	1,829.7	1,841.8	773.4	537.7	145.8	33.3	519.6	144.9	5,826.2	192.4	23.3	6,041.9

242

Table VII-9-4a. *Uruguay's Exports to LAFTA Countries, 1962—Raw Materials*
(Thousands of U.S. Dollars)

	Argentina	Brazil	Chile	Colombia	Ecuador	Mexico	Paraguay	Peru	Total LAFTA	Bolivia	Venezuela	TOTAL
ANIMAL												
1a. Live	29.5	1,640.4					16.0	26.2	1,712.1		10.1	1,722.2
1b. Fibers		857.8	779.7	1,976.1	119.7	4.6	40.8	15.8	3,794.5	159.2		3,953.7
1c. Fish												
1d. Other												
AGRICULTURAL												
1a. Grains			14.3						14.3			14.3
1b. Fibers	4.6								4.6			4.6
1c. Fruits	2.8	4.3							7.1			7.1
1d. Seeds												
1e. Other												
FORESTRY												
1a. Plants												
MINERAL												
1a. Metals												
1b. Oil												
1c. Stone	433.0	2.3							435.3			435.3
1d. Non-metals												
1e. Other												
TOTAL RAW MATERIALS	469.9	2,504.8	794.0	1,976.1	119.7	4.6	56.8	42.0	5,967.9	159.2	10.1	6,137.2

Source: Banco de la República Oriental del Uruguay, Departamento de Negocios con el Exterior, *Exportaciones Cumplidas, 1962*, Montevideo, 1963.

213

Table VII.9-4b. *Uruguay's Exports to LAFTA Countries, 1962—Semi-Processed*
(Thousands of U.S. Dollars)

	Argentina	Brazil	Chile	Colombia	Ecuador	Mexico	Paraguay	Peru	Total LAFTA	Bolivia	Venezuela	TOTAL
ANIMAL												
2a. Hides	6.2		9.2						15.4		17.0	32.4
2b. Fat								27.3	27.3			27.3
2c. Meat												
2d. Pelts												
2e. Other												
AGRICULTURAL												
2a. Flour												
2b. Grains		265.4							265.4			265.4
2c. Sugar												
2d. Fruits												
2e. Coffee												
2f. Other	5.3								5.3			5.3
FORESTRY												
2a. Lumber	0.3								0.3			0.3
2b. Extracts												
MINERAL												
2a. Metals	558.5								558.5			558.5
2b. Oil												
TOTAL SEMI-PROCESSED	570.3	265.4	9.2					27.3	872.2		17.0	889.2

244

Table VII-9-4c. *Uruguay's Exports to LAFTA Countries, 1962—Processed or Manufactured*
(Thousands of U.S. Dollars)

	Argentina	Brazil	Chile	Colombia	Ecuador	Mexico	Paraguay	Peru	Total LAFTA	Bolivia	Venezuela	TOTAL
ANIMAL												
3a. Leather												
3b. Canned												
3c. Dairy	25.1	0.2	1.7					1.9	28.9	12.1		41.0
3d. Meal												
3e. Seafood		4.7							4.7			4.7
3f. Other								1.5	1.5			1.5
AGRICULTURAL												
3a. Food												
3b. Tobacco												
3c. Beverage												
3d. Oils		6.5							6.5			6.5
3e. Textiles	42.9				12.0		15.5		70.4			70.4
3f. Sugar												
3g. Other												
FORESTRY												
3a. Wood												
3b. Paper	24.9								24.9			24.9
MINERAL												
3a. Metals							0.1		0.1			0.1
3b. Machinery	14.5	8.2	3.4	6.6		1.6	18.4	7.2	59.9			59.9
3c. Vehicles												
3d. Cement	12.6	32.1					10.7		55.4			55.4
3e. Chemicals	3.9		5.4				2.2	1.1	12.6			12.6
3f. Glass		172.6					47.4		220.0			220.0
MISCELLANEOUS MANUFACTURES	463.2	11.5	111.0		1.0	29.9	74.8	0.3	691.7	0.3	8.5	700.5
TOTAL PROCESSED	587.1	235.8	121.5	6.6	13.0	31.5	169.1	12.0	1,176.6	12.4	8.5	1,197.5
TOTAL EXPORTS	1,627.3	3,006.0	924.7	1,982.7	132.7	36.1	225.9	81.3	8,016.7	171.6	35.6	8,223.9

Table VII-9-5a. *Uruguay's Exports to LAFTA Countries, 1963 — Raw Materials*
(Thousands of U.S. Dollars)

	Argentina	Brazil	Chile	Colombia	Ecuador	Mexico	Paraguay	Peru	Total LAFTA	Bolivia	Venezuela	TOTAL
ANIMAL												
1a. Live	7.3	2,543.2			1.4		25.2	0.7	2,577.8		8.6	2,586.4
1b. Fibers	13.5	2,727.4	10.5	1,615.5		50.7	20.7		4,438.3	34.0		4,472.3
1c. Fish												
1d. Other	0.8								0.8			0.8
AGRICULTURAL												
1a. Grains		2,631.7	799.7				57.6	324.0	3,813.0			3,813.0
1b. Fibers												
1c. Fruits	8.0							0.1	8.1			8.1
1d. Seeds												
1e. Other	0.7	947.8			198.1				1,146.6			1,146.6
FORESTRY												
1a. Plants												
MINERAL												
1a. Metals												
1b. Oil												
1c. Stone	254.5								254.5			254.5
1d. Non-metals	130.2								130.2			130.2
1e. Other	0.2	17.5							17.7			17.7
TOTAL RAW MATERIALS	415.2	8,867.6	810.2	1,615.5	199.5	50.7	103.5	324.8	12,387.0	34.0	8.6	12,429.6

Source: Banco de la República Oriental del Uruguay, Departamento de Negocios con el Exterior, *Exportaciones Cumplidas, 1963,* Montevideo, 1964.

246

Table VII-9-5b. *Uruguay's Exports to LAFTA Countries, 1963—Semi-Processed*
(Thousands of U.S. Dollars)

	Argen-tina	Brazil	Chile	Colom-bia	Ecuador	Mexico	Para-guay	Peru	Total LAFTA	Bolivia	Vene-zuela	TOTAL
ANIMAL												
2a. Hides			156.0					24.9	180.9			180.9
2b. Fat	27.7							19.1	46.8			46.8
2c. Meat												
2d. Pelts												
2e. Other												
AGRICULTURAL												
2a. Flour							31.3		31.3			31.3
2b. Grains		277.2							277.2			277.2
2c. Sugar												
2d. Fruits												
2e. Coffee												
2f. Other		21.4							21.4			21.4
FORESTRY												
2a. Lumber												
2b. Extracts												
MINERAL												
2a. Metals							1.0		1.0			1.0
2b. Oil												
TOTAL SEMI-PROCESSED	27.7	298.6	156.0				32.3	44.0	558.6			558.6

Table VII-9-5c. Uruguay's Exports to LAFTA Countries, 1963—Processed or Manufactured
(Thousands of U.S. Dollars)

	Argentina	Brazil	Chile	Colombia	Ecuador	Mexico	Paraguay	Peru	Total LAFTA	Bolivia	Venezuela	TOTAL
ANIMAL												
3a. Leather	24.0	9.7	5.6			1.4			40.7			40.7
3b. Canned						19.2		36.5	55.7			55.7
3c. Dairy												
3d. Meal												
3e. Seafood		51.8							51.8			51.8
3f. Other								1.3	1.3			1.3
AGRICULTURAL												
3a. Food												
3b. Tobacco												
3c. Beverage					14.9		5.8		20.7			20.7
3d. Oils		247.9		37.8					285.7			285.7
3e. Textiles		27.7							27.7			27.7
3f. Sugar												
3g. Other								2.6	2.6			2.6
FORESTRY												
3a. Wood												
3b. Paper												
MINERAL												
3a. Metals	8.3	40.0	20.0			2.2	55.0	66.2	191.7			191.7
3b. Machinery												
3c. Vehicles												
3d. Cement		73.5					12.4		85.9			85.9
3e. Chemicals	1.8			2.6		3.8	0.2	40.3	48.7		1.9	50.6
3f. Glass		75.2					43.3		118.5			118.5
MISCELLANEOUS MANUFACTURES	436.1	1.9	479.3	1.6	22.4	11.4	120.8	46.9	1,120.4	39.7	6.6	1,166.7
TOTAL PROCESSED	470.2	527.7	504.9	42.0	37.3	38.0	237.5	193.8	2,051.4	39.7	8.5	2,099.6
TOTAL EXPORTS	913.1	9,693.9	1,471.1	1,657.5	236.8	88.7	373.3	562.6	14,997.0	73.7	17.1	15,087.8

Table VII-10-1a. *Bolivia's Exports to LAFTA Countries, 1959—Raw Materials*
(Thousands of U.S. Dollars)

	Argen- tina	Brazil	Chile	Colom- bia	Ecuador	Mexico	Para- guay	Peru	Uruguay	Total LAFTA	Vene- zuela	TOTAL
ANIMAL												
1a. Live		55.5	3.9					4.4		63.8		63.8
1b. Fibers												
1c. Fish												
1d. Other												
AGRICULTURAL												
1a. Grains			1.6							1.6		1.6
1b. Fibers												
1c. Fruits		79.1	8.2					0.1		87.4		87.4
1d. Seeds	3.0							42.6		45.6		45.6
1e. Other												
FORESTRY												
1a. Plants			1.2							1.2		1.2
MINERAL												
1a. Metals	1,048.2	383.0				425.1		30.2		1,886.5		1,886.5
1b. Oil	3,076.1		14.1							3,090.2		3,090.2
1c. Stone			0.1							0.1		0.1
1d. Non-metals	0.1									0.1		0.1
1e. Other	0.4									0.4		0.4
TOTAL RAW MATERIALS	4,127.8	517.6	29.1			425.1		77.3		5,176.9		5,176.9

Source: Dirección Nacional de Estadística y Censos, *Comercio Exterior*, La Paz, 1960.

Table VII-10-1b. *Bolivia's Exports to LAFTA Countries, 1959—Semi-Processed*

(Thousands of U.S. Dollars)

	Argentina	Brazil	Chile	Colombia	Ecuador	Mexico	Paraguay	Peru	Uruguay	Total LAFTA	Venezuela	TOTAL
ANIMAL												
2a. Hides	3.5		37.3					127.7		168.5		168.5
2b. Fat		6.2	7.8					38.6		52.6		52.6
2c. Meat												
2d. Pelts												
2e. Other	101.5	2.8	2.7					0.3		107.3		107.3
AGRICULTURAL												
2a. Flour												
2b. Grains												
2c. Sugar												
2d. Fruits			0.2							0.2		0.2
2e. Coffee	0.2		40.8				17.2	206.0		264.2		264.2
2f. Other	21.0		1.0					0.2		22.2		22.2
FORESTRY												
2a. Lumber	356.4	1.0	2.5						75.0	434.9		434.9
2b. Extracts		984.8						78.6		1,063.4		1,063.4
MINERAL												
2a. Metals												
2b. Oil			7.2				11.7			18.9		18.9
TOTAL SEMI-PROCESSED	482.6	994.8	99.5				28.9	451.4	75.0	2,132.2		2,132.2

Table VII-10-1c. *Bolivia's Exports to LAFTA Countries, 1959—Processed or Manufactured*
(Thousands of U.S. Dollars)

	Argentina	Brazil	Chile	Colombia	Ecuador	Mexico	Paraguay	Peru	Uruguay	Total LAFTA	Venezuela	TOTAL
ANIMAL												
3a. Leather												
3b. Canned												
3c. Dairy												
3d. Meal												
3e. Seafood												
3f. Other												
AGRICULTURAL												
3a. Food												
3b. Tobacco												
3c. Beverage			0.3							0.3		0.3
3d. Oils	3.1	3.7	1.9	0.5	0.1	0.5	0.1		2.6	12.6	0.4	13.0
3e. Textiles			1.4							1.4		1.4
3f. Sugar												
3g. Other												
FORESTRY												
3a. Wood			0.3							0.3		0.3
3b. Paper			0.2							0.2		0.2
MINERAL												
3a. Metals												
3b. Machinery												
3c. Vehicles												
3d. Cement			0.1							0.1		0.1
3e. Chemicals												
3f. Glass												
MISCELLANEOUS MANUFACTURES	0.1	0.3	15.5					17.7		33.6		33.6
TOTAL PROCESSED	3.2	4.0	19.7	0.5	0.1	0.5	0.1	17.8	2.6	48.5	0.4	48.9
TOTAL EXPORTS	4,613.6	1,516.4	148.3	0.5	0.1	425.6	29.0	546.5	77.6	7,357.6	0.4	7,358.0

Table VII-10-2a. *Bolivia's Exports to LAFTA Countries, 1960—Raw Materials*
(Thousands of U.S. Dollars)

	Argentina	Brazil	Chile	Colombia	Ecuador	Mexico	Paraguay	Peru	Uruguay	Total LAFTA	Venezuela	TOTAL
ANIMAL												
1a. Live	46.4		0.1					12.0		58.5		58.5
1b. Fibers			0.9							0.9		0.9
1c. Fish												
1d. Other												
AGRICULTURAL												
1a. Grains			2.4							2.4		2.4
1b. Fibers												
1c. Fruits		1.0	18.3					0.1		19.4		19.4
1d. Seeds		871.7	0.4					1.8		873.9		873.9
1e. Other												
FORESTRY												
1a. Plants		0.2								0.2		0.2
MINERAL												
1a. Metals	49.9	2,174.7	14.9			58.1				2,297.6		2,297.6
1b. Oil	3,320.2		24.5				4.8			3,349.5		3,349.5
1c. Stone			0.3							0.3		0.3
1d. Non-metals			48.6							48.6		48.6
1e. Other												
TOTAL RAW MATERIALS	3,370.1	3,094.0	110.4			58.1	4.8	13.9		6,651.3		6,651.3

Source: Dirección Nacional de Estadística y Censos, Comercio Exterior, La Paz, 1961.

252

Table VII-10-2b. *Bolivia's Exports to LAFTA Countries, 1960—Semi-Processed*
(Thousands of U.S. Dollars)

	Argen-tina	Brazil	Chile	Colom-bia	Ecuador	Mexico	Para-guay	Peru	Uruguay	Total LAFTA	Vene-zuela	TOTAL
ANIMAL												
2a. Hides	18.0		0.6					51.2		69.8		69.8
2b. Fat												
2c. Meat		6.5	1.6					1.7		9.8		9.8
2d. Pelts	80.9	1.1	25.3							107.3		107.3
2e. Other												
AGRICULTURAL												
2a. Flour			0.1							0.1		0.1
2b. Grains			0.3							0.3		0.3
2c. Sugar												
2d. Fruits		2.5	0.4							2.9		2.9
2e. Coffee	6.4		1.4					3.4		11.2		11.2
2f. Other	142.7		1.8							144.5		144.5
FORESTRY												
2a. Lumber	314.1	1.2	0.5							315.8		315.8
2b. Extracts	1.9	852.7	0.3					6.2		861.1		861.1
MINERAL												
2a. Metals							13.4			13.4		13.4
2b. Oil			119.8							119.8		119.8
TOTAL SEMI-PROCESSED	564.0	864.0	152.1				13.4	62.5		1,656.0		1,656.0

Table VII-10-2c. *Bolivia's Exports to LAFTA Countries, 1960—Processed or Manufactured*

(Thousands of U.S. Dollars)

	Argen-tina	Brazil	Chile	Colom-bia	Ecuador	Mexico	Para-guay	Peru	Uruguay	Total LAFTA	Vene-zuela	TOTAL
ANIMAL												
3a. Leather												
3b. Canned												
3c. Dairy			0.1							0.1		0.1
3d. Meal												
3e. Seafood												
3f. Other												
AGRICULTURAL												
3a. Food												
3b. Tobacco												
3c. Beverage			0.4							0.4		0.4
3d. Oils												
3e. Textiles	1.8	1.0	1.8	0.1	1.3	0.2		0.5	0.2	6.9	0.2	7.1
3f. Sugar			1.2							1.2		1.2
3g. Other												
FORESTRY												
3a. Wood			9.5					0.1		9.6		9.6
3b. Paper			0.2							0.2		0.2
MINERAL												
3a. Metals												
3b. Machinery												
3c. Vehicles												
3d. Cement												
3e. Chemicals		0.2	16.4					5.0		21.6		21.6
3f. Glass												
MISCELLANEOUS MANUFACTURES	0.1	0.7	7.7					0.3		8.8		8.8
TOTAL PROCESSED	1.9	1.9	37.3	0.1	1.3	0.2		5.9	0.2	48.8	0.2	49.0
TOTAL EXPORTS	3,936.0	3,959.9	299.8	0.1	1.3	58.3	18.2	82.3	0.2	8,356.1	0.2	8,356.3

Table VII-10-3a. *Bolivia's Exports to LAFTA Countries, 1961—Raw Materials*
(Thousands of U.S. Dollars)

	Argen-tina	Brazil	Chile	Colom-bia	Ecuador	Mexico	Para-guay	Peru	Uruguay	Total LAFTA	Vene-zuela	TOTAL
ANIMAL												
1a. Live	88.6									88.6		88.6
1b. Fibers			2.5					9.7		12.2		12.2
1c. Fish												
1d. Other												
AGRICULTURAL												
1a. Grains			2.4							2.4		2.4
1b. Fibers												
1c. Fruits	0.4							0.6		8.6		8.6
1d. Seeds	3.5	192.0	7.6					14.2		209.7		209.7
1e. Other												
FORESTRY												
1a. Plants												
MINERAL												
1a. Metals	114.8	1,279.6	30.1					6.1		1,400.5		1,400.5
1b. Oil	1,878.6									1,908.7		1,908.7
1c. Stone												
1d. Non-metals			154.0							154.0		154.0
1e. Other												
TOTAL RAW MATERIALS	1,997.3	1,560.2	196.6					30.6		3,784.7		3,784.7

Source: Dirección Nacional de Estadística y Censos, *Comercio Exterior*, La Paz, 1962.

255

Table VII-10-3b. *Bolivia's Exports to LAFTA Countries, 1961—Semi-Processed*
(Thousands of U.S. Dollars)

	Argentina	Brazil	Chile	Colombia	Ecuador	Mexico	Paraguay	Peru	Uruguay	Total LAFTA	Venezuela	TOTAL
ANIMAL												
2a. Hides	4.2	1.2						43.0		48.4		48.4
2b. Fat		0.9								0.9		0.9
2c. Meat								0.8		0.8		0.8
2d. Pelts	0.4	0.9								1.3		1.3
2e. Other												
AGRICULTURAL												
2a. Flour		0.7								0.7		0.7
2b. Grains												
2c. Sugar												
2d. Fruits			0.1					6.0		6.1		6.1
2e. Coffee	26.8		1.3					6.3		34.4		34.4
2f. Other	186.4		4.4							190.8		190.8
FORESTRY												
2a. Lumber	383.6		2.9					1.2		387.7		387.7
2b. Extracts	0.3	773.5						24.5		798.3		798.3
MINERAL												
2a. Metals												
2b. Oil			217.9				9.3			227.2		227.2
TOTAL SEMI-PROCESSED	601.7	777.2	226.6				9.3	81.8		1,696.6		1,696.6

Table VII-10-3c. *Bolivia's Exports to LAFTA Countries, 1961—Processed or Manufactured*

(Thousands of U.S. Dollars)

	Argentina	Brazil	Chile	Colombia	Ecuador	Mexico	Paraguay	Peru	Uruguay	Total LAFTA	Venezuela	TOTAL
ANIMAL												
3a. Leather												
3b. Canned												
3c. Dairy			0.1							0.1		0.1
3d. Meal												
3e. Seafood												
3f. Other												
AGRICULTURAL												
3a. Food												
3b. Tobacco												
3c. Beverage												
3d. Oils	4.0									4.0		4.0
3e. Textiles	1.3	2.0	2.1	0.2	0.2	0.3		0.6	0.5	7.2	0.2	7.4
3f. Sugar												
3g. Other			0.9							0.9		0.9
FORESTRY												
3a. Wood	0.5	0.3	1.1							1.9		1.9
3b. Paper												
MINERAL												
3a. Metals												
3b. Machinery												
3c. Vehicles												
3d. Cement								7.7		7.7		7.7
3e. Chemicals												
3f. Glass												
MISCELLANEOUS MANUFACTURES	6.7	3.2	20.5	0.2				1.6		32.2		32.2
TOTAL PROCESSED	12.5	5.5	24.7	0.4	0.2	0.3	9.3	9.9	0.5	54.0	0.2	54.2
TOTAL EXPORTS	2,611.5	2,342.9	447.9	0.4	0.2	0.3	9.3	122.3	0.5	5,535.3	0.2	5,535.5

257

Table VII-10-4a. *Bolivia's Exports to LAFTA Countries, 1962—Raw Materials*
(Thousands of U.S. Dollars)

	Argen-tina	Brazil	Chile	Colom-bia	Ecuador	Mexico	Para-guay	Peru	Uruguay	Total LAFTA	Vene-zuela	TOTAL
ANIMAL												
1a. Live		92.6								92.6		92.6
1b. Fibers			1.7							1.7		1.7
1c. Fish												
1d. Other												
AGRICULTURAL												
1a. Grains								1.0		1.0		1.0
1b. Fibers	2.1	0.8	2.2							5.1		5.1
1c. Fruits												
1d. Seeds		20.9	0.2							21.1		21.1
1e. Other			0.1							0.1		0.1
FORESTRY												
1a. Plants												
MINERAL												
1a. Metals	115.3		0.5					5.9		121.7		121.7
1b. Oil	1,282.1		1.8				5.8			1,289.7		1,289.7
1c. Stone			0.2							0.2		0.2
1d. Non-metals		12.4	169.5							181.9		181.9
1e. Other												
TOTAL RAW MATERIALS	1,399.5	126.7	176.2				5.8	6.9		1,715.1		1,715.1

Source: Dirección Nacional de Estadística y Censos, *Comercio Exterior*, La Paz, 1963.

Table VII-10-4b. *Bolivia's Exports to LAFTA Countries, 1962—Semi-Processed*
(Thousands of U.S. Dollars)

	Argentina	Brazil	Chile	Colombia	Ecuador	Mexico	Paraguay	Peru	Uruguay	Total LAFTA	Venezuela	TOTAL
ANIMAL												
2a. Hides	2.7	0.4						34.2		37.3		37.3
2b. Fat		25.0								25.0		25.0
2c. Meat												
2d. Pelts												
2e. Other												
AGRICULTURAL												
2a. Flour												
2b. Grains												
2c. Sugar												
2d. Fruits								8.1		8.1		8.1
2e. Coffee	7.4		56.2					18.6		82.2		82.2
2f. Other												
FORESTRY												
2a. Lumber	238.4	4.2						0.1		242.7		242.7
2b. Extracts	0.7	588.9						63.4		653.0		653.0
MINERAL												
2a. Metals	125.0		26.5				11.5			163.0		163.0
2b. Oil												
TOTAL SEMI-PROCESSED	374.2	618.5	82.7				11.5	124.4		1,211.3		1,211.3

Table VII-10-4c. *Bolivia's Exports to LAFTA Countries, 1962—Processed or Manufactured*

(Thousands of U.S. Dollars)

	Argentina	Brazil	Chile	Colombia	Ecuador	Mexico	Paraguay	Peru	Uruguay	Total LAFTA	Venezuela	TOTAL
ANIMAL												
3a. Leather												
3b. Canned												
3c. Dairy												
3d. Meal												
3e. Seafood	0.1									0.1		0.1
3f. Other												
AGRICULTURAL												
3a. Food												
3b. Tobacco												
3c. Beverage												
3d. Oils												
3e. Textiles	0.2									0.2		0.2
3f. Sugar												
3g. Other			0.1							0.1		0.1
FORESTRY												
3a. Wood		0.1								0.1		0.1
3b. Paper												
MINERAL												
3a. Metals												
3b. Machinery												
3c. Vehicles												
3d. Cement												
3e. Chemicals	105.1		0.2					3.0		108.3		108.3
3f. Glass												
MISCELLANEOUS **MANUFACTURES**	0.9	5.7	3.3	0.2			0.1	2.2		12.4	0.2	12.6
TOTAL PROCESSED	106.3	5.8	3.6	0.2			0.1	5.2		121.2	0.2	121.4
TOTAL EXPORTS	1,880.0	751.0	262.5	0.2			17.4	136.5		3,047.6	0.2	3,047.8

Table VII-11-1a. *Venezuela's Exports to LAFTA Countries, 1959—Raw Materials*

(Thousands of U.S. Dollars)

	Argentina	Brazil	Chile	Colombia	Ecuador	Mexico	Paraguay	Peru	Uruguay	Total LAFTA	Bolivia	TOTAL
ANIMAL												
1a. Live			50.0	1.5						51.5		51.5
1b. Fibers												
1c. Fish												
1d. Other												
AGRICULTURAL												
1a. Grains												
1b. Fibers	4.5									4.5		4.5
1c. Fruits												
1d. Seeds												
1e. Other												
FORESTRY												
1a. Plants												
MINERAL												
1a. Metals	0.6	0.1		180.6				0.1	2.1	183.5		183.5
1b. Oil	67,111.9	53,278.1	7,854.9	32.5	519.2	59.9			13,302.2	142,158.7		142,158.7
1c. Stone												
1d. Non-metals												
1e. Other	106.3	1,808.4								1,914.7		1,914.7
TOTAL RAW MATERIALS	67,223.3	55,086.6	7,904.9	214.6	519.2	59.9		0.1	13,304.3	144,312.9		144,312.9

Source: República de Venezuela, Ministerio de Fomento, Dirección General de Estadística y Censos Nacionales, <u>Boletín de Comercio Exterior</u>, December, 1959.

261

Table VII-11-1b. *Venezuela's Exports to LAFTA Countries, 1959—Semi-Processed*
(Thousands of U.S. Dollars)

	Argentina	Brazil	Chile	Colombia	Ecuador	Mexico	Paraguay	Peru	Uruguay	Total LAFTA	Bolivia	TOTAL
ANIMAL												
2a. Hides												
2b. Fat												
2c. Meat												
2d. Pelts												
2e. Other												
AGRICULTURAL												
2a. Flour												
2b. Grains												
2c. Sugar												
2d. Fruits												
2e. Coffee			7.7							7.7		7.7
2f. Other												
FORESTRY												
2a. Lumber												
2b. Extracts			0.2					16.9		18.7		18.7
MINERAL												
2a. Metals												
2b. Oil	18,125.1	29,755.1	382.0	305.5	2,208.7	176.7	61.4	239.4	1,172.2	52,426.1		52,426.1
TOTAL SEMI-PROCESSED	18,125.1	29,755.1	389.9	307.1	2,208.7	176.7	61.4	256.3	1,172.2	52,452.5		52,452.5

Table VII-11-1c. *Venezuela's Exports to LAFTA Countries, 1959—Processed or Manufactured*
(Thousands of U.S. Dollars)

	Argentina	Brazil	Chile	Colombia	Ecuador	Mexico	Paraguay	Peru	Uruguay	Total LAFTA	Bolivia	TOTAL
ANIMAL												
3a. Leather												
3b. Canned												
3c. Dairy												
3d. Meal												
3e. Seafood												
3f. Other				4.7						4.7		4.7
AGRICULTURAL												
3a. Food	3.0			0.1						3.1		3.1
3b. Tobacco												
3c. Beverage												
3d. Oils												
3e. Textiles				0.6				0.2		0.8		0.8
3f. Sugar												
3g. Other			0.6	0.2						0.8		0.8
FORESTRY												
3a. Wood	2.6			17.2		2.0		0.2		22.0		22.0
3b. Paper			0.2	0.2						0.4		0.4
MINERAL												
3a. Metals												
3b. Machinery												
3c. Vehicles	394.9	10.0	51.1	196.8	77.3	23.3		51.1	7.2	811.7	1.7	813.4
3d. Cement		128.9		659.4	6.8	15.0		18.6		828.7		828.7
3e. Chemicals	0.4		0.1			2.8		0.8		4.1		4.1
3f. Glass		39.8		1.1						40.9		40.9
MISCELLANEOUS MANUFACTURES	394.9	6.1	5.9	1,844.0	1,138.8	165.6		25.0	3.5	3,583.8	1.8	3,585.6
TOTAL PROCESSED	795.8	184.8	57.9	2,724.3	1,222.9	208.7		95.9	10.7	5,301.0	3.5	5,304.5
TOTAL EXPORTS	86,144.2	85,026.5	8,352.7	3,246.0	3,950.8	445.3	61.4	352.3	14,487.2	202,066.4	3.5	202,069.9

263

Table VII-11-2a. *Venezuela's Exports to LAFTA Countries, 1960—Raw Materials*
(Thousands of U.S. Dollars)

	Argentina	Brazil	Chile	Colombia	Ecuador	Mexico	Paraguay	Peru	Uruguay	Total LAFTA	Bolivia	TOTAL
ANIMAL												
1a. Live												
1b. Fibers												
1c. Fish												
1d. Other												
AGRICULTURAL												
1a. Grains				1.0						1.0		1.0
1b. Fibers												
1c. Fruits				1.4	0.1					1.5		1.5
1d. Seeds												
1e. Other												
FORESTRY												
1a. Plants	0.4									0.4		0.4
MINERAL												
1a. Metals	42.0	33.4	3.1	175.2	3.1	22.2		158.2		437.2		437.2
1b. Oil	48,112.6	45,979.4	8,597.2		2,997.2				21,745.0	127,431.4		127,431.4
1c. Stone				0.1						0.1		0.1
1d. Non-metals												
1e. Other	331.4	2,871.0								3,202.4		3,202.4
TOTAL RAW MATERIALS	48,486.4	48,883.8	8,600.3	177.7	3,000.4	22.2		158.2	21,745.0	131,074.0		131,074.0

Source: República de Venezuela, Ministerio de Fomento, Dirección General de Estadística y Censos Nacionales, Boletín de Comercio Exterior, December, 1960.

Table VII-11-2b. *Venezuela's Exports to LAFTA Countries, 1960—Semi-Processed*
(Thousands of U.S. Dollars)

	Argentina	Brazil	Chile	Colombia	Ecuador	Mexico	Paraguay	Peru	Uruguay	Total LAFTA	Bolivia	TOTAL
ANIMAL												
2a. Hides												
2b. Fat				1.6						1.6		1.6
2c. Meat												
2d. Pelts												
2e. Other												
AGRICULTURAL												
2a. Flour				7.1						7.1		7.1
2b. Grains												
2c. Sugar												
2d. Fruits												
2e. Coffee												
2f. Other												
FORESTRY												
2a. Lumber												
2b. Extracts												
MINERAL												
2a. Metals												
2b. Oil	18,779.4	34,861.2	347.4	391.5			3,482.1	1,330.9	1,331.1	60,523.6		60,523.6
TOTAL SEMI-PROCESSED	18,779.4	34,861.2	347.4	400.2			3,482.1	1,330.9	1,331.1	60,532.3		60,532.3

265

Table VII-11-2c. *Venezuela's Exports to LAFTA Countries, 1960—Manufactured or Processed*
(Thousands of U.S. Dollars)

	Argentina	Brazil	Chile	Colombia	Ecuador	Mexico	Paraguay	Peru	Uruguay	Total LAFTA	Bolivia	TOTAL
ANIMAL												
3a. Leather								0.4		0.4		0.4
3b. Canned												
3c. Dairy	1.8			0.2						2.1		2.1
3d. Meal												
3e. Seafood				18.0						18.0		18.0
3f. Other	0.2							0.1		0.3		0.3
AGRICULTURAL												
3a. Food				8.8			0.2	0.1		9.1		9.1
3b. Tobacco												
3c. Beverage												
3d. Oils												
3e. Textiles								0.2		0.2		0.2
3f. Sugar		0.1								0.1		0.1
3g. Other				2.0						2.0		2.0
FORESTRY												
3a. Wood	1.6		0.2		0.1			20.2		22.1		22.1
3b. Paper								0.1		0.1		0.1
MINERAL												
3a. Metals												
3b. Machinery												
3c. Vehicles	298.3	244.1	58.4	80.6	23.9	21.8		51.6	3.0	781.7	1.4	783.1
3d. Cement		78.9		277.7	12.3	3.4		93.7		466.0		466.0
3e. Chemicals			0.1	8.0	0.1	2.9		9.3		20.4		20.4
3f. Glass				1.9						1.9		1.9
MISCELLANEOUS MANUFACTURES	584.5	632.1	399.3	761.0	30.5	143.0	0.1	189.1	0.1	2,739.7	3.2	2,742.9
TOTAL PROCESSED	886.4	955.2	458.0	1,158.2	66.9	171.2	0.3	364.8	3.1	4,064.1	4.6	4,068.7
TOTAL EXPORTS	68,152.2	84,700.2	9,405.7	1,736.1	3,067.3	193.4	3,482.4	1,853.9	23,079.2	195,670.4	4.6	195,675.0

Table VII-11-3a. *Venezuela's Exports to LAFTA Countries, 1961—Raw Materials*

(Thousands of U.S. Dollars)

	Argentina	Brazil	Chile	Colombia	Ecuador	Mexico	Paraguay	Peru	Uruguay	Total LAFTA	Bolivia	TOTAL
ANIMAL												
1a. Live												
1b. Fibers												
1c. Fish												
1d. Other								0.1		0.1		0.1
AGRICULTURAL												
1a. Grains				18.2						18.2		18.2
1b. Fibers												
1c. Fruits				0.7						0.7		0.7
1d. Seeds												
1e. Other												
FORESTRY												
1a. Plants												
MINERAL												
1a. Metals	1.0	14.6	6,458.7	0.4		4.5		29.3		6,508.5		6,508.5
1b. Oil	28,467.9	60,071.3		230.6	1,899.0			118.0	9,743.2	100,530.0		100,530.0
1c. Stone				1.5		2.0				3.5		3.5
1d. Non-metals												
1e. Other		303.0								303.0		303.0
TOTAL RAW MATERIALS	28,468.9	60,388.9	6,458.7	251.4	1,899.0	6.5		147.4	9,743.2	107,364.0		107,364.0

Source: República de Venezuela, Ministerio de Fomento, Dirección General de Estadística y Censos Nacionales, Boletín de Comercio Exterior, December, 1961.

267

Table VII-11-3b. *Venezuela's Exports to LAFTA Countries, 1961—Semi-Processed*
(Thousands of U.S. Dollars)

	Argentina	Brazil	Chile	Colombia	Ecuador	Mexico	Paraguay	Peru	Uruguay	Total LAFTA	Bolivia	TOTAL
ANIMAL												
2a. Hides												
2b. Fat												
2c. Meat				31.7						31.7		31.7
2d. Pelts												
2e. Other												
AGRICULTURAL												
2a. Flour				62.6						62.6		62.6
2b. Grains				2.8						2.8		2.8
2c. Sugar												
2d. Fruits												
2e. Coffee												
2f. Other												
FORESTRY												
2a. Lumber				0.1						0.1		0.1
2b. Extracts												
MINERAL												
2a. Metals								0.2		0.2		0.2
2b. Oil	23,287.4	21,596.7	288.1	1,207.6	530.8		621.3	1,346.6	1,255.1	50,133.6		50,133.6
TOTAL SEMI-PROCESSED	23,287.4	21,596.7	288.1	1,304.8	530.8		621.3	1,346.8	1,255.1	50,231.0		50,231.0

268

Table VII-11-3c. *Venezuela's Exports to LAFTA Countries, 1961—Manufactured or Processed*
(Thousands of U.S. Dollars)

	Argentina	Brazil	Chile	Colombia	Ecuador	Mexico	Paraguay	Peru	Uruguay	Total LAFTA	Bolivia	TOTAL
ANIMAL												
3a. Leather												
3b. Canned												
3c. Dairy												
3d. Meal												
3e. Seafood				25.1						25.1		25.1
3f. Other												
AGRICULTURAL												
3a. Food												
3b. Tobacco												
3c. Beverage						0.1				0.1		0.1
3d. Oils												
3e. Textiles				0.1						0.1		0.1
3f. Sugar												
3g. Other				2.0		0.1				2.1		2.1
FORESTRY												
3a. Wood				0.1				0.1		0.2		0.2
3b. Paper								0.1		0.1		0.1
MINERAL												
3a. Metals												
3b. Machinery	389.2	36.4	21.3	65.2	147.9	29.8	3.9	35.1		728.8		728.8
3c. Vehicles		34.2		4.8	4.1			198.8	18.4	260.3		260.3
3d. Cement												
3e. Chemicals		5.3	0.1	0.4		0.4			0.1	6.3		6.3
3f. Glass				0.5						0.5		0.5
MISCELLANEOUS MANUFACTURES	926.6	1.7	27.6	905.5	127.9	25.2		52.5	6.3	2,073.3	0.9	2,074.2
TOTAL PROCESSED	1,315.8	77.6	49.0	1,003.7	279.9	55.6	3.9	286.6	24.8	3,096.9	0.9	3,097.8
TOTAL EXPORTS	53,072.1	82,063.2	6,795.8	2,559.9	2,709.7	62.1	625.2	1,780.8	11,023.1	160,691.9	0.9	160,692.8

Table VII-II-4a. *Venezuela's Exports to LAFTA Countries, 1962—Raw Materials*
(Thousands of U.S. Dollars)

	Argen-tina	Brazil	Chile	Colom-bia	Ecuador	Mexico	Para-guay	Peru	Uruguay	Total LAFTA	Bolivia	TOTAL
ANIMAL												
1a. Live												
1b. Fibers												
1c. Fish												
1d. Other						0.1				0.1		0.1
AGRICULTURAL												
1a. Grains												
1b. Fibers												
1c. Fruits												
1d. Seeds				0.2						0.2		0.2
1e. Other												
FORESTRY												
1a. Plants												
MINERAL												
1a. Metals						57.3				57.3		57.3
1b. Oil	15,039.0	88,096.3	10,743.9		2,704.4			1,351.9	11,885.2	129,820.7		129,820.7
1c. Stone		12.6		3.2						15.8		15.8
1d. Non-metals		89.3								89.3		89.3
1e. Other												
TOTAL RAW MATERIALS	15,039.0	88,198.2	10,743.9	3.4	2,704.4	57.4		1,351.9	11,885.2	129,983.4		129,983.4

Source: República de Venezuela, Ministerio de Fomento, Dirección General de Estadística y Censos Nacionales, Boletín de Comercio Exterior, December, 1962.

270

Table VII-11-4b. *Venezuela's Exports to LAFTA Countries, 1962—Semi-Processed*
(Thousands of U.S. Dollars)

	Argentina	Brazil	Chile	Colombia	Ecuador	Mexico	Paraguay	Peru	Uruguay	Total LAFTA	Bolivia	TOTAL
ANIMAL												
2a. Hides												
2b. Fat				48.1						48.1		48.1
2c. Meat												
2d. Pelts												
2e. Other												
AGRICULTURAL												
2a. Flour												
2b. Grains												
2c. Sugar				2.3						2.3		2.3
2d. Fruits												
2e. Coffee												
2f. Other			0.1							0.1		0.1
FORESTRY												
2a. Lumber				5.0						5.0		5.0
2b. Extracts												
MINERAL												
2a. Metals												
2b. Oil	19,539.0	10,187.9	274.7	436.7	501.6		473.8	754.8	858.8	33,027.3		33,027.3
TOTAL SEMI-PROCESSED	19,539.0	10,187.9	274.8	492.1	501.6		473.8	754.8	858.8	33,082.8		33,082.8

Table VII-11-4c. *Venezuela's Exports to LAFTA Countries, 1962–Processed or Manufactured*
(Thousands of U.S. Dollars)

	Argentina	Brazil	Chile	Colombia	Ecuador	Mexico	Paraguay	Peru	Uruguay	Total LAFTA	Bolivia	TOTAL
ANIMAL												
3a. Leather												
3b. Canned												
3c. Dairy												
3d. Meal												
3e. Seafood												
3f. Other				66.3						66.3		66.3
AGRICULTURAL												
3a. Food												
3b. Tobacco												
3c. Beverage												
3d. Oils				3.1						3.1		3.1
3e. Textiles	0.1									0.1		0.1
3f. Sugar												
3g. Other												
FORESTRY												
3a. Wood	0.1									0.1		0.1
3b. Paper	3.0	0.2	0.1	0.1	0.2	0.1		0.1		3.8	0.1	3.9
MINERAL												
3a. Metals								441.2		441.2		441.2
3b. Machinery	69.5	9.0	9.6	86.7	12.8	7.1	16.8		7.8	219.3		219.3
3c. Vehicles		9.6	48.5	154.7				54.7		267.5		267.5
3d. Cement												
3e. Chemicals					0.6	2.5	1.0	0.7		4.8		4.8
3f. Glass												
MISCELLANEOUS MANUFACTURES	38.1	1.3	9.5	671.0	42.6	88.0	2.5	111.9	7.7	972.6	6.4	979.0
TOTAL PROCESSED	110.8	20.1	67.7	981.9	56.2	97.7	20.3	608.6	15.5	1,978.8	6.5	1,985.3
TOTAL EXPORTS	34,688.8	98,406.2	11,086.4	1,477.4	3,262.2	155.1	494.1	2,715.3	12,759.5	165,045.0	6.5	165,051.5

Table VII-11-5a. *Venezuela's Exports to LAFTA Countries, 1963—Raw Materials*

(Thousands of U.S. Dollars)

	Argentina	Brazil	Chile	Colombia	Ecuador	Mexico	Paraguay	Peru	Uruguay	Total LAFTA	Bolivia	TOTAL
ANIMAL												
1a. Live				4.8				0.1		4.9		4.9
1b. Fibers												
1c. Fish												
1d. Other												
AGRICULTURAL												
1a. Grains												
1b. Fibers												
1c. Fruits												
1d. Seeds												
1e. Other				1.5						1.5		1.5
FORESTRY												
1a. Plants												
MINERAL												
1a. Metals	4.5		38.0	30.3	0.4	6.7		190.2	6.6	276.7		276.7
1b. Oil	10,642.9	74,871.0	5,928.4		2,708.7	255.7		1,161.7	9,660.3	105,228.7		105,228.7
1c. Stone				1.2						1.2		1.2
1d. Non-metals								0.1		0.1		
1e. Other		114.9		5.1						120.0		120.0
TOTAL RAW MATERIALS	10,647.4	74,985.9	5,966.4	42.9	2,709.1	262.4		1,352.1	9,666.9	105,633.1		105,633.1

Source: República de Venezuela, Ministerio de Fomento, Dirección General de Estadística y Censos Nacionales, Boletín de Comercio Exterior, December, 1963.

273

Table VII-11-5b. *Venezuela's Exports to LAFTA Countries, 1963—Semi-Processed*
(Thousands of U.S. Dollars)

	Argentina	Brazil	Chile	Colombia	Ecuador	Mexico	Paraguay	Peru	Uruguay	Total LAFTA	Bolivia	TOTAL
ANIMAL												
2a. Hides												
2b. Fat				34.4						34.4		34.4
2c. Meat												
2d. Pelts												
2e. Other												
AGRICULTURAL												
2a. Flour												
2b. Grains								0.3		0.3		0.3
2c. Sugar												
2d. Fruits												
2e. Coffee				0.1						0.1		0.1
2f. Other												
FORESTRY												
2a. Lumber				2.1						2.1		2.1
2b. Extracts												
MINERAL												
2a. Metals	669.6			71.4			170.5	0.1		741.1		741.1
2b. Oil	4,057.9	10,039.1	277.8	561.0	13.2			2,633.2	478.4	18,231.1		18,231.1
TOTAL SEMI-PROCESSED	4,727.5	10,039.1	277.8	669.0	13.2		170.5	2,633.6	478.4	19,009.1		19,009.1

Table VII-11-5c. Venezuela's Exports to LAFTA Countries, 1963—Processed or Manufactured
(Thousands of U.S. Dollars)

	Argentina	Brazil	Chile	Colombia	Ecuador	Mexico	Paraguay	Peru	Uruguay	Total LAFTA	Bolivia	TOTAL
ANIMAL												
3a. Leather												
3b. Canned												
3c. Dairy												
3d. Meal												
3e. Seafood				22.9						22.9		22.9
3f. Other												
AGRICULTURAL												
3a. Food				0.9						0.9		0.9
3b. Tobacco												
3c. Beverage			0.1							0.1		0.1
3d. Oils												
3e. Textiles					15.3	1.8		3.8		20.9		20.9
3f. Sugar				0.8				2.1		2.9		2.9
3g. Other												
FORESTRY												
3a. Wood				0.2					2.4	2.6		2.6
3b. Paper	0.1					0.5		0.6		1.2	0.1	1.3
MINERAL												
3a. Metals			14.6							14.6		14.6
3b. Machinery	72.9	0.1		68.0	3.8	3.4		22.8		171.0		171.0
3c. Vehicles			0.4	10.1				150.5		161.0		161.0
3d. Cement			0.1	148.1	0.5			1.9		150.6		150.6
3e. Chemicals				0.1				0.1		0.2		0.2
3f. Glass												
MISCELLANEOUS MANUFACTURES	22.8		30.3	198.2	7.1	88.1		38.8	1.3	386.6	4.4	391.0
TOTAL PROCESSED	95.8	0.1	45.5	449.3	26.7	93.8		220.6	3.7	935.5	4.5	940.0
TOTAL EXPORTS	15,470.7	85,025.1	6,289.7	1,161.2	2,749.0	356.2	170.5	4,206.3	10,149.0	125,577.7	4.5	125,582.2

Summary Basic Tables

Table VIII-a. *LAFTA Countries' Share of Intra-LAFTA Exports, 1938-1963*

(Percent)

Country	1938	1948	1952	1954	1956	1958	1959	1960	1961	1962	1963
Argentina	45.2	35.1	21.3	35.4	31.4	31.8	42.5	47.9	33.6	40.0	43.3
Brazil	19.9	35.0	31.8	29.1	27.8	38.4	23.2	25.5	32.0	21.4	18.0
Chile	5.0	6.5	16.1	11.4	11.7	8.8	12.0	8.6	11.7	11.1	11.6
Colombia	0.2	0.5	0.7	0.7	0.9	0.8	0.9	1.4	2.0	2.1	1.6
Ecuador	2.8	2.0	1.8	2.4	2.0	2.0	2.4	1.5	2.3	1.7	1.8
Mexico	0.7	1.5	1.3	1.3	1.5	0.9	1.5	1.5	2.4	4.5	6.1
Paraguay	1.7	2.7	2.7	3.6	4.1	3.7	2.3	2.6	3.3	3.1	2.4
Peru	15.3	13.1	16.8	8.1	13.1	10.2	14.4	9.8	10.6	13.8	11.6
Uruguay	9.1	3.5	7.4	7.9	7.5	3.4	0.8	1.0	2.0	2.3	3.6
Total	100	100	100	100	100	100	100	100	100	100	100
Total intra-LAFTA exports (Millions of U.S. dollars)	89.7	422.1	394.2	495.5	358.3	372.9	323.7	339.1	297.3	353.8	424.6

Sources: Tables VI-1 to VI-11.

Table VIII-b. *LAFTA Countries' Share of Intra-LAFTA Imports, 1938-1963*

(Percent)

Country	1938	1948	1952	1954	1956	1958	1959	1960	1961	1962	1963
Argentina	26.0	37.7	39.2	33.8	34.5	43.8	30.5	28.5	35.5	24.6	19.2
Brazil	40.0	20.7	22.0	28.4	28.7	26.6	33.3	29.1	12.6	30.7	31.3
Chile	12.1	15.1	17.1	17.8	14.9	11.6	15.5	21.8	26.4	19.1	22.9
Colombia	0.8	5.5	3.3	2.9	3.6	1.8	2.6	1.8	2.9	3.1	4.1
Ecuador	0.3	0.7	0.7	0.7	1.1	0.5	0.7	0.7	0.4	1.0	1.0
Mexico	0.5	0.6	0.4	0.4	0.7	0.8	1.1	1.0	1.2	1.5	2.1
Paraguay	3.0	2.0	1.4	2.3	2.4	2.0	2.2	2.0	2.4	1.3	1.5
Peru	5.8	7.8	4.4	3.9	5.0	5.1	5.9	7.3	8.9	10.8	11.8
Uruguay	11.4	10.0	11.4	9.7	9.0	7.7	8.2	7.8	9.7	7.9	6.1
Total	100	100	100	100	100	100	100	100	100	100	100
Total intra-LAFTA imports (Millions of U.S. dollars)	102.2	497.1	396.2	539.2	407.9	400.6	351.3	373.6	354.8	419.0	524.5

Sources: Tables VI-1 to VI-11.

Table IX-1a. *Raw Materials as a Percentage of Exports of Argentina to LAFTA Countries, Bolivia and Venezuela, 1959-1963*

	Exports of Argentina				
Importing Country	1959	1960	1961	1962	1963
Argentina					
Brazil	92.7	90.4	76.8	86.3	73.5
Chile	54.6	71.0	56.1	66.5	46.1
Colombia	52.4	51.3	33.8	78.8	71.3
Ecuador	16.3	72.2	46.0	78.3	70.1
Mexico	13.5	9.0	5.6	6.5	10.4
Paraguay	63.1	62.9	57.7	44.6	40.7
Peru	48.5	80.0	67.1	83.1	83.5
Uruguay	72.4	47.1	27.3	39.4	16.6
Bolivia	23.2	10.3	21.4	57.7	37.9
Venezuela	32.7	37.2	45.4	57.0	26.7

Source: Table VII-1.

Note to Table IX: The sum of the percentages for raw materials, semi-processed, and processed goods corresponding to the same importing country and the same year for each exporting country equals 100 per cent.

278

Table IX-1b. *Semi-Processed Commodities as a Percentage of Exports of Argentina to LAFTA Countries, Bolivia and Venezuela, 1959-1963*

Importing Country	Exports of Argentina				
	1959	1960	1961	1962	1963
Argentina					
Brazil	5.8	6.3	14.4	8.2	10.7
Chile	33.8	18.5	22.0	27.5	27.4
Colombia	13.1	24.4	19.3	13.4	16.7
Ecuador	13.1	2.5	1.9	2.8	2.0
Mexico	42.7	38.2	41.1	30.1	11.2
Paraguay	2.4	4.8	3.3	9.1	13.2
Peru	33.6	9.3	23.6	13.2	11.1
Uruguay	23.2	11.6	8.7	11.2	45.9
Bolivia	52.1	16.0	39.4	23.8	24.9
Venezuela	12.2	5.8	7.3	5.4	8.7

Source: Table VII-1.

Table IX-1c. *Processed and Manufactured Commodities as a Percentage of Exports of Argentina to LAFTA Countries, Bolivia and Venezuela, 1959-1963*

Importing Country	Exports of Brazil				
	1959	1960	1961	1962	1963
Argentina	12.0	9.2	8.0	10.1	1.2
Brazil					
Chile	10.9	0.1	69.5	2.4	3.7
Colombia	3.5	--	2.5	--	9.6
Ecuador	--	--	0.5	--	--
Mexico	2.0	57.5	5.5	2.7	4.2
Paraguay	1.4	0.5	1.8	2.1	1.6
Peru	0.8	0.1	0.7	1.6	4.1
Uruguay	30.4	8.7	35.1	11.1	13.2
Bolivia	--	12.1	14.2	4.9	8.7
Venezuela	20.5	2.5	56.4	10.3	0.2

Source: Table VII-2.

280

Table IX-2a. *Raw Materials as a Percentage of Exports of Brazil to LAFTA Countries, Bolivia and Venezuela, 1959-1963*

Importing Country	Exports of Argentina				
	1959	1960	1961	1962	1963
Argentina					
Brazil	1.5	3.3	8.8	5.5	14.0
Chile	11.6	10.5	21.9	6.0	26.5
Colombia	34.6	24.3	46.9	7.8	12.0
Ecuador	70.6	25.3	52.1	18.9	27.9
Mexico	43.8	52.8	53.3	63.4	78.4
Paraguay	34.5	32.3	39.0	49.3	46.1
Peru	17.9	10.7	9.3	3.7	5.4
Uruguay	4.4	41.3	64.0	49.4	37.5
Bolivia	24.7	73.7	39.2	18.5	37.2
Venezuela	55.1	57.0	47.3	37.6	64.6

Source: Table VII-1.

Table IX-2b. *Semi-Processed Commodities as a Percentage of Exports of Brazil to LAFTA Countries, Bolivia and Venezuela, 1959-1963*

	Exports of Brazil				
Importing Country	1959	1960	1961	1962	1963
Argentina	84.9	84.2	81.8	76.7	82.6
Brazil					
Chile	73.7	93.3	20.0	83.7	79.4
Colombia	--	2.9	79.8	1.7	14.7
Ecuador	--	1.0	0.8	2.5	3.0
Mexico	1.3	2.2	1.0	4.0	46.2
Paraguay	45.0	40.7	4.5	18.5	2.0
Peru	12.2	39.3	73.3	80.2	54.1
Uruguay	67.1	76.8	47.2	72.7	55.9
Bolivia	--	7.0	4.9	4.9	5.8
Venezuela	28.4	52.5	14.8	5.5	0.2

Source: Table VII-2.

Table IX-2c. *Processed and Manufactured Commodities as a Percentage of Exports of Brazil to LAFTA Countries, Bolivia and Venezuela, 1959-1963*

Importing Country	Exports of Brazil				
	1959	1960	1961	1962	1963
Argentina	3.1	6.6	10.2	13.2	5.4
Brazil					
Chile	15.4	6.7	10.4	13.9	16.9
Colombia	96.5	97.1	17.7	98.3	75.7
Ecuador	99.9	99.0	98.6	97.5	97.0
Mexico	96.7	40.2	93.5	93.3	49.6
Paraguay	53.6	58.8	93.8	79.4	96.4
Peru	87.0	60.6	26.0	18.2	41.8
Uruguay	2.5	14.5	17.7	16.2	30.9
Bolivia	99.9	80.9	80.9	90.1	85.4
Venezuela	51.0	45.0	28.8	84.3	99.6

Source: Table VII-2.

283

Table IX-3a. *Raw Materials as a Percentage of Exports of Chile to LAFTA Countries, Bolivia and Venezuela, 1959-1963*

	Exports of Chile				
Importing Country	1959	1960	1961	1962	1963
Argentina	15.0	14.4	15.5	24.3	21.4
Brazil	42.6	31.7	52.0	13.7	9.6
Chile					
Colombia	35.7	41.2	32.4	3.1	23.7
Ecuador	12.9	43.9	23.2	33.7	22.2
Mexico	33.5	92.1	98.6	54.1	34.9
Paraguay	5.4	95.5	0.4	--	35.4
Peru	30.0	34.6	33.2	38.0	26.2
Uruguay	49.4	4.2	2.0	7.2	15.7
Bolivia	0.6	1.2	1.7	13.5	7.3
Venezuela	43.6	21.2	20.6	7.9	10.2

Source: Table VII-3.

284

Table IX-3b. *Semi-Processed Commodities as a Percentage of Exports of Chile to LAFTA Countries, Bolivia and Venezuela, 1959-1963*

Importing Country	Exports of Chile				
	1959	1960	1961	1962	1963
Argentina	33.5	64.4	13.5	32.2	39.9
Brazil	10.4	18.1	1.8	77.9	76.4
Chile					
Colombia	--	16.5	11.2	3.6	3.2
Ecuador	46.4	1.7	3.6	0.4	--
Mexico	0.1	0.1	0.3	0.3	0.9
Paraguay	--	--	--	--	--
Peru	23.6	26.3	11.5	5.3	6.0
Uruguay	--	18.3	1.6	1.1	11.5
Bolivia	6.2	2.9	7.4	2.3	15.0
Venezuela	0.7	27.4	38.2	--	--

Source: Table VII-3.

285

Table IX-3c. *Processed and Manufactured Commodities as a Percentage of Exports of Chile to LAFTA Countries, Bolivia and Venezuela, 1959-1963*

	Exports of Chile				
Importing Country	1959	1960	1961	1962	1963
Argentina	51.5	21.2	71.0	43.5	38.7
Brazil	47.0	50.2	46.2	8.4	14.0
Chile					
Colombia	64.3	42.3	56.4	93.3	73.1
Ecuador	40.7	54.4	73.2	65.9	77.8
Mexico	66.4	7.8	1.1	45.6	64.2
Paraguay	94.5	4.5	99.6	99.9	64.6
Peru	46.4	39.1	55.3	56.7	67.8
Uruguay	50.6	77.5	96.4	91.7	72.8
Bolivia	93.2	95.9	90.9	84.2	77.7
Venezuela	55.7	51.4	41.2	92.1	89.8

Source: Table VII-3.

286

Table IX-4a. *Raw Materials as a Percentage of Exports of Colombia to LAFTA Countries, Bolivia and Venezuela, 1959-1963*

	Exports of Colombia				
Importing Country	1959	1960	1961	1962	1963
Argentina	--	--	--	10.3	52.8
Brazil	--	--	0.2	--	--
Chile	--	--	79.0	6.1	36.2
Colombia					
Ecuador	--	0.2	57.4	23.4	34.9
Mexico	3.6	1.5	--	--	9.1
Paraguay	--	--	--	--	--
Peru	--	--	--	--	0.1
Uruguay	0.6	--	5.5	--	--
Bolivia	8.3	--	7.6	--	--
Venezuela	9.9	5.6	15.6	9.6	10.3

Source: Table VII-4.

Table IX-4b. *Semi-Processed Commodities as a Percentage of Exports of Colombia to LAFTA Countries, Bolivia and Venezuela, 1959-1963*

Importing Country	Exports of Colombia				
	1959	1960	1961	1962	1963
Argentina	93.6	73.1	86.1	87.4	40.3
Brazil	--	--	--	--	22.1
Chile	98.0	77.0	10.1	88.8	51.9
Colombia					
Ecuador	0.7	--	1.3	0.2	2.0
Mexico	34.6	57.2	71.2	51.0	17.9
Paraguay	--	--	--	--	--
Peru	91.2	97.5	80.4	85.9	55.0
Uruguay	88.1	--	9.1	--	0.1
Bolivia	18.8	--	--	23.1	0.7
Venezuela	4.0	1.2	0.7	0.8	0.5

Source: Table VII-4.

Table IX-4c. *Processed and Manufactured Commodities as a Percentage of Exports of Colombia to LAFTA Countries, Bolivia and Venezuela, 1959-1963*

Importing Country	Exports of Colombia				
	1959	1960	1961	1962	1963
Argentina	6.4	26.9	13.9	2.3	6.9
Brazil	99.9	99.9	99.8	99.9	77.9
Chile	2.0	23.0	10.9	5.1	11.9
Colombia					
Ecuador	99.3	99.8	41.3	76.4	63.1
Mexico	61.8	41.3	28.8	49.0	73.0
Paraguay	--	--	--	99.9	99.9
Peru	8.8	2.5	19.6	14.1	44.9
Uruguay	11.3	99.9	85.4	99.9	99.9
Bolivia	72.9	99.9	92.3	76.9	99.3
Venezuela	86.1	93.2	83.7	89.6	89.2

Source: Table VII-4.

289

Table IX-5a. *Raw Materials as a Percentage of Exports of Ecuador to LAFTA Countries, Bolivia and Venezuela, 1959-1963*

	Exports of Ecuador				
Importing Country	1959	1960	1961	1962	1963
Argentina	--	4.0	--	82.3	74.7
Brazil	--	--	3.0	--	23.0
Chile	94.8	96.5	94.3	99.1	85.0
Colombia	0.1	0.1	0.3	--	0.2
Ecuador					
Mexico	--	--	--	--	--
Paraguay	--	--	--	--	--
Peru	93.0	87.6	90.7	81.8	91.8
Uruguay	--	--	--	--	--
Bolivia	--	--	--	--	0.4
Venezuela	76.3	98.1	--	22.6	32.7

Source: Table VII-5.

290

Table IX-5b. *Semi-Processed Commodities as a Percentage of Exports of Ecuador to LAFTA Countries, Bolivia and Venezuela, 1959-1963*

Importing Country	Exports of Ecuador				
	1959	1960	1961	1962	1963
Argentina	99.6	67.4	62.7	16.3	23.9
Brazil	--	--	95.0	--	14.8
Chile	4.6	3.2	5.3	0.8	11.8
Colombia	84.3	56.3	74.9	71.7	79.3
Ecuador					
Mexico	--	--	--	--	--
Paraguay	--	--	--	--	--
Peru	0.2	1.2	4.9	16.8	1.6
Uruguay	84.1	87.5	--	--	90.0
Bolivia	--	38.5	--	--	--
Venezuela	20.6	--	95.4	--	0.3

Source: Table VII-5.

291

Table IX-5c. *Processed and Manufactured Commodities as a Percentage of Exports of Ecuador to LAFTA Countries, Bolivia and Venezuela, 1959-1963*

	Exports of Ecuador				
Importing Country	1959	1960	1961	1962	1963
Argentina	0.4	28.6	37.3	1.4	1.4
Brazil	--	99.9	2.0	99.9	62.2
Chile	0.5	0.3	0.3	0.1	3.2
Colombia	15.6	43.6	24.8	28.3	20.5
Ecuador					
Mexico	99.9	99.9	99.9	99.9	99.9
Paraguay	99.9	99.9	99.9	99.9	99.9
Peru	6.7	11.1	4.4	1.4	6.6
Uruguay	15.9	12.5	99.9	99.9	10.0
Bolivia	99.9	61.4	99.9	99.9	99.6
Venezuela	3.1	1.9	4.6	77.4	67.0

Source: Table VII-5.

292

Table IX-6a. *Raw Materials as a Percentage of Exports of Mexico to LAFTA Countries, Bolivia and Venezuela, 1959-1963*

Importing Country	Exports of Mexico				
	1959	1960	1961	1962	1963
Argentina	33.0	3.7	2.2	2.2	8.5
Brazil	65.6	44.3	5.7	8.3	38.3
Chile	82.3	41.5	0.2	23.7	28.9
Colombia	35.3	18.3	7.6	9.7	8.0
Ecuador	0.4	1.0	0.8	1.2	4.0
Mexico					
Paraguay	--	36.2	--	2.0	--
Peru	7.7	8.9	0.7	5.1	1.3
Uruguay	43.3	1.3	--	28.1	20.0
Bolivia	--	--	--	--	0.8
Venezuela	21.9	10.9	12.8	10.7	21.4

Source: Table VII-6.

Table IX-6b. *Semi-Processed Commodities as a Percentage of Exports of Mexico to LAFTA Countries, Bolivia and Venezuela, 1959-1963*

Importing Country	Exports of Mexico				
	1959	1960	1961	1962	1963
Argentina	5.3	41.3	35.0	17.5	25.6
Brazil	10.1	37.9	73.0	40.0	24.5
Chile	5.0	13.7	53.6	8.1	13.1
Colombia	3.8	5.5	21.5	15.0	20.4
Ecuador	--	--	0.3	--	0.1
Mexico					
Paraguay	--	--	14.9	--	--
Peru	1.3	5.8	1.1	2.6	1.4
Uruguay	--	24.5	44.8	15.2	10.6
Bolivia	--	--	3.9	--	--
Venezuela	1.2	3.3	10.0	22.4	7.6

Source: Table VII-6.

294

Table IX-6c. *Processed and Manufactured Commodities as a Percentage of Exports of Mexico to LAFTA Countries, Bolivia and Venezuela, 1959-1963*

Importing Country	Exports of Mexico				
	1959	1960	1961	1962	1963
Argentina	61.7	55.0	62.8	80.3	65.9
Brazil	24.3	17.7	21.2	51.7	37.2
Chile	12.6	44.8	46.2	68.1	58.0
Colombia	60.9	76.2	70.9	75.3	71.6
Ecuador	99.7	98.9	98.8	98.8	95.9
Mexico					
Paraguay	99.9	63.7	85.1	98.0	99.9
Peru	90.9	85.3	98.2	92.3	97.3
Uruguay	56.7	74.2	55.2	56.8	69.5
Bolivia	99.9	99.9	96.1	99.9	99.2
Venezuela	76.9	85.9	77.2	66.9	71.0

Source: Table VII-6.

295

Table IX-7a. *Raw Materials as a Percentage of Exports of Paraguay to LAFTA Countries, Bolivia and Venezuela, 1959-1963*

Importing Country	Exports of Paraguay				
	1959	1960	1961	1962	1963
Argentina	5.2	4.4	4.9	4.6	10.3
Brazil	12.6	46.0	6.4	6.5	--
Chile	--	--	--	8.2	--
Colombia	--	--	--	--	--
Ecuador	--	--	--	--	--
Mexico	--	--	--	--	--
Paraguay					
Peru	--	--	--	--	--
Uruguay	6.9	0.8	8.5	23.5	15.9
Bolivia	1.6	--	--	--	--
Venezuela	--	--	--	--	--

Source: Table VII-7.

296

Table IX-7b. *Semi-Processed Commodities as a Percentage of Exports of Paraguay to LAFTA Countries, Bolivia and Venezuela, 1959-1963*

Importing Country	Exports of Paraguay				
	1959	1960	1961	1962	1963
Argentina	85.3	90.0	88.5	88.5	78.0
Brazil	65.0	26.1	49.0	40.6	21.0
Chile	99.9	--	--	2.7	1.8
Colombia	--	--	--	--	--
Ecuador	--	--	--	--	--
Mexico	--	--	--	--	--
Paraguay					
Peru	--	--	--	--	--
Uruguay	65.7	74.9	57.4	54.1	56.4
Bolivia	93.1	99.9	99.9	--	--
Venezuela	--	--	--	--	--

Source: Table VII-7.

297

Table IX-7c. *Processed and Manufactured Commodities as a Percentage of Exports of Paraguay to LAFTA Countries, Bolivia and Venezuela, 1959-1963*

Importing Country	Exports of Paraguay				
	1959	1960	1961	1962	1963
Argentina	9.4	5.6	6.6	6.8	11.7
Brazil	22.4	27.9	44.6	53.0	79.0
Chile	--	--	--	89.0	98.2
Colombia	--	--	--	--	--
Ecuador	--	--	--	--	--
Mexico	--	--	--	99.9	99.9
Paraguay					
Peru	--	99.9	--	--	--
Uruguay	27.3	24.3	34.I	22.4	15.9
Bolivia	5.3	--	--	99.9	--
Venezuela	--	--	--	--	--

Source: Table VII-7.

298

Table IX-8a. *Raw Materials as a Percentage of Exports of Peru to LAFTA Countries, Bolivia and Venezuela, 1959-1963*

Importing Country	Exports of Peru				
	1959	1960	1961	1962	1963
Argentina	98.3	78.8	81.8	83.4	95.8
Brazil	97.0	72.0	32.1	15.6	16.0
Chile	36.1	27.9	74.0	81.3	49.8
Colombia	75.0	75.4	55.7	46.2	32.3
Ecuador	7.3	15.1	18.9	22.0	42.6
Mexico	1.0	4.0	0.9	0.3	0.1
Paraguay	--	--	--	--	--
Peru					
Uruguay	76.8	38.8	87.7	75.1	47.9
Bolivia	2.6	4.5	8.2	18.4	14.3
Venezuela	7.7	1.2	26.1	52.0	77.6

Source: Table VII-8.

Table IX-8b. *Semi-Processed Commodities as a Percentage of Exports of Peru to LAFTA Countries, Bolivia and Venezuela, 1959-1693*

Importing Country	Exports of Peru				
	1959	1960	1961	1962	1963
Argentina	0.7	0.3	3.4	6.3	1.7
Brazil	2.2	19.3	60.1	73.0	76.3
Chile	62.0	70.0	21.4	13.8	44.4
Colombia	2.7	7.5	21.5	--	0.5
Ecuador	33.1	23.0	8.5	13.5	6.7
Mexico	--	--	--	--	1.0
Paraguay	--	--	--	--	1.5
Peru					
Uruguay	22.9	59.2	11.5	6.8	49.4
Bolivia	8.8	78.7	30.5	23.4	2.0
Venezuela	25.4	11.9	8.8	3.4	0.2

Source: Table VII-8.

Table IX-8c. *Processed and Manufactured Commodities as a Percentage of Exports of Peru to LAFTA Countries, Bolivia and Venezuela, 1959-1963*

Importing Country	Exports of Peru				
	1959	1960	1961	1962	1963
Argentina	1.0	20.9	14.8	10.3	2.5
Brazil	0.1	8.7	7.8	11.4	7.7
Chile	1.9	2.1	4.6	4.9	5.8
Colombia	22.3	17.1	22.8	53.8	67.2
Ecuador	59.6	61.9	72.6	64.5	50.7
Mexico	99.0	96.0	99.1	99.7	98.9
Paraguay	99.9	99.9	99.9	99.9	98.5
Peru					
Uruguay	0.3	2.0	0.8	18.1	2.7
Bolivia	88.6	16.8	61.3	58.2	83.7
Venezuela	66.9	86.9	65.1	44.6	22.2

Source: Table VII-8.

301

Table IX-9a. *Raw Materials as a Percentage of Exports of Uruguay to LAFTA Countries, Bolivia and Venezuela, 1959-1963*

Importing Country	Exports of Uruguay				
	1959	1960	1961	1962	1963
Argentina	16.5	12.5	26.4	28.9	45.5
Brazil	99.7	96.7	96.8	83.3	91.5
Chile	--	97.8	97.4	85.9	55.1
Colombia	99.9	99.8	99.9	99.7	97.5
Ecuador	99.9	97.1	99.9	90.2	84.2
Mexico	--	--	58.6	12.7	57.2
Paraguay	55.2	33.3	21.4	25.2	27.7
Peru	99.7	55.1	87.1	51.7	57.7
Uruguay					
Bolivia	99.9	99.6	99.3	92.8	46.1
Venezuela	21.9	58.6	54.5	28.4	50.3

Source: Table VII-9.

Table IX-9b. *Semi-Processed Commodities as a Percentage of Exports of Uruguay to LAFTA Countries, Bolivia and Venezuela, 1959-1963*

Importing Country	Exports of Uruguay				
	1959	1960	1961	1962	1963
Argentina	4.3	0.3	1.8	35.0	3.0
Brazil	--	--	0.1	8.8	3.1
Chile	--	--	--	1.0	10.6
Colombia	--	--	--	--	--
Ecuador	--	--	--	--	--
Mexico	--	--	--	--	--
Paraguay	--	--	--	--	8.7
Peru	--	4.3	4.9	33.6	7.8
Uruguay					
Bolivia	--	--	0.1	--	--
Venezuela	76.1	--	45.5	47.8	--

Source: Table VII-9.

Table IX-9c. *Processed and Manufactured Commodities as a Percentage of Exports of Uruguay to LAFTA Countries, Bolivia and Venezuela, 1959-1963*

Importing Country	Exports of Uruguay				
	1959	1960	1961	1962	1963
Argentina	79.2	87.2	71.8	36.1	51.5
Brazil	0.3	3.3	3.1	7.9	5.4
Chile	99.9	2.2	2.6	13.1	34.3
Colombia	--	0.2	--	0.3	2.5
Ecuador	--	2.9	0.1	9.8	15.8
Mexico	99.9	99.9	41.4	87.3	42.8
Paraguay	44.8	66.7	78.6	74.8	63.6
Peru	0.3	41.6	8.0	14.7	34.5
Uruguay					
Bolivia	--	0.4	0.6	7.2	53.9
Venezuela	2.0	41.4	--	23.8	49.7

Source: Table VII-9.

Table IX-10a. *Raw Materials as a Percentage of Exports of Bolivia to LAFTA Countries and Venezuela, 1959-1962*

| Importing Country | Exports of Bolivia | | | |
	1959	1960	1961	1962
Argentina	89.5	85.6	76.5	74.4
Brazil	34.1	78.1	66.6	16.9
Chile	19.6	36.8	43.9	67.1
Colombia	--	--	--	--
Ecuador	--	--	--	--
Mexico	99.9	99.7	--	--
Paraguay	--	26.4	--	33.3
Peru	14.1	16.9	25.0	5.1
Uruguay	--	--	--	--
Bolivia				
Venezuela	--	--	--	--

Source: Table VII-10.

Table IX-10b. *Semi-Processed Commodities as a Percentage of Exports of Bolivia to LAFTA Countries and Venezuela, 1959-1962*

Importing Country	Exports of Bolivia			
	1959	1960	1961	1962
Argentina	10.5	14.3	23.0	19.9
Brazil	65.6	21.8	33.2	82.3
Chile	67.1	50.7	50.6	31.5
Colombia	--	--	--	--
Ecuador	--	--	--	--
Mexico	--	--	--	--
Paraguay	99.7	73.6	100.0	66.1
Peru	82.6	75.9	66.9	91.1
Uruguay	96.6	--	--	--
Bolivia				
Venezuela	--	--	--	--

Source: Table VII-10.

306

Table IX-10c. *Processed and Manufactured Commodities as a Percentage of Exports of Bolivia to LAFTA Countries and Venezuela, 1959-1962*

	Exports of Bolivia			
Importing Country	1959	1960	1961	1962
Argentina	--	0.1	0.5	5.7
Brazil	0.3	0.1	0.2	0.8
Chile	13.3	12.5	5.5	1.4
Colombia	99.9	99.9	99.9	99.9
Ecuador	99.9	99.9	99.9	--
Mexico	0.1	0.3	99.9	--
Paraguay	0.3	--	--	0.6
Peru	3.3	7.2	8.1	3.8
Uruguay	3.4	99.9	99.9	--
Bolivia				
Venezuela	99.9	99.9	99.9	99.9

Source: Table VII-10.

Table IX-11a. *Raw Materials as a Percentage of Exports of Venezuela to LAFTA Countries and Bolivia, 1959-1963*

	Exports of Venezuela				
Importing Country	1959	1960	1961	1962	1963
Argentina	78.0	71.2	53.6	43.4	68.8
Brazil	64.8	57.7	73.6	89.6	88.2
Chile	94.6	91.4	95.0	96.9	94.9
Colombia	6.6	10.2	9.8	0.2	3.7
Ecuador	13.1	97.8	70.1	82.9	98.5
Mexico	13.5	11.5	10.5	37.0	73.7
Paraguay	--	--	--	--	--
Peru	--	8.5	8.3	49.8	32.2
Uruguay	91.8	94.2	88.4	93.1	95.3
Bolivia	--	--	--	--	--
Venezuela					

Source: Table VII-11.

Table IX-11b. *Semi-Processed Commodities as a Percentage of Exports of Venezuela to LAFTA Countries and Bolivia, 1959-1963*

Importing Country	Exports of Venezuela				
	1959	1960	1961	1962	1963
Argentina	21.1	27.5	43.9	56.3	30.6
Brazil	35.0	41.2	26.3	10.3	11.8
Chile	4.7	3.7	4.2	2.5	4.4
Colombia	9.5	23.1	51.0	33.3	57.6
Ecuador	55.9	--	19.6	15.4	0.5
Mexico	39.7	--	--	--	--
Paraguay	99.9	99.9	99.4	95.9	99.9
Peru	72.8	71.8	75.6	27.8	62.6
Uruguay	8.1	5.7	11.4	6.7	4.7
Bolivia	--	--	--	--	--
Venezuela					

Source: Table VII-11.

Table IX-11c. *Processed and Manufactured Commodities as a Percentage of Exports of Venezuela to LAFTA Countries and Bolivia, 1959-1963*

Importing Country	Exports of Venezuela				
	1959	1960	1961	1962	1963
Argentina	0.9	1.3	2.5	0.3	0.6
Brazil	0.2	1.1	0.1	0.1	--
Chile	0.7	4.9	0.8	0.6	0.7
Colombia	83.9	66.7	39.2	66.5	38.7
Ecuador	31.0	2.2	10.3	1.7	1.0
Mexico	46.8	88.5	89.5	63.0	26.3
Paraguay	--	0.1	0.6	4.1	--
Peru	27.2	19.7	16.1	22.4	5.2
Uruguay	0.1	0.1	0.2	0.2	--
Bolivia	99.9	99.9	99.9	99.9	99.9
Venezuela					

Source: Table VII-11.

Table Xa. *Raw Materials as a Percentage of Total Exports Going to LAFTA Countries, Bolivia and Venezuela, by Country, 1959-1963*

Country	Year				
	1959	1960	1961	1962	1963
Argentina	76.1	76.8	57.7	74.9	62.2
Brazil	16.7	7.8	18.6	8.9	10.2
Chile	23.3	21.1	22.7	19.5	15.3
Colombia	3.6	1.2	15.4	7.2	20.7
Ecuador	37.5	62.5	36.0	46.2	40.3
Mexico	32.7	19.6	6.0	10.0	22.6
Paraguay	5.2	4.3	5.3	6.7	12.2
Peru	46.0	40.8	62.6	59.4	46.4
Uruguay	82.6	38.3	68.9	74.6	82.4
Bolivia	70.4	79.6	68.4	56.3	
Venezuela	71.4	67.0	66.8	78.8	84.1

Source: Table VII.

Note to Table X: The sum of the percentages of raw materials, semi-processed, and processed goods corresponding to the same country and the same year equals 100 per cent.

Table Xb. *Semi-Processed Commodities as a Percentage of Total Exports Going to LAFTA Countries, Bolivia and Venezuela, by Country, 1959-1963*

Country	Year				
	1959	1960	1961	1962	1963
Argentina	14.7	10.2	19.0	14.0	16.6
Brazil	76.5	81.9	68.3	73.7	69.4
Chile	24.2	42.9	11.1	45.8	52.5
Colombia	53.3	65.5	47.3	57.7	21.5
Ecuador	52.7	19.8	49.2	38.4	46.1
Mexico	2.6	12.9	30.3	23.3	16.0
Paraguay	83.7	87.5	84.8	84.2	71.6
Peru	41.2	42.3	19.9	24.4	37.4
Uruguay	5.7	0.3	0.9	10.8	3.7
Bolivia	29.0	19.8	30.6	39.7	
Venezuela	26.0	30.9	31.3	20.0	15.1

Source: Table VII.

Table Xc. *Processed and Manufactured Commodities as a Percentage of Total Exports Going to LAFTA Countries, Bolivia and Venezuela, by Country, 1959-1963*

Country	Year				
	1959	1960	1961	1962	1963
Argentina	9.2	13.0	23.3	11.0	21.2
Brazil	6.8	10.3	13.1	17.4	20.4
Chile	52.5	36.0	66.2	34.7	32.2
Colombia	43.1	33.3	37.3	35.1	57.8
Ecuador	9.8	17.7	14.8	15.4	13.6
Mexico	64.7	67.5	63.7	66.7	61.4
Paraguay	11.1	8.2	9.9	9.1	16.2
Peru	12.8	16.9	17.5	16.2	16.2
Uruguay	11.7	61.4	30.2	14.6	13.9
Bolivia	0.6	0.6	1.0	4.0	
Venezuela	2.6	2.1	1.9	1.2	0.8

Source: Table VII.

Table XI-1. *Percentage of Total Trade to LAFTA Countries, Bolivia and Venezuela, by Country; 1959*

Exporting Country	Importing Country											
	Argentina	Brazil	Chile	Colombia	Ecuador	Mexico	Paraguay	Peru	Uruguay	LAFTA	Bolivia	Venezuela
Argentina	--	59.8	16.9	0.2	--	0.5	5.6	5.6	4.1	92.7	3.5	3.8
Brazil	56.2	--	12.9	0.3	--	0.1	1.1	0.3	27.2	98.1	0.3	1.6
Chile	57.0	19.4	--	2.0	2.4	3.1	--	7.1	2.9	93.8	4.0	2.1
Colombia	1.4	0.7	20.0	--	7.7	0.8	--	33.4	0.4	64.4	0.1	35.5
Ecuador	0.5	--	21.9	55.8	--	--	0.1	1.9	0.1	80.3	0.2	19.5
Mexico	5.0	3.3	15.0	13.6	3.8	--	0.8	8.8	1.0	51.3	0.3	48.4
Paraguay	82.2	0.4	2.2	--	--	--	--	--	10.9	95.7	4.3	--
Peru	17.8	2.7	61.3	2.4	5.4	1.2	--	--	1.5	92.3	6.5	1.2
Uruguay	12.0	46.1	--	8.0	3.4	0.7	2.6	18.3	--	93.0	2.0	6.9
Bolivia	62.7	20.6	2.0	--	--	5.8	0.4	7.4	1.1	99.9	--	--
Venezuela	42.6	42.1	4.1	1.6	2.0	0.2	--	0.2	7.2	99.9	--	--

Sources: Table VII-1 to Table VII-11. Total of exports of each country to each country and to LAFTA as a whole taken as a percentage of grand total to LAFTA plus Bolivia and Venezuela.

Note to Table XI: The LAFTA percentage plus the percentages to Bolivia and Venezuela in each row of Tables XI-1 to XI-5 add to 100 per cent.

Table XI-2. *Percentage of Total Trade to LAFTA Countries, Bolivia and Venezuela, by Country, 1960*

Exporting Country	Importing Country											
	Argentina	Brazil	Chile	Colombia	Ecuador	Mexico	Paraguay	Peru	Uruguay	LAFTA	Bolivia	Venezuela
Argentina	--	48.6	24.5	0.2	--	0.4	5.0	9.1	7.6	95.5	1.4	3.2
Brazil	63.9	--	13.1	0.3	0.1	0.2	1.1	0.4	18.8	97.9	0.7	1.4
Chile	54.4	17.7	--	3.0	2.1	1.1	0.2	10.2	3.2	92.0	5.4	2.6
Colombia	2.3	0.8	15.5	--	6.0	1.1	--	52.3	0.2	78.2	--	21.8
Ecuador	0.3	--	26.6	32.7	--	1.6	0.1	2.9	0.1	64.3	0.7	35.0
Mexico	7.1	13.7	15.2	14.0	4.9	--	0.3	7.9	1.6	64.7	2.8	32.5
Paraguay	85.4	0.9	--	--	--	--	--	--	13.0	99.3	0.7	--
Peru	25.8	5.8	45.3	1.7	8.1	2.3	--	--	1.8	90.8	7.8	1.4
Uruguay	65.1	8.4	7.0	3.8	3.5	0.3	3.8	2.3	--	94.2	5.0	0.8
Bolivia	47.1	47.4	3.6	--	--	0.7	0.2	1.0	--	99.9	--	--
Venezuela	34.8	43.3	4.8	0.9	1.6	0.1	1.8	0.9	11.8	99.9	--	--

Source: Table VII-1 to Table VII-11. Total of exports of each country to each country and to LAFTA as a whole taken as a percentage of grand total to LAFTA plus Bolivia and Venezuela.

315

Table XI-3. *Percentage of Total Trade to LAFTA Countries, Bolivia and Venezuela, by Country, 1961*

Exporting Country	Importing Country											
	Argentina	Brazil	Chile	Colombia	Ecuador	Mexico	Paraguay	Peru	Uruguay	LAFTA	Bolivia	Venezuela
Argentina	--	23.8	38.3	0.3	0.1	1.0	7.7	12.7	5.2	89.1	6.7	4.2
Brazil	69.3	--	9.0	1.2	0.1	0.2	0.6	1.3	16.2	97.9	0.4	1.7
Chile	61.3	16.6	--	0.7	1.3	0.8	--	7.6	3.8	92.1	5.1	2.8
Colombia	2.4	2.9	4.0	--	16.3	2.9	--	52.8	1.0	82.3	0.2	17.5
Ecuador	0.8	0.3	33.2	51.9	--	0.3	0.1	4.9	0.1	91.6	0.4	8.0
Mexico	10.5	16.7	13.8	14.9	5.6	--	0.3	7.7	2.0	71.7	0.4	28.0
Paraguay	88.0	0.7	--	--	--	--	--	--	11.1	99.8	0.2	--
Peru	24.5	11.6	42.7	2.8	5.0	2.7	0.1	--	4.2	93.6	3.8	2.4
Uruguay	30.3	30.5	12.8	8.9	2.4	0.6	8.6	2.4	--	96.5	3.2	0.4
Bolivia	47.2	42.3	8.1	--	--	--	0.2	2.2	--	99.9	--	--
Venezuela	33.0	51.1	4.2	1.6	1.7	--	0.4	1.1	6.9	99.9	--	--

Source: Table VII-1 to Table VII-11. Total of exports of each country to each country and to LAFTA as a whole taken as a percentage of grand total to LAFTA plus Bolivia and Venezuela.

Table XI-4. *Percentage of Total Trade to LAFTA Countries, Bolivia and Venezuela, by Country, 1962*

Exporting Country	Importing Country											
	Argentina	Brazil	Chile	Colombia	Ecuador	Mexico	Paraguay	Peru	Uruguay	LAFTA	Bolivia	Venezuela
Argentina	--	44.3	20.5	1.5	0.1	0.6	3.6	16.6	4.4	91.5	4.9	3.6
Brazil	63.0	--	12.2	0.2	--	0.4	2.8	1.6	18.2	98.4	1.1	0.5
Chile	35.0	43.6	--	1.6	1.1	1.6	0.1	7.3	2.5	92.8	4.1	3.2
Colombia	7.6	0.2	14.3	--	18.5	1.2	0.2	43.8	1.7	87.6	0.3	12.3
Ecuador	3.2	--	36.7	50.4	--	--	--	8.7	--	99.0	0.4	0.6
Mexico	10.6	35.1	11.0	9.0	3.1	--	0.1	7.8	2.5	79.2	0.3	20.6
Paraguay	88.2	1.0	0.2	--	--	--	--	--	10.5	99.9	0.1	--
Peru	16.1	21.6	45.2	1.9	2.7	3.5	--	--	2.8	93.8	2.8	3.3
Uruguay	19.8	36.6	11.2	24.1	1.6	0.4	2.7	1.0	--	97.4	2.1	0.4
Bolivia	61.7	24.6	8.6	--	--	--	0.6	4.5	--	99.9	--	--
Venezuela	21.0	59.6	6.7	0.9	2.0	0.1	0.3	1.6	7.7	99.9	--	--

Source: Table VII-1 to Table VII-11. Total of exports of each country to each country and to LAFTA as a whole taken as a percentage of grand total to LAFTA plus Bolivia and Venezuela.

Table XI-5. *Percentage of Total Trade to LAFTA Countries, Bolivia and Venezuela, by Country, 1963*

Exporting Country	Importing Country											
	Argentina	Brazil	Chile	Colombia	Ecuador	Mexico	Paraguay	Peru	Uruguay	LAFTA	Bolivia	Venezuela
Argentina	--	39.2	21.0	4.1	0.2	1.3	4.8	18.0	4.9	93.5	2.3	4.2
Brazil	59.0	--	11.8	0.7	--	1.7	2.5	1.3	17.2	94.2	1.4	4.3
Chile	28.3	52.7	--	1.7	1.4	2.3	0.1	7.2	2.7	96.4	1.0	2.7
Colombia	7.8	1.9	3.9	--	38.7	3.2	0.6	26.3	4.2	86.6	0.2	13.3
Ecuador	3.3	--	25.8	52.5	--	0.1	--	17.0	0.3	99.0	0.3	0.5
Mexico	7.7	31.5	15.5	12.9	2.9	--	0.2	9.3	1.5	81.5	0.6	17.9
Paraguay	80.7	3.7	1.5	--	--	0.1	--	--	14.0	100.0	--	--
Peru	11.8	18.7	45.9	3.3	2.7	4.6	--	--	4.6	91.6	2.8	5.7
Uruguay	6.1	64.2	9.8	11.0	1.6	0.6	2.5	3.7	--	99.5	0.5	0.1
Bolivia												
Venezuela	12.3	67.7	5.0	0.9	2.2	0.3	0.1	3.3	8.1	99.9	--	--

Source: Table VII-1 to Table VII-11. Total of exports of each country to each country and to LAFTA as a whole taken as a percentage of grand total to LAFTA plus Bolivia and Venezuela.

Table XII. *National Income by LAFTA Countries, Bolivia and Venezuela, 1950-1962*[a]

Country	1950	1952	1954	1956	1958	1960	1962
Argentina (billions of pesos)	51.9	83.8	106.3	150.9	271.2	626.0	905.6
Bolivia[b] (millions of U.S. dollars)	311.5	364.7	318.5	348.0	351.2	369.5	397.0
Brazil (billions of cruzieros)	212.6	292.6	451.3	726.7	1,046.2	1,879.2	--
Chile (millions of 1961 escudos)	3,136	3,510	3,742	3,814	4,188	4,114	4,669
Colombia (billions of pesos)	6.8	8.2	11.0	12.7	16.5	21.8	28.2
Ecuador (millions of sucres)	6,032	7,335	8,663	9,304	10,280	11,697	13,628
Mexico (billions of pesos)	37.5	52.0	59.2	84.0	114.7	139.1	160.5
Paraguay (billions of guaranies)	1.2	4.4	9.0	14.2	19.1	22.8	27.3
Peru (billions of soles)	12.0	16.1	19.8	24.4	29.4	41.4	49.4
Venezuela (billions of bolivares)	7.7	9.8	12.2	14.7	18.3	19.5	20.9

Sources: International Monetary Fund, International Financial Statistics, Vol. 14, No. 1 (Jan., 1961) and Vol. 18, No. 2 (February, 1965); National Planning Board of Bolivia, Memo to the Committee of Nine, 1963. Corporacion de Fomento de la Produccion, Dept. de Investigaciones Economicas, Cuentas Nacionales de Chile, 1940-1962, Santiago, 1963.

[a] Figures for Uruguay not available in a form which allows comparison with foreign trade figures.

[b] Figures for Bolivia are gross national product.

Table XIII-a. *Total Exports of LAFTA Countries, Bolivia and Venezuela, by Country, 1950-1962*[a]

Country	1950	1952	1954	1956	1958	1960	1962
Argentina (billions of pesos)	5.4	4.4	6.8	18.1	28.6	89.2	137.1
Bolivia (millions of U.S. dollars) b/	75.2	106.7	70.3	81.3	50.1	51.5	57.4
Brazil (billions of cruzieros)	24.9	26.1	43.0	59.5	63.8	147.1	307.1
Chile (millions of 1961 escudos)	435.9	456.8	412.3	426.1	473.0	548.8	496.0
Colombia (millions of pesos)	771	1,083	1,579	1,660	2,322	2,597	3,032
Ecuador (millions of sucres)	1,110	1,526	1,922	1,817	2,062	2,281	2,503
Mexico (billions of pesos)	4.5	5.7	7.3	11.0	9.2	9.6	11.6
Paraguay (millions of guaranies)	167.7	298.2	813.0	2,076.6	3,730.0	3,284.9	4,142.3
Peru (billions of soles)	2.8	3.6	4.7	5.9	6.6	11.7	14.4
Venezuela (millions of bolivares)	3,889	4,858	5,661	7,090	7,777	8,147	8,689

Sources: International Monetary Fund, International Financial Statistics, Vol. 14, No. 1 (Jan., 1961) and Vol. 17, No. 7 (July, 1964); National Planning Board of Bolivia, Memo to the Committee of Nine, 1963. Corporacion de Fomento de la Produccion, Dept. de Investigaciones Economicas, Cuentas Nacionales de Chile, 1940-1962, Santiago, 1963. Table XII, above.

a/
    Figures for Uruguay not available in a form which allows comparison with national income figures.

b/
    Valued at FOB (IMF Export Series B).

Table XIII-b. *Total Imports of LAFTA Countries, Bolivia and Venezuela, by Country, 1950-1962*[a]

Country	1950	1952	1954	1956	1958	1960	1962
Argentina (billions of pesos)	4.8	8.4	7.1	18.3	35.0	103.3	153.6
Bolivia (millions of U.S. dollars)	55.8	92.6	72.9	84.1	79.6	71.5	97.5
Brazil (billions of cruzieros)	20.3	37.2	55.2	71.6	103.3	201.2	511.7
Chile (millions of 1961 escudos)	308.5	382.4	380.4	445.1	457.8	677.4	602.0
Colombia (millions of pesos)	711	1,038	1,679	1,643	2,811	3,420	3,683
Ecuador (millions of sucres)	620	879	1,520	1,361	1,402	1,520	1,731
Mexico (billions of pesos)	4.8	7.0	8.9	13.4	14.1	14.8	14.3
Paraguay (millions of guaranies)	84.8	278.4	992.4	1,465.1	3,332.2	3,866.4	4,285.8
Peru (billions of soles)	2.7	4.5	4.9	6.9	7.8	10.2	14.4
Venezuela (millions of bolivares)	1,995	2,528	3,063	3,736	4,783	3,552	3,871

Sources: International Monetary Fund, International Financial Statistics, Vol. 14, No. 1 (Jan., 1961) and Vol. 17, No. 7 (July, 1964); National Planning Board of Bolivia, Memo to the Committee of Nine, 1963. Corporacion de Fomento de la Produccion, Dept. de Investigaciones Economicas, Cuentas Nacionales de Chile, 1940-1962, Santiago, 1963. Table XII, above.

a/
Figures for Uruguay not available in a form which allows comparison with national income figures.

Table XIV-a. *Total Exports of LAFTA Countries, Bolivia and Venezuela as a Percentage of National Income, 1950-1962*[a]

Country	1950	1952	1954	1956	1958	1960	1962
Argentina	10.4	5.2	6.4	12.0	10.5	14.2	15.1
Bolivia [b]	24.2	30.0	22.0	23.4	14.3	14.0	14.5
Brazil	11.7	8.9	9.5	8.2	6.1	7.8	--
Chile	13.9	13.0	11.0	11.2	11.2	13.3	10.6
Colombia	11.2	13.1	14.2	13.1	14.1	11.9	10.8
Ecuador	18.4	20.8	22.1	19.5	20.0	19.5	18.4
Mexico	12.0	10.9	12.4	13.1	8.0	6.9	7.2
Paraguay	14.2	6.8	9.0	14.6	19.5	14.4	15.2
Peru	23.4	22.4	23.9	24.1	22.4	28.3	29.1
Venezuela	50.6	49.5	46.6	48.2	42.5	41.8	41.5

Sources: International Monetary Fund, International Financial Statistics, Vol. 14, No. 1 (Jan., 1961) and Vol. 18, No. 2 (February, 1965); National Planning Board of Bolivia, Memo to the Committee of Nine, 1963. Corporacion de Fomento de la Produccion, Dept. de Investigaciones Economicas, Cuentas Nacionales de Chile, 1940-1962, Santiago, 1963. Table XII, above.

a/
   Figures for Uruguay not available in a form which allows comparison with national income figures.

b/
   Percentages of national income are underestimated because of use of gross national product.

Table XIV-b. *Total Imports of LAFTA Countries, Bolivia and Venezuela as a Percentage of National Income, 1950-1962*[a]

Country	1950	1952	1954	1956	1958	1960	1962
Argentina	9.3	10.0	6.7	12.1	12.9	16.5	17.0
Bolivia [b]	17.9	26.1	22.8	24.2	22.7	19.3	24.6
Brazil	9.6	12.7	12.2	9.8	9.9	10.7	--
Chile	9.8	10.9	10.2	11.6	10.9	16.4	12.8
Colombia	10.4	12.6	15.3	13.0	17.1	15.7	13.1
Ecuador	10.2	11.9	17.5	14.6	13.6	12.9	12.7
Mexico	12.8	13.4	15.1	15.9	12.3	10.6	8.9
Paraguay	7.2	6.3	11.0	10.3	17.4	17.0	15.7
Peru	22.4	27.7	24.8	28.4	26.6	24.5	29.1
Venezuela	25.9	25.8	25.1	25.4	26.1	18.2	18.5

Sources: International Monetary Fund, International Financial Statistics, Vol. 14, No. 1 (Jan., 1961) and Vol. 18, No. 2 (February, 1965); National Planning Board of Bolivia, Memo to the Committee of Nine, 1963. Corporacion de Fomento de la Produccion, Dept. de Investigaciones Economicas, Cuentas Nacionales de Chile, 1940-1962, Santiago, 1963. Table XII, above.

a/
Figures for Uruguay not available in a form which allows comparison with national income figures.

b/
Percentages of national income are underestimated because of use of gross national product.

Table XV. *Imports Per Capita of LAFTA Countries, Bolivia and Venezuela, by Country, 1960*

(U.S. dollars)

Exporting Country	Importing Country										
	Argentina	Bolivia	Brazil	Chile	Colombia	Ecuador	Mexico	Paraguay	Peru	Uruguay	Venezuela
Argentina		1.13	1.34	5.19	0.02	---	0.03	4.24	1.63	3.47	0.76
Bolivia	0.23		0.04	0.03	---	---	---	---	0.02	---	---
Brazil	3.17	0.19		3.17	0.01	---	---	---	0.05	5.41	0.18
Chile	0.96	0.70	0.12		0.09	0.16	0.03	---	0.30	0.64	0.10
Colombia	0.01	---	---	---		0.09	0.01	---	0.32	0.04	0.20
Ecuador	---	---	---	0.54	0.16		---	---	0.14	---	0.45
Mexico	0.04	---	0.02	0.22	0.06	---		---	0.07	---	0.49
Paraguay	0.45	---	0.01	---	---	---	---		---	0.50	---
Peru	0.59	0.73	0.04	2.91	0.07	0.37	0.03	---		0.21	0.10
Uruguay	0.09	---	0.01	0.04	0.02	---	0.01	0.06	0.01		0.01
Venezuela	4.52	---	1.61	0.04	0.11	0.02	0.01	---	0.12	13.26	
Total Imports Per Capita from LAFTA Countries, Bolivia and Venezuela	10.06	2.75	3.19	12.14	0.54	0.64	0.12	4.30	2.66	23.53	2.29

Source: Table VI. Population census by country, 1960.

324

Bibliography

Acta Final de la Conferencia Regional de los Paises de la Plata. Montevideo, February 6, 1941.

Allen, Roy G. D., and Edward Ely (eds.). *International Trade Statistics,* New York: Wiley; London: Chapman and Hall, 1953.

American Bankers Association, Commission on Commerce and Marine. *The South American West Coast,* New York, 1925.

Angulo, Enrique. "Ante la Reunión de la ALAMAR," *Comercio Exterior* (Mexico), November 1963.

Banco Central de Ecuador. *Comercio Exterior Ecuatoriano* (Quito), October-November-December, 1959; October-November-December, 1960; October-November-December, 1961.

Banco Central de Paraguay. Departmento de Estudios Económicos, *Boletín Estadístico Mensual* (Asunción), December 1963; December 1964.

Banco Comercial. *Información Económica del Uruguay* (Montevideo), June 1960; June 1961; June 1962.

Banco de la República Oriental del Uruguay, Departmento de Negocios con el Exterior. *Exportaciones Cumplidas, 1962.* Montevideo, 1963; *Exportaciones Cumplidas, 1963.* Montevideo, 1964.

Behrendt, Richard F. *Inter-Amercan Economic Relations.* New York: The Committee on International Economic Policy, 1948.

Brown, Robert. *Transport and the Economic Development of Latin America.* Washington, D.C.: The Brookings Institution (to be published in 1965).

Burgin, Miron. *The Economic Aspects of Argentine Federalism.* Cambridge, Massachusetts: Harvard University Press, 1946.

Cairncross, Alexander K. "World Trade in Manufactures Since 1900." *Economia Internazionale* (Genoa), Vol. 8, No. 4, November 1955.

Dell, Sidney. "Economic Integration and the American Example." *Economic Journal* (London), Vol. 69, No. 273, March 1959.

—————. *Problemas de un mercado común en América Latina.* Mexico, D.F.: Centro de Estudios Monetarios Latinoamericanos, 1959.

Estados Unidos de Brasil, Ministerio da Fazenda, Servicio de Estatística Económica e Financiera. *Comercio Exterior do Brasil,* Rio de Janeiro, Brazil. The following years are used in this study: 1959, 1960, 1961, 1962, 1963.

Estados Unidos de México, Secretaria de Industria y Comercio, Dirección General de Estadística. *Anuario Estadístico del Comercio Exterior de los*

Estados Unidos Mexicanos, Mexico, D.F. The following years are used in this study: 1959, 1960, 1961, 1962, 1963.

Furtado, Celso. *The Economic Growth of Brazil.* Berkeley and Los Angeles: University of California Press, 1963.

García Reynoso, Plácido. "Probables efectos del tratado de Montevideo en la industrialización de América Latina." *El Trimestre Económico* (Mexico), Vol. XXVI, No. 106, 1960.

General Agreements on Tariffs and Trade (GATT). *Basic Instruments and Selected Documents*, Vol. I. Geneva, May 1952.

—————. *Basic Instruments and Selected Documents*, Vol. III: *Text of the General Agreements in Force, 1958.* Geneva, 1958.

—————. *Information Paper on the Procedures for Accession to the General Agreement on Tariffs and Trade and the Advantages for Less-Developed Countries.* Prepared by the Executive Secretary to the Contracting Parties for the United Nations Economic Commission for Africa. New York, 1960. United Nations Doc. E/CN.14/61.

—————. *The Possible Impact of the European Economic Community, in Particular the Common Market, Upon World Trade.* Geneva, 1957 (Trade Intelligence Paper No. 6).

—————. *Trends in International Trade: A Report by a Panel of Experts.* Geneva, 1958.

Goormaghtigh, John. "European Coal and Steel Community." *International Conciliation.* New York: Carnegie Endowment for International Peace, May 1955 (No. 503).

Hamilton, Earl J. *American Treasure and Price Revolution in Spain.* Cambridge: Harvard University Press, 1934.

Hanson, Simon G. *Argentine Meat and the British Market.* Stanford, California: Stanford University Press, 1938.

Herring, Hubert. *A History of Latin America* (2nd ed.). New York: Alfred A. Knopf, 1962.

Inman, Samuel Guy. *Latin America—Its Place in World Life* (rev. ed.). New York: Harcourt, Brace & Co., 1942.

International Monetary Fund. *International Financial Statistics.* Washington, D.C., January and February, 1965.

————— and International Bank for Reconstruction and Development. *Direction of Trade.* Washington, D.C., Annual, 1958-62 and May-December, 1964.

James, Herman and Martin, Percy A. *The Republics of Latin America.* New York and London: Harper and Brothers, 1923.

Levin, J. *The Export Economies.* Cambridge: Harvard University Press, 1960.

Meade, James E. *Problems of Economic Union.* London: Allen and Unwin; Chicago: University of Chicago Press, 1953.

Meier, Gerald M. "International Trade and International Inequality." *Oxford Economic Papers* (Oxford), n.s., Vol. 10, No. 3, October 1958.

Mikesell, Raymond F. "The Movement Toward Regional Trading Groups in Latin America," in Albert Hirschman, ed. *Latin American Issues.* New York: Twentieth Century Fund, 1961.

Myint, Hla. "The 'Classical Theory' of International Trade and the Underdeveloped Countries," *Economic Journal* (London), Vol. 68, No. 270, June 1958.

Nurske, Ragnar. *Patterns of Trade and Development.* Oxford: Basil Blackwell, 1959.

Pan American Union. *The Peruvian Economy.* Washington, D.C., 1950.

Pollock, David. "The Development of Commodity Trade Between Latin America and the United States." United Nations, Economic Commission for Latin America, *Economic Bulletin for Latin America,* Vol. VI, No. 2, October 1961.

Prebisch, Raúl. "Commercial Policy in the Underdeveloped Countries." *American Economic Review,* Vol. 49, No. 2, May 1959.

—————. "The Economic Development of Latin America and Its Principal Problems." United Nations, Economic Commission for Latin America, *Economic Bulletin for Latin America,* Vol. VII, No. 1, February 1962.

—————. *Toward a Dynamic Development Policy for Latin America.* New York: United Nations, April 14, 1963.

República de Argentina, Secretaria de Estado de Hacienda, Dirección Nacional de Estadística y Censo. *Comercio Exterior,* Buenos Aires, Argentina. The following years are used in this study: 1959, 1960, 1961, 1962, 1963.

República de Bolivia, Dirección Nacional de Estadística y Censos. *Comercio Exterior.* La Paz, Bolivia. The following years are used in this study: 1960, 1961, 1962, 1963.

República de Bolivia, National Planning Board of Bolivia. *Memo to the Committee of Nine.* La Paz, 1963.

República de Chile, Cámara de Comercio de Santiago de Chile. *Comercio Exterior de Chile, 1963.* Santiago, April 1964.

República de Chile, Corporación de Fomento de la Producción, Departamento de Investigaciones Económicas. *Cuentas Nacionales de Chile, 1960-1962.* Santiago, 1963.

República de Chile, Dirección Nacional de Estadística y Censos. *Comercio Exterior.* Santiago. The following years are used in this study: 1960, 1961, 1962, 1963.

República de Colombia, Departamento Administrativo Nacional de Estadística. *Anuario de Comercio Exterior.* Bogotá, Colombia. The following years are used in this study: 1959, 1960, 1961, 1692, 1963.

República de Ecuador, Ministerio de Finanzas. Dirección de Financiamiento y Asesoría Fiscal. *Anuario de Comercio Exterior.* Quito, Ecuador. The following years are used in this study: 1962, 1963.

República de Perú, Ministerio de Hacienda y Comercio, Superintendencia General de Aduanas. *Estadística del Comercio Exterior*. Lima, Perú. The following years are used in this study: 1959, 1960, 1961, 1962, 1963.

República de Venezuela, Ministerio de Fomento, Dirección General de Estadística y Censos Nacionales. *Boletín de Comercio Exterior*. Caracas, December 1958, December 1960, December 1961, December 1962, December 1963.

Robertson, William Spence. *History of Latin American Nations* (3rd ed.). New York: D. Appleton-Century Co., 1943.

Sammons, Robert L. "Proposals for a Common Market in Latin America." *Public Policy*, Graduate School of Public Administration, Harvard University, Vol. 10, 1960.

Sannwald, Rolf and Stohler, Jacques. *Economic Integration: Theoretical Assumptions and Consequences of European Unification*. Princeton, New Jersey: Princeton University Press, 1959.

United Nations, Department of Economic and Social Affairs. *Commodity Trade and Economic Development*. New York, 1953.

————. *Instability in Export Markets of Underdeveloped Countries in Relation to Their Ability to Obtain Foreign Exchange from Exports of Primary Commodities, 1901-1950*. New York, 1952.

————. *Inter-Latin American Trade—Current Problems*. New York, January 1957.

————. *Study of the Prospects of Inter-Latin American Trade* (Southern Zone of the Region), New York, 1954.

United Nations, Economic Commission for Latin America. "The Achievement of Coordination in Latin American Trade Policy: Relations With the European Economic Community," *Economic Bulletin for Latin America*, Vol. VII, No. 2, October 1962.

————. *The Economic Development of Latin America in the Post-War Period*, Vol. II, New York, 1964.

————. *Economic Survey of Latin America, 1949*. New York, 1950.

————. *Foreign Private Investments in the Latin American Free Trade Area*. New York, 1961.

————. "The Free Trade Area." *Economic Bulletin for Latin America*, Vol. V, No. 1, March 1960.

————. *Influence of the Common Market on Latin American Economic Development*, Doc. E/CN.12/C.1/13, New York, April 14, 1959. (See ECLA, *The Latin American Common Market*, Part B.)

————. *The Latin American Common Market*. New York, 1959.

————. *The Latin American Movement Towards Multilateral Economic Cooperation*, Doc. E/CN.12/567. Santiago, Chile, March 1961.

————. "Latin America's Foreign Trade in the Early Months of 1957." *Economic Bulletin for Latin America*, Vol. II, No. 2, October 1957.

—————. "Latin America's Foreign Trade in the First Half of 1958." *Economic Bulletin for Latin America*, Vol. III, No. 2, October 1958.

—————. "Progress Towards the Latin American Common Market." *Economic Bulletin for Latin America*, Vol. IV, No. 1, March 1959.

—————. *Report of the Central American Economic Cooperation Committee, 25 February 1957 to 10 June 1958.* Mexico, 1959.

—————. *Role of Agricultural Commodities in a Latin American Regional Market.* Panama, 1959.

—————. *The Role of Agriculture in the Latin American Common Market and Free Trade Area Arrangements.* Caracas 1961.

—————. *Study of Inter-Latin American Trade.* New York, 1957.

—————. *A Study of Trade Between Latin America and Europe.* Geneva, 1963.

—————. "Tenth Session of the Economic Commission for Latin America, Mar del Plata, Argentina, May 6-17, 1963." *Economic Bulletin for Latin America*, Vol. VIII, No. 2, October 1963.

—————. "The United Nations Conference on Trade and Development." *Economic Bulletin for Latin America*, Vol. VIII, No. 2, October 1963.

United Nations, International Monetary Fund, and International Bank for Reconstruction and Development. *Direction of International Trade*, Washington, Series T, Vol. VI, No. 9 (1955), Vol. VII, No. 6 (1956), Vol. VIII, No. 7 (1957), Vol. IX, No. 10 (1958).

Urquidi, Victor L. *Free Trade and Economic Integration.* University of California Press, Berkeley and Los Angeles, 1962.

—————. "The Idea of the Latin American Common Market." *Economics and Statistics Review of Puerto Rico.* The Puerto Rican Economics and Statistics Association, San Juan, Vol. II, No. 1, 1961.

Viner, Jacob. *The Customs Union Issue.* New York: Carnegie Endowment for International Peace, 1950; Washington, D.C.: Anderson Kramer Associates, 1961.

—————. *International Trade and Economic Development.* Lectures delivered at the National University of Brazil. Glencoe, Illinois: Free Press, 1952; Oxford: Clarendon Press, 1953.

Wionczek, Miguel. (ed.) *Integración de América Latina—Experiencias y Perspectivas.* Mexico, D.F.: Fondo de Cultura Económica, 1964.

—————. "Latin American Free Trade Association." *International Conciliation.* New York: Carnegie Endowment for International Peace, January 1965 (no. 551).

Yates, Paul L. *Forty Years of Foreign Trade: A Statistical Handbook With Special Reference to Primary Products and Underdeveloped Countries.* London: Allen and Unwin; New York: Macmillan, 1959.